Marketing for Farmers

Gene A. Futrell

DOANE WESTERN

Doane-Western, Inc./8900 Manchester Road/St. Louis, Missouri 63144

Copyright©1982 by
Doane-Western, Inc.
St. Louis, Missouri

All Rights Reserved. No part of this book may be reproduced in any way, or by any means, without permission in writing from the publisher.

Library of Congress Catalog Card Number: 82-70257
ISBN: 0-932250-18-1

Printed in U.S.A.

The Editor

Gene A. Futrell is Professor of Economics and Extension Economist in Market Price Analysis and Outlook at Iowa State University. He was reared on an Iowa farm and has graduate degrees from Iowa State and Ohio State Universities.

Dr. Futrell is well known around the United States as a livestock analyst and marketing specialist. He has served as consultant for market analysis and outlook with several agricultural publications. His present duties bring him in close contact with farmers and ranchers through the various educational meetings he conducts.

In his role as editor of this book, Dr. Futrell contributed substantially to its writing, as well as assuming overall responsibility for the concept, organization, and preparation of the manuscript.

Contributing Authors

Gerald R. Campbell is Associate Professor of Agricultural Economics at the University of Wisconsin. Dr. Campbell has teaching, research, and extension responsibilities in agricultural marketing. He was reared on an Ohio farm.

Kenneth E. Egertson is Professor and Extension Marketing Economist in the Department of Agricultural Economics, University of Minnesota. Professor Egertson's responsibilities include extension education, teaching, and research in livestock marketing and prices.

Marvin L. Hayenga is Associate Professor of Economics at Iowa State University, with responsibilities for research and teaching in agricultural marketing. Dr. Hayenga grew up on an Illinois farm and has industry experience as a corporate Agricultural Economist.

Donald M. Hofstrand is Area Farm Management Specialist for the Extension Service, Iowa State University. He was reared on a grain and livestock farm. He has done very effective work in grain marketing with northern Iowa farmers.

Robert J. Reierson is an economic consultant on the livestock and meat industry. Dr. Reierson was previously Corporate Economist for Monfort of Colorado, Project Leader for the Western Livestock Marketing Information Project, and Extension Economist at the University of Wisconsin.

J. Marvin Skadberg is Professor and Extension Economist at Iowa State University. Dr. Skadberg has both extension and research responsibilities in livestock marketing and has also had experience in industry as a research and planning economist. Professor Skadberg was reared on a farm in North Dakota.

Gary F. Stasko is Extension Economist at Iowa State University. He was reared on an Illinois farm and has experience as a soybean and oil/meal merchandiser in industry.

J. William Uhrig is Professor of Agricultural Economics at Purdue University and has responsibilities in extension, teaching, and research. He has over 10 years farming experience plus economic research experience in industry. Dr. Uhrig was reared on a central Illinois grain and livestock farm and has become well known for his work in grain marketing and outlook.

J. Hugh Winn is Professor of Economics and Extension Marketing Specialist at Colorado State University. Professor Winn's extension work has focused on livestock and meat marketing. Born in Texas, he has also been closely involved with the Western Livestock Marketing Information Project for many years.

Robert N. Wisner is Professor of Economics and Extension Economist at Iowa State University. Dr. Wisner is widely known for his work in grain marketing and grain market analysis. He was reared on a grain and livestock farm in southeastern Michigan.

★ ★ ★ ★

It's midmorning in early December. You've just come into the house to warm yourself and to gulp down a cup of coffee before returning to work on that offset disc that's been needing repairs all year. Hundreds of miles distant in Chicago, what seems like controlled chaos has just begun for the day. In a huge room, men push, yell, and make frantic hand signals.

Amazingly, out of that frenzied activity, new commodity prices are instantly spewed forth to widespread locations. Their implications are pondered by countless thousands of people. "February cattle, off thirty . . . March corn, up two and a half."

That afternoon in another city, a handful of executives gather in a boardroom. Decisions are to be made. It all seems so far away—so unrelated to that gray morning at the kitchen table; but those key decisions and that hubbub in Chicago are helping to determine the wages you will earn for a full year's work.

A light snow begins to fall later that evening. That's good, the wheat can use it. At the same time, far away in Brazil, the hot sun is beating down on fields of soybeans starved for moisture. This situation will soon begin affecting prices in Chicago and at your local elevator. In turn, the decisions you make on your own farm will be influenced. That back eighty may well end up in beans next spring because of what's happening in the world's Southern Hemisphere.

Farm Marketing has changed. In the early-1970s, agriculture found itself off and running pell-mell in a new era of market volatility. New and more powerful forces pushed and pulled price charts into jagged lines. As world demand expanded and farm production raced to keep up, global weather and international politics began to exert profound influences on conditions down on the farm. The government tried to adapt its farm programs to the new environment, often with limited success.

Conditions suddenly *demanded* something more. Being good at farming or ranching was no longer enough. Simply producing and then selling your products could easily get you caught in the "sawteeth" of prices that often changed more in one day than during a full season in years past. Terms like "marketing strategy" and "risk management" were heard more frequently.

Farm marketing. That's what this book is about. It is a term that covers so much that it's difficult to pin down a meaning. But for you, an operating farmer or rancher, the meaning can be simplified. For you, marketing means negotiating the best deal possible for what you do as an agricultural producer. Your labor, skills, money, talents . . . all those things that go into putting grain in the bin or livestock on the truck are on the line.

The marketing job includes making those planting decisions next spring, as well as determining how and when to sell the crop. It requires that you have some understanding of what goes on in the large room in Chicago and how it affects you. It means that you should learn all you can about the network of interrelated factors which determine farm prices. The job is your responsibility alone.

MARKETING FOR FARMERS is written for you. This is not a book on marketing theory, but a practical guide to help you make those decisions so crucial to your livelihood.

Editor Gene Futrell and the other authors contributing to this book have kept your needs firmly in mind in the pages that follow. All are recognized for their knowledge and experience in given areas of agricultural marketing. Equally important, theirs is a *practical* orientation which is joined with an ability to communicate important information in a simple, straightforward way.

Notice that grain and livestock marketing are handled separately, each in a series of chapters. After a grounding in the marketing system, you are challenged to access your marketing objectives and to formulate a plan. The mechanics of how you can better analyze markets and carry out your objectives are then presented in a concise, understandable way. We think you will find this book valuable as a reference, even after the first reading.

THE DOANE-WESTERN EDITORS

Contents

Chapter 1   **The Changing Market Challenge** 1
A Changing Market, 1; Prices More Variable, 2; Marketing Choices, 3.

Chapter 2   **The Grain Marketing System** 7
Grain Production Characteristics, 7; The Demand for U.S. Grain, 8; Grain Marketing Channels, 12; Grain Pricing, 13; The System in Perspective, 16.

Chapter 3   **Determining Your Grain Marketing Objectives** .. 17
Objectives, 17; Marketing Plans, 20; Developing a Marketing Plan, 22; Financial Conditions, 25; Seasonal Price Patterns, 33; Price Outlook, 33; Marketing Tools, 34.

Chapter 4   **Grain Storage as a Marketing Strategy** 39
Drying and Conditioning Grain for Storage, 40; When to Sell, 41; Seasonality of Grain Prices, 43; Probability of a Storage Return, 45; Economics of Drying Corn, 46; Economics of Drying Soybeans, 58.

Chapter 5   **Selling through Cash Contracts** 75
Why Cash Forward Contracts, 76; Contracting Alternatives, 77; Contracting Guidelines, 83; Cash Contracts versus Hedging with the Futures, 83.

Chapter 6   **Futures Markets for Grain** 87
Farmer Use of Futures, 88; Commodity Exchanges, 88; Futures Traders, 90; Costs of Futures Trading, 93; Basis, 96; Futures Price Movement, 102; Futures Prices as Forecasts, 103; Tax Treatment of Futures Transactions, 104; How to Hedge, 104; Choosing a Broker, 110; Sample Problems, 112; Hedging Matrix, 114.

Chapter 7   **Grain Markets: Sources of Information and Market Factors** 121
The USDA Market Information System, 122; Export Demand Indicators, 126; Analysis of Grain Market Information, 128; Role of Advisory Services, 132.

Chapter 8   **How Livestock Are Marketed** 135
Livestock Marketing Channels and Patterns, 137; Methods of Marketing, 144; Market Supervision, 149; The Future, 150.

Chapter	9	**Developing a Livestock Marketing Plan** 151

Establishing Goals and Objectives, 151; Selecting a Market, 153; A Timing Strategy, 158; Market Discounts, 163; Market Premiums, 163; Cost of Gain, 166; Marketing Formulas, 167; Developing a Pricing Plan, 169.

Chapter	10	**Using Livestock Futures** 173

General Characteristics of Livestock Futures, 173; General Hedging Considerations, 175; Analysis of Expected Hedge Returns, 176; Evaluating a Potential Hedge, 179; Localized Futures Prices vs. Basis, 180; Hedging Examples, 181; Removing a Hedge, 188; Limitations of Livestock Hedges, 190; Livestock Basis, 194.

Chapter	11	**Livestock Markets: Sources of Information and Market Factors** 201

Supply, 201; Demand, 203; Data and Its Sources, 205; Interpreting Livestock Statistics, 210; Seasonal Supply and Price Considerations, 213; Cyclical Supply and Price Tendencies, 218; Development of Price Expectations, 221.

Chapter	12	**Technical Price Analysis** 225

Volume and Open Interest, 226; Bar Chart Analysis, 229; Summary, 246

Appendix A	**Hedger's Glossary** 251
Appendix B	**Livestock Futures Contract Specifications** 263
Appendix C	**Commodity Price Data** 268
Index	 285

CHAPTER **1**

The Changing Market Challenge

Marketing decisions have become an increasingly important part of the overall job of managing your farm business. Successful managers have always had to make the right decisions regarding what and how to produce; historically, that has been the most critical area of farm management. While using up-to-date production technology and making sound production decisions are still necessary, that alone is no longer sufficient to assure success in farming. Now, effective management of capital and marketing have become the key areas of successful farm business management.

Farmers have long been faced with decisions on such things as which marketing method to use (direct negotiation with buyers, auction selling, terminal markets, forward contracts, etc.), where to sell, when to sell, and in some cases, what form of product to sell (selling at heavy or light weights, at what quality grade, or at what moisture level). These same decisions must still be made. But, the timing of product pricing and the selection of the most appropriate marketing strategy for particular situations have taken on new and greater significance.

A Changing Market

The increased importance of marketing decisions results in part from changes in the food and agricultural sector. It's made up of larger and more specialized operations throughout the production, processing and distribution system. Changing lifestyles have created demands for new and more convenient-to-use forms of many food products. There has been a sharp rise in away from home eating-in restaurants, and in fast-food and drive-in establishments. This has brought more pressure from these buyers for larger volumes of product of a specified and consistent quality or form. In some cases this has created a need for new pricing mechanisms and marketing arrangements to fit the changing needs of these major customers for your commodities.

Prices More Variable

Greater volatility of commodity prices has sharply increased the impact that commodity marketing (or purchasing) decisions have on farm business profits. Grain markets no longer linger near government price support levels; and price volatility in livestock markets has also increased in recent years.

Figures 1-1 and 1-2 illustrate the variability of commodity markets. The bars show how much prices changed during each year since 1965. Price fluctuations have usually been much wider since the early seventies. Soybeans have been particularly volatile, with changes of $2 to $4 or more in most recent years. Cattle and hog prices are also much more variable than they were in the sixties. Under these conditions, selecting the best time to price your farm products can have a big impact on your returns. Only 20¢ per bushel more for corn, on a farm producing 30,000 bushels of corn per year, would mean an extra $6,000. And a dollar per hundredweight increase in the sale price of hogs would make a difference of about $4,500 on a two-thousand head per year operation.

Smaller U.S. and world grain stocks and a tighter supply/demand balance are part of the explanation for more volatile grain prices. We are in an international market where prices are highly sensitive to weather and crop conditions in this country and other major producing nations. Weather, too, has been somewhat more variable in the past decade, contributing to wider swings in world grain and oilseed production.

Greater volatility of livestock markets reflects some of the same influences as in grains. Feed is usually the most important and costly single input of livestock production. When feed prices were stable and predictable they were not a major factor in changes in livestock profitability. Now, volatile grain and oilseed markets are a major influence on changes in the profitability of livestock operations.

The less predictable commodity prices have also attracted greater participation in commodity futures markets—both by speculators and by hedgers seeking to reduce price uncertainty in their businesses. While this makes the futures markets potentially more useful to farmer-hedgers because of increased market volume, it may also add to the short-term price volatility in some commodities.

As a consequence of these changes, opportune timing of crop and livestock sales (or of pricing) can offer you a much greater payoff than was previously possible. The same is true on the purchase side with respect to feed needs and feeder livestock. But you must be increasingly well-informed about market supply and demand conditions. You must be able to use those cash and futures marketing systems that offer the greatest marketing efficiency and flexibility in a volatile and risky environment.

Marketing Choices

Some new or modified market alternatives which offer you more options have been developed in many commodity marketing systems. Through forward contracting, you can establish an exact or approximate market price for your product before a crop is planted, a pig is born, or cattle or hogs are put in the feedlot. Either you, the producer, or the buyer of grain or livestock can use the futures market to establish market price levels or offset price risk.

You can often sell direct to processors or handlers, negotiating the price or taking their bid price; or you can sell through marketing agencies such as auctions or terminal markets. You may elect to sell storable commodities at harvest or store them in your own or someone else's storage facility. So there can be a number of marketing options depending upon the commodities being produced.

With more factors influencing markets, developing accurate price forecasts is more difficult. You may have to do more forward pricing and accept prices that are profitable on part of your production when those prices are available—even when there's a possibility of higher prices later.

The amount of price risk an individual can realistically manage is now an important part of the marketing picture. Financial condition and cash-flow needs of individual farmers must be considered by each farmer in deciding a marketing strategy. An established farmer with large assets can reasonably follow marketing strategies that are higher risk than can one with more limited net worth. Many farmers have become more dependent upon purchased inputs and outside sources of capital as they've entered into or expanded a farming operation. The resulting large debt repayments required each year make them more susceptible to bad crops, death losses in livestock, or poor commodity marketing decisions.

In the sections which follow, several commodity marketing specialists will discuss the marketing alternatives available to producers of the most important livestock and crops.

Certainly, this is not all you need to know about marketing. However, you can benefit by knowing what some of these new marketing approaches are, whether they might adapt to your situation, and how they might eliminate some undesirable risks or enhance long term profitability for you.

The Changing Market Challenge 5

Figure 1-1. Annual Price Variation on Grains.

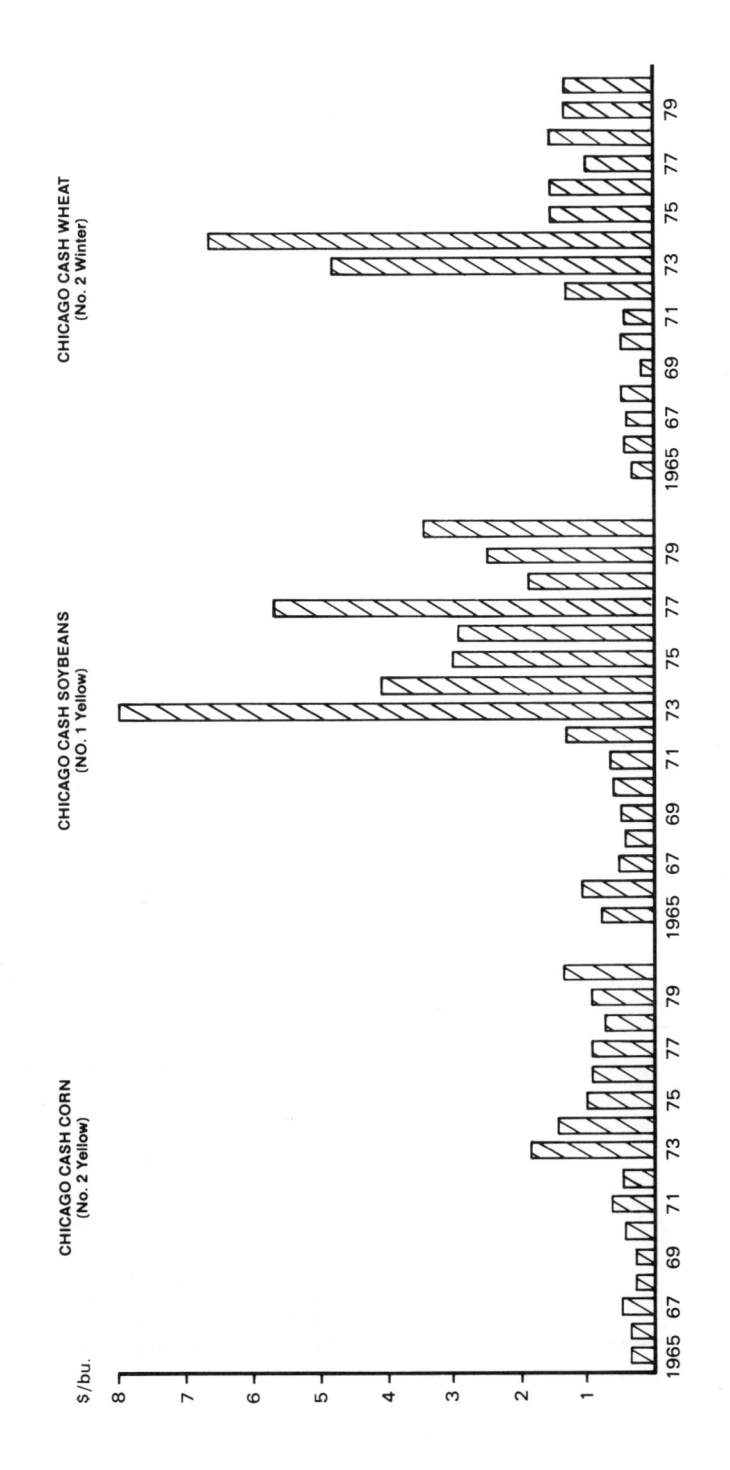

Figure 1-2. Annual Price Variation on Hogs and Cattle.

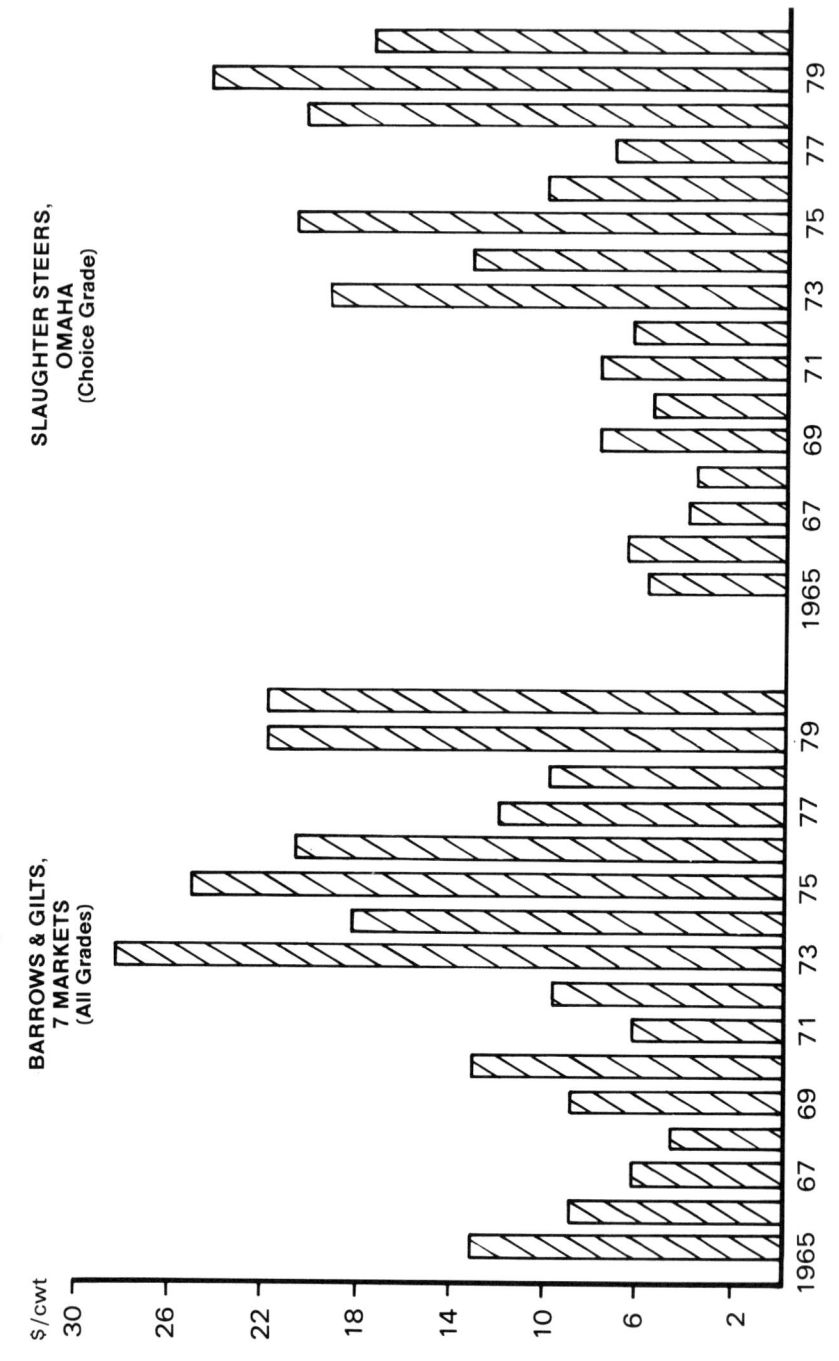

CHAPTER **2**

The Grain Marketing System

In recent years the U.S. grain marketing system has grown more complex. New uses for grain in the production of alcohol and other industrial products are taking an increasing share of production each year. More grain is going to foreign buyers. Understanding the system has become more difficult.

On the input supply side, inflation has been severe. Fuel, fertilizer, seed and machinery prices have increased at or above the general rate of inflation. This is likely to continue because of the concentrated structure of the input supply industries. At the same time, grain prices are subject to volatile stress of world supply and demand. Price can move higher or lower in very brief time frames—and input costs have no direct bearing on short-term market fluctuations.

It's important for you to understand your role in the overall system. Many of the important factors shaping your prices and profits occur in other parts of the system. This chapter describes the U.S. grain marketing system. It will provide you with the background you need to see how you fit into the overall picture.

Grain Production Characteristics

Grain is generally produced in an annual production cycle. One of the grain marketing system's fundamental problems is the need to allocate the grain inventory over the entire consumption year.

A second characteristic that is important to the marketing system is the land-extensive nature of grain production. It takes large amounts of land to produce grain. Thus, grain is produced over a wide geographic area. As a result of growing export markets and a decline in livestock production in parts of the Corn Belt, an increasing share of grain is consumed some distance from where it is produced. Grain must be moved from the widely dispersed production areas to widely dispersed users at home and abroad.

The Demand For U.S. Grain

The demand for most grain products is derived from their value as a food for either livestock (corn, oats, sorghum, soybean meal and barley) or people (wheat, rice, soybeans, and sunflowers). In addition to food uses, grains provide many industrial products such as oils and starches. In recent years grains are being looked to as a source of fuel through the conversion of starch into alcohol. Figures 2-1 through 2-3 indicate the most important uses for our major grain crops.

The most important development in the grain marketing system in recent years is the growth in exports. With this growth have come major changes in several parts of the grain marketing system including pricing, transportation, and grading. Figure 2-4 indicates the importance of exports as a share of domestic production. Exports have accounted for more than half of U.S. production of wheat and soybeans in most years. In coarse grains (corn, sorghum, barley), exports have grown in importance from about 10% of domestic production in the early 1970's to nearly 30% in recent years.

International markets are more important in determining U.S. grain prices than they were a few years ago. We now must be aware of the developments in other producing and consuming nations as we try to forecast price movements. The international market system compounds the problem of getting accurate information many times over.

Export growth has elevated the importance of grain to our national economy. As our balance of payments deficit grew in the early 1970's, grain became an important source of earnings to offset the deficit. In addition, we have become the world's major source of grain imports. Thus, we can expect that grain will continue to be viewed as an important element in the development of trade and strategic policies in the next decade.

The Grain Marketing System

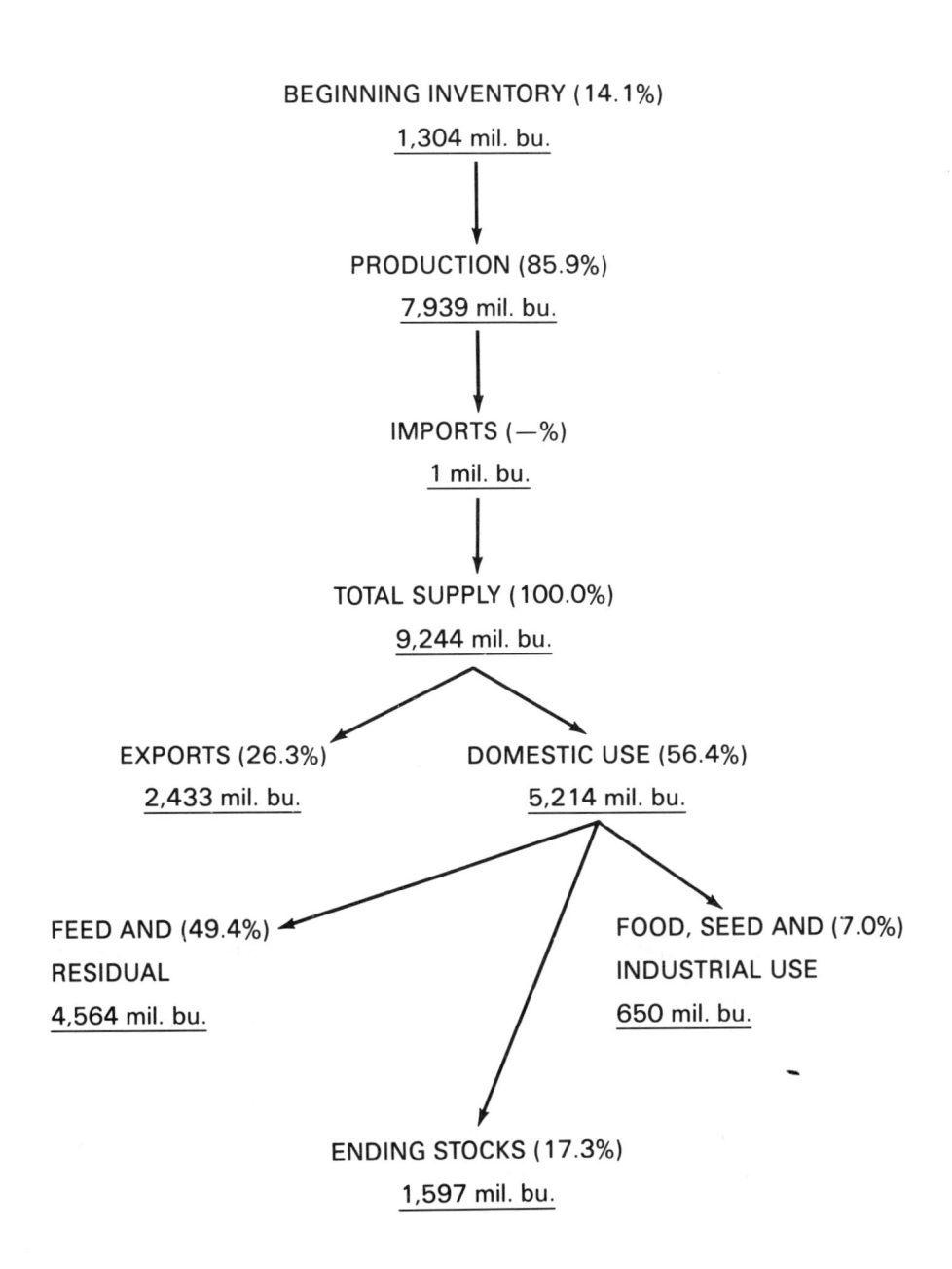

Figure 2-1. Major Supply and Use Categories for Corn, Oct. 1, 1978-Sept. 30, 1980. (Share of Total Supply Shown in Parentheses.)

BEGINNING INVENTORY (14.1%)

1,304 mil. bu.

↓

PRODUCTION (85.9%)

7,939 mil. bu.

↓

IMPORTS (—%)

1 mil. bu.

↓

TOTAL SUPPLY (100.0%)

9,244 mil. bu.

EXPORTS (26.3%)   DOMESTIC USE (56.4%)

2,433 mil. bu.   5,214 mil. bu.

FEED AND (49.4%)   FOOD, SEED AND (7.0%)
RESIDUAL   INDUSTRIAL USE
4,564 mil. bu.   650 mil. bu.

ENDING STOCKS (17.3%)

1,597 mil. bu.

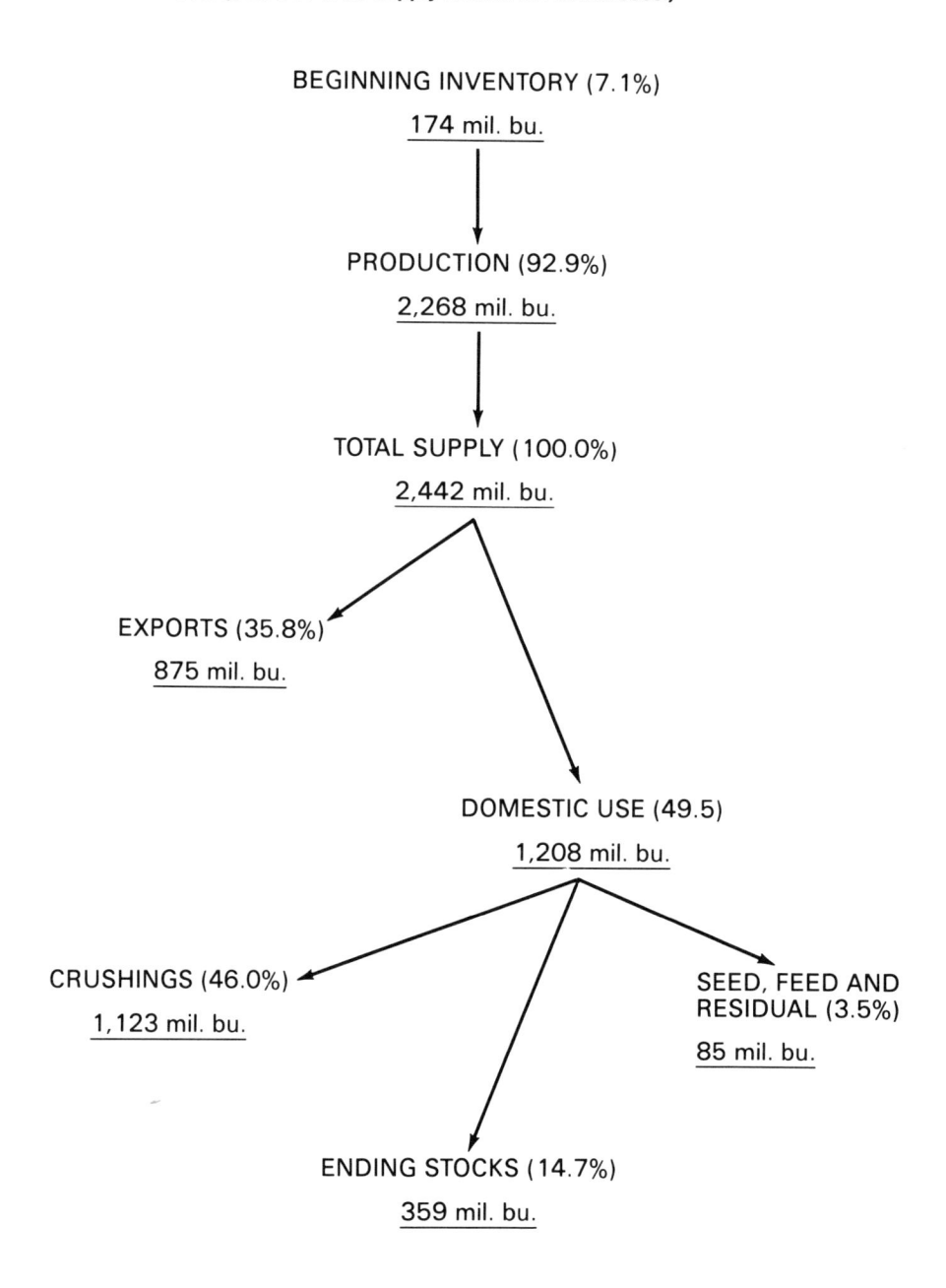

Figure 2-2. Major Supply and Use Categories for Soybeans, Sept. 1, 1979-August 31, 1980. (Share of Total Supply Shown in Parentheses.)

BEGINNING INVENTORY (7.1%)
174 mil. bu.

PRODUCTION (92.9%)
2,268 mil. bu.

TOTAL SUPPLY (100.0%)
2,442 mil. bu.

EXPORTS (35.8%)
875 mil. bu.

DOMESTIC USE (49.5)
1,208 mil. bu.

CRUSHINGS (46.0%)
1,123 mil. bu.

SEED, FEED AND RESIDUAL (3.5%)
85 mil. bu.

ENDING STOCKS (14.7%)
359 mil. bu.

The Grain Marketing System

Figure 2-3. Major Supply and Use Categories for Wheat, June 1, 1979-May 31, 1980. (Share of Total Supply Shown in Parentheses.)

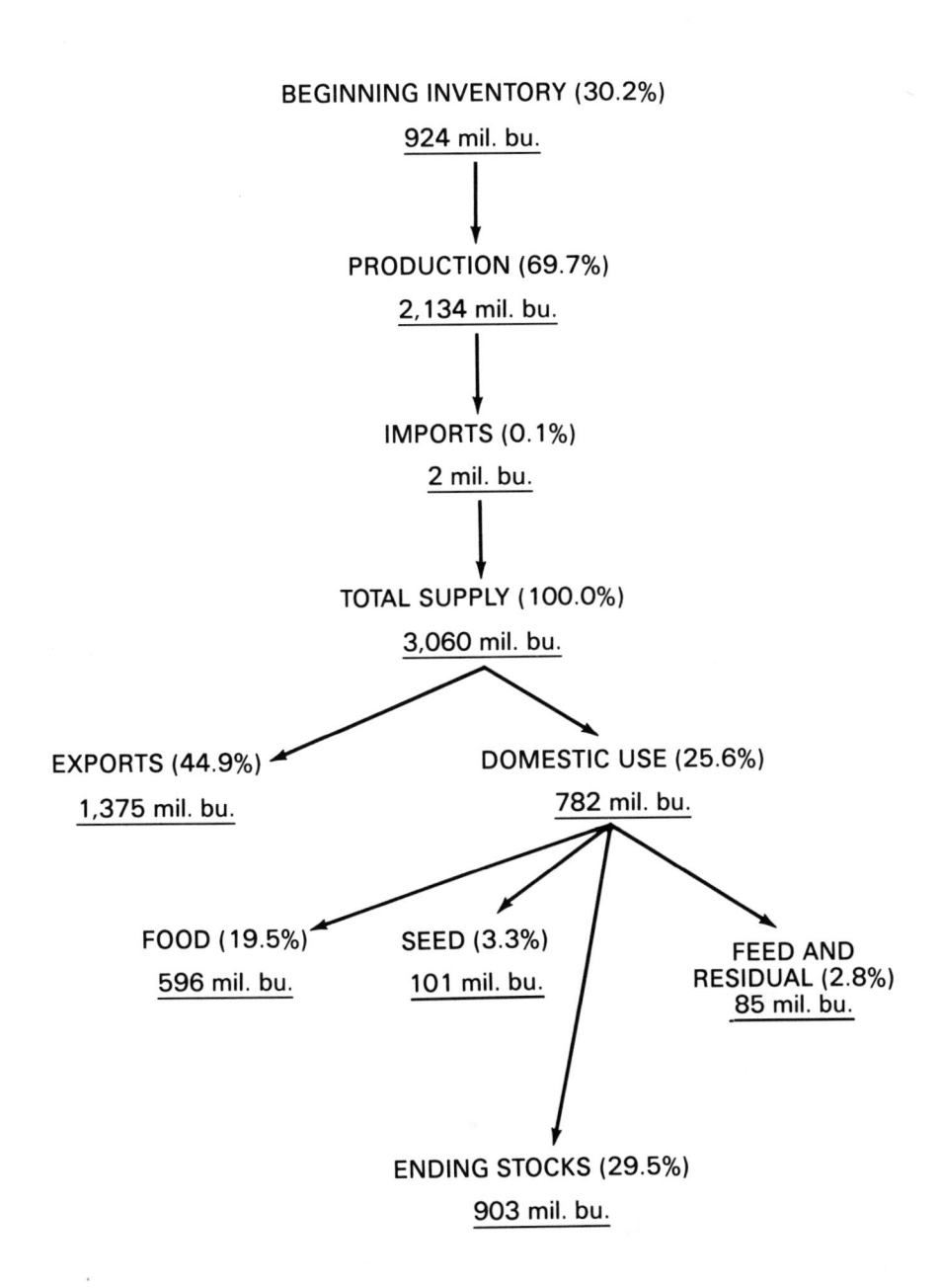

BEGINNING INVENTORY (30.2%)
924 mil. bu.
↓
PRODUCTION (69.7%)
2,134 mil. bu.
↓
IMPORTS (0.1%)
2 mil. bu.
↓
TOTAL SUPPLY (100.0%)
3,060 mil. bu.

EXPORTS (44.9%)
1,375 mil. bu.

DOMESTIC USE (25.6%)
782 mil. bu.

FOOD (19.5%)
596 mil. bu.

SEED (3.3%)
101 mil. bu.

FEED AND RESIDUAL (2.8%)
85 mil. bu.

ENDING STOCKS (29.5%)
903 mil. bu.

GRAIN MARKETING CHANNELS

Our major grain crops follow similar patterns in their movement from farms to ultimate consumers. As we pointed out earlier, grains are produced annually while grain consumption occurs more or less evenly over time. This means that a major market activity is storage. The first step in the marketing channel is the movement from field to storage.

Local elevators—Most of our grain crop moves from storage to a local elevator for grading, sorting and, in some cases, further storage. The local elevator concentrates the grain from many farms. In the process grain is sorted and blended into uniform grade lots, then dried and conditioned as required before shipment. The local elevator is generally the first pricing point. It sells and arranges for shipment of grain to terminal elevators, processors, farmers and other users. In areas where livestock are produced the local elevator may also process grain into formulated mixed feeds.

Subterminal elevators—Shipment of grain from local elevators to subterminal elevators generally occurs by truck or rail. In areas such as the Wheat Belt where local elevators are dispersed over long distances, rail is the predominant transport mode. In the Corn Belt, where production is denser and local elevators are smaller and more closely grouped, trucks play a bigger role. In either case, it is important to note that transportation is a major part of the cost of linking subterminals to local elevators. In general, the subterminal elevator concentrates grain into larger lots for further shipment by rail, barge or ship. Storage is usually only an incidental aspect of the subterminal elevator operation. The emphasis here is on having sufficient storage to temporarily hold grain until a sufficient quantity is available for further shipment. Many subterminal elevators purchase no grain from farmers and often only have receiving facilities for rail or other large volume shipment modes.

Terminal elevators—Inland terminal elevators look mainly to processing and export markets as outlets for their grain. Shipments from inland terminals usually move by rail or water into export and processing markets. A recent Minnesota study showed that about 37% of the inland terminals are owned by exporting companies. Multiple region terminal elevator companies operated 14% of the inland terminal elevators and single region terminal companies operated the remaining 49% of the companies.

Export terminal elevators—While Gulf of Mexico ports receive the major attention in discussions of grain exports, East Coast, Great Lakes and Pacific Coast ports are also important. Export terminals differ somewhat in their activity. This is especially true for the Great Lakes ports, where the severe winter closes the St. Lawrence Seaway for about three months each year. Great Lakes port elevators are used for storage during the winter when the St. Lawrence Seaway is closed. In the other major ports, especially the Gulf ports, terminal facilities function as transfer points for grain to export vessels. The Gulf Coast ports have the most modern facilities with the highest utilization rates.

In 1976 about 54% of port elevator capacity was owned by what were then the "big five" exporters (Cargill, Continental, Bunge, Louis Dreyfus, and Cook). Flour millers owned about 6.5% of port elevator capacity. Farmer Cooperatives owned just under 15%. About 7.5% of capacity was owned by public elevators and the remaining 20.5% was accounted for by independent elevator and warehouse companies. While the popular press refers to "government grain deals," the international grain companies handle the actual sales and shipping arrangements for international transactions. The companies are usually closely-held corporations or private companies which operate in many foreign markets. While there has been some growth in recent years in farmer cooperative participation in the export markets, private companies continue to account for nearly 80% of export sales.

GRAIN PRICING

The physical grain distribution system is paralleled by a pricing system which transfers title to the grain and establishes values at various levels. The pricing system also serves to provide incentives for the movement of grain into different uses and toward different geographic regions.

A central feature of the pricing system for grain in the United States is the commodity futures markets. These markets act as central barometers of grain values. They also serve to focus and widely distribute information on grain prices and changing domestic and international supply and demand conditions.

Figure 2-4. U.S. Exports: Share of Domestic Production and World Trade.

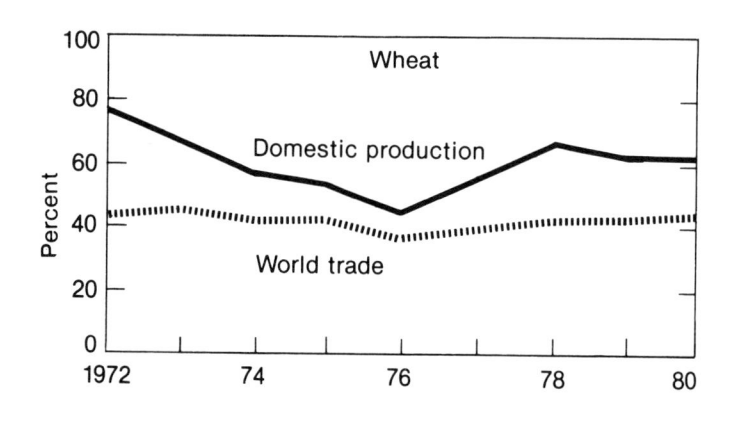

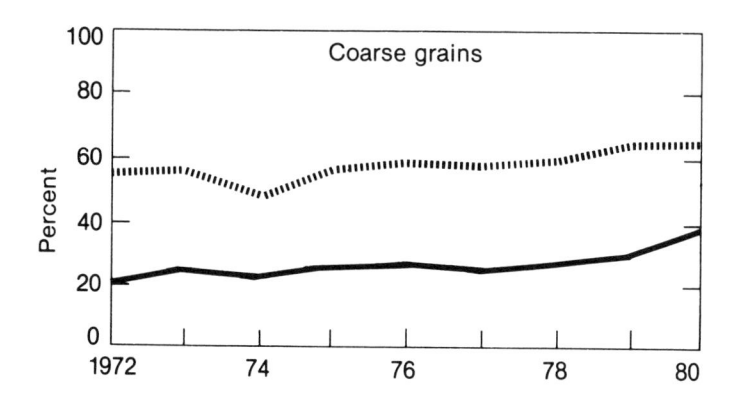

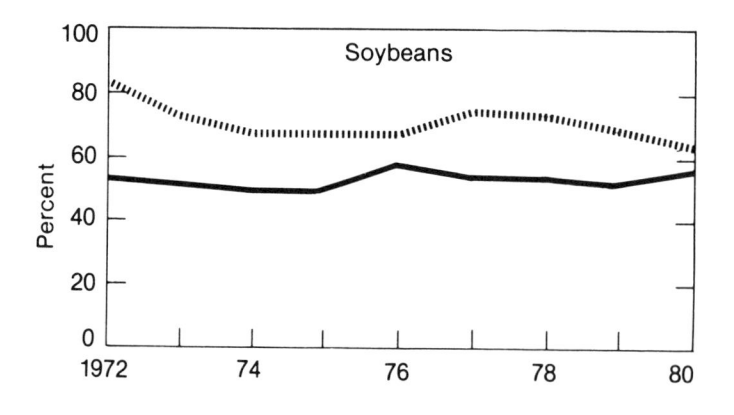

Prices at the subterminal and local elevator level are generally developed from the base established in futures markets. Local prices reflect differences associated with transportation costs, quality, holding costs, local supply and demand conditions and the extent of competition in the local market.

The overall level of grain prices is also influenced by government programs. In recent years the USDA food and feedgrain programs have used a target price concept. This price is a minimum net price to be received by producers who participate in the program. The programs also established a loan rate, the maximum value that can be loaned to producers using their grain as collateral. Under these programs participating producers receive deficiency payments whenever the average market price is below the target price. The volume of grain on which deficiency payments can be received is limited by the determination of the producer's normal crop acreage. During the 1970's, deficiency payments were seldom necessary since the average market price was generally above the target price level.

The farmer-held reserve program has also influenced prices since the late 1970's. This program allowed producers to contractually commit grain to a three year storage program. The reserve program was designed to isolate supplies from the market and build a strategic reserve of grain for years of short supply. Producers who participate in the reserve program are paid an annual storage payment and are eligible to obtain long term loans at favorable interest rates. The reserve program establishes a minimum price at which grain can be sold from the reserve and the loans be repaid. The release price is a critical part of the price determination process. When market prices reach this level, traders watch closely in anticipation of additional grain entering the marketplace.

Perhaps the most controversial aspect of government involvement has been in the export sector. The USDA negotiated several international grain agreements during the 1970's and early 1980's. The agreement with the Soviet Union was the largest and most discussed of these bilateral agreements. The controversial element in these agreements concerns the tradeoff between export stability, increased exports, and reduced flexibility in export trade.

An embargo of grain shipments from the United States was decreed several times during the 1970's. In some cases these embargoes barred all shipments of particular grains. However, the 1980-81 embargo affected grain shipments only to the Soviet Union. It limited shipments above the minimum agreed to in the existing bilateral agreement with the Soviets. Generally embargoes at least temporarily lower grain prices in the United States, making them extremely unpopular with grain producers.

The growing share of U.S. grain going into export markets means that foreign policy, national security and domestic economic concerns will continue to provide signals which may trigger embargoes. As the grain marketing system has developed export markets, it has inherited the risk of political decisions both in Washington, D.C. and in foreign capitals.

The System in Perspective

The United States grain marketing system is highly complex. The prices you receive at your local elevator are affected by actions and events at all levels of the system. As you develop your marketing strategy for the current year and your long term production and marketing plans, you need to consider the potential system changes which will affect you. Transportation systems; new grain uses; export market developments; local, national, and international market competition; U.S. and foreign grain policy; and input supply developments are all important parts of your grain marketing environment.

The 1970's saw many changes in the grain system. The future will likely see additional changes. Critical factors on the horizon include more efficient transportation systems, further export market development, use of grain as an energy source, government programs to insure adequate grain supplies and deal with occasional surplus production, improved grading systems, high costs of holding grain inventories, and improved safety in grain handling at terminal and port elevators. You have a stake in the direction these changes take.

CHAPTER **3**

Determining Your Grain Marketing Objectives

Successful grain marketing is one of the most difficult and frustrating challenges facing farmers. Gone are the days when markets were relatively stable and the penalty for poor marketing amounted to only a few cents a bushel. You are now faced with roller-coaster markets whose underlying impetus can completely change in a short time. Forces that drive markets upward can quickly disappear, resulting in rapidly falling prices. The market remains at the lower level until the next force comes to break the calm.

Widely fluctuating markets have provided substantial returns for the astute marketer. These same markets have led to dismal returns for others. Those who are disappointed try their luck again, however, because there's no other choice. Marketing is an indispensible part of the farm business and must be dealt with daily.

OBJECTIVES

The first step toward good marketing is to determine what you want from your marketing program. Indecision about marketing objectives often leads to failure. Some objectives commonly considered to be important by many producers are presented below.

Sell at highest price of the year is a common objective of many grain producers. All energies are focused on whether the present price is the high or if the price will go higher.

Attempting to sell at the high price of the year tends to be self-defeating. Regardless of the price level, there will be optimistic farmers and market analysts predicting even higher prices. Consequently, the high price of the year may be passed by in anticipation of even higher prices.

The goal of selling at the high price of the year may also be rather unrealistic. Trying to predict future price movements is difficult at best. As a result, the goal of selling at the high price often leads to failure. This sense of failure can be both economic and personal.

Sell above the average price is a much more achievable goal than selling at the high for the year. Inherent in this goal are the assumptions that much of what happens in the market is beyond our control and that our ability to predict future price movements is poor at best. Selling at a price above the average may seem like a rather easy goal for the aggressive marketer, but for others it is not. The goal is not realistic for the producer who consistently sells at prices below the average.

Bear in mind that selling at a price above the average will not guarantee a profit. It is possible for prices during most of the year to be below the price needed to cover costs. Consequently, selling at a price above the average may not be a suitable goal in some situations.

Net selling price above average price as a goal takes into account the costs associated with holding grain past harvest. These are the cost of storing grain and the interest on the money invested in stored grain.

This goal involves attempting to sell when the net price (selling price minus storage and interest costs) is above the average price for the year. The longer grain is stored, the larger these costs become. As a consequence, the longer grain is stored after harvest, the greater the difference between selling price and net price.

Selling above the mid-point involves attempting to sell at prices above the mid-point between the high and the low prices of the year.

The mid-point price is often above the average price. This can be shown in a hypothetical example of grain price movement in Figure 3-1. When price approaches a high point, it often moves rapidly to a peak and then abruptly turns downward. When price approaches a low point, it gradually recedes until the low point is reached then slowly begins to rise. The price pattern appears similar to a mountain range with steep, pointed peaks and broad, flat valleys. The average price is below the mid-point price because price levels during much of the year are closer to the low point than the high point.

Making a profit is a goal of every farmer. Looking at potential profit levels shifts attention away from the market and toward the farm business. Typically, farmers spend a disproportionately large amount of time looking at market conditions and a small amount of time analyzing the effect that changing market conditions have on the farm business.

Figure 3-1. Grain Price Patterns.

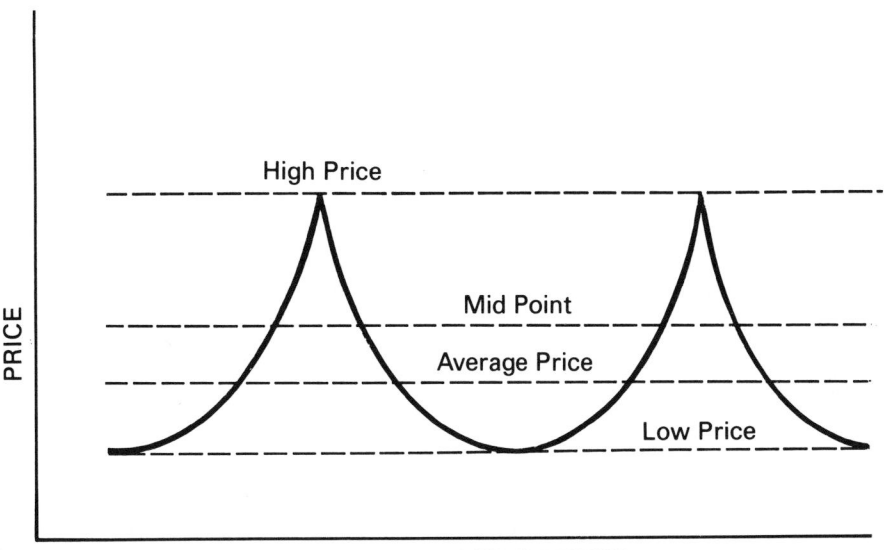

You should calculate potential profit levels from various sale prices. If you don't, selling at a seemingly good grain price may actually result in a loss. This is especially important for farmers with highly leveraged businesses who have large debt payments. It is also important when cost levels per bushel are high because of poor yields.

For others, calculating profit levels may be less important. Price may be above the level needed to cover costs during the entire marketing period. This is especially true for high equity farmers who consistently achieve high yields. They have relatively low cost break-even price levels.

Most farmers have not been satisfied with simply making a profit, but try to make the largest profit possible. The goal of maximizing profits often pays large dividends when producing the crop. But, when the crop is marketed, this goal becomes one of selling at the high price. As mentioned earlier, strict adherence to a goal of selling at the high price of the year is often not feasible in an uncertain market environment.

Cash-flow needs of the business are important marketing considerations. Having sufficient cash to cover upcoming expenses and payments is sound financial management. But, selling to meet cash-flow needs is marketing by default. It's simply selling grain when payments are due and is nothing more than hauling grain to the elevator and getting paid. This approach may occur because the producer is not willing to take the time to project his cash-flow in advance.

Although cash-flow needs of the business should not dominate your marketing program, they cannot be ignored. Grain sales need not occur immediately prior to the due date; they can be at any time from the beginning of the marketing period to the time of payment.

Minimizing risk requires foresight. In recent years, volatile markets have produced large dividends from selling toward the top of the market. They have also resulted in substantial losses when grain has to be sold toward the bottom. Price risk is of special concern to farmers who are highly leveraged financially.

Much of the success of modern farmers is their ability to manage risk. In marketing, managing risks essentially means not losing sight of the financial consequences of a grain sale. Possibly more important, it means not losing sight of the potential financial consequences of not selling grain.

Obviously, a successful marketing program embodies more than one of the goals listed above. In fact, it may involve several. You must develop the proper mix of goals to suit your situation. After goals have been determined, a marketing plan can be developed to achieve the goals.

MARKETING PLANS

Farmers are generally good planners in the production aspects of raising a crop. They develop weed control, fertilizer, and tillage programs and coordinate these with their financial resources into a comprehensive production plan. They may modify plans because of changing conditions such as an abnormally wet spring or an unexpected pest problem.

The approach many farmers take to marketing is quite different. Planning is either oversimplified or non-existent. Often the marketing plan is to simply put the grain in storage and see what happens. After several months, a portion may be sold to meet cash-flow payments. The rest is either abruptly sold because someone said the market was going down, or held into the following summer. If market price has not risen during the year, the grain is finally sold because storage facilities must be emptied to make room for the new crop.

A carefully implemented production plan has been followed by a poorly developed marketing plan.

A marketing plan is one of when to price grain. Grain can be priced before, during or after harvest (Figure 3-2). The planning horizon for pricing a grain crop ranges from well before harvest until almost a year after harvest. It covers almost two years. The planning period begins with the start of trading of the first futures contract for delivery of grain in the new crop year. The period ends when the grain must be removed from storage to make room for the harvest of a new crop. Some farmers have sufficient storage facilities to store more than one year's crop and thus extend the planning period even further.

Figure 3-2. Grain Pricing Planning Horizon.

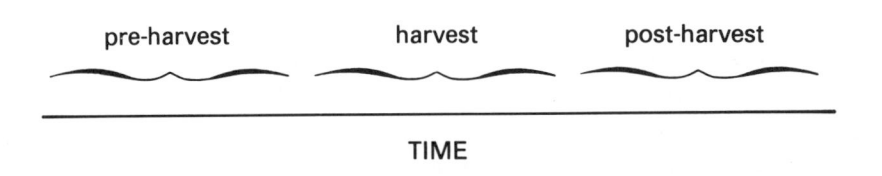

So during this period, you must make the decision of when to price your grain—before, during or after harvest. The plan may involve pricing during only one of these periods or all three.

Pre-harvest pricing is becoming more popular with producers. Grain is priced with either a hedge or an elevator contract.

Pricing a crop that has not been produced involves a certain amount of risk. Weather vagaries may severely reduce yields, so that the amount of grain produced may be less than the amount priced. Factors to consider in determining susceptibility to production risk include the possibility of drouth, hail or early frost. You can guard against these risks with crop insurance and by selling only a portion of the potential crop until yield prospects are firm.

Harvest pricing has decreased in importance among grain farmers, but a large amount of grain is still priced during this period. Either farm storage facilities do not exist or elevator storage is filled to capacity. Harvest pricing is usually accomplished by a cash sale, although it may also involve more complex marketing tools such as a hedge or an elevator contract.

Post-harvest pricing. After harvest is the most common period for pricing grain. Post-harvest pricing can occur relatively soon after harvest or eight to ten months or more later.

Grain may be priced once during the period or several times. For example, the post-harvest period may be divided into quarters and one-fourth of the grain priced each quarter; or the year can be divided into ten or more periods with grain priced monthly.

Several marketing tools can be used to price grain after harvest. The most common method is simply to store the grain and price it with a cash sale. The futures market or elevator contracts are also used.

DEVELOPING A MARKETING PLAN

Four major factors are important in developing a viable marketing plan. First, you must consider your personal feelings and attitudes about marketing. Next, the financial needs of the business must be taken into account. Seasonal price patterns are another factor. Finally, the price outlook is an important consideration.

The first three factors usually do not change substantially during the marketing period. But, the price outlook is likely to change frequently during the pricing period. A poor crop or a bumper crop somewhere in the world, for example, may change the supply situation dramatically, making it advisable to modify the marketing plan. However, the basic plan, although modified, should be adhered to throughout the pricing period.

Personal Considerations

Marketing is far from an exact science. The market is filled with information, including some that is ambiguous at times and often conflicting. Markets react to rumors only to have these rumors dispelled. World governments change their trade policies abruptly and often without warning.

Much of your success in marketing depends on your ability to effectively function in this uncertain climate. Specific decisions must be made with vague and conflicting information. You must carefully weigh the factors and information involved in making the decision. If you are not aware of your feelings and attitudes toward marketing, they can tip the decision-making scale and result in wrong decisions.

Speculator vs. businessman. You must determine if your attitudes toward marketing are similar to those of a speculator or a businessman. The word "speculator" conjures up images of a wheeler-dealer standing in the pits of the Chicago Board of Trade, rapidly buying and selling futures contracts in hope of making a fast profit. The word businessman brings to mind the image of a person whose energies are directed toward the survival and growth of a business. In agriculture we generally think of the farmer as being a businessman.

Forget these stereotypes. The Board of Trade is filled with businessmen whose primary purpose is the long-term profitability of their companies. Conversely, the rural areas are filled with speculating farmers whose primary purpose is to make a fast dollar by hitting the high of the market. The farmer is usually speculating with stored grain instead of futures contracts.

Second, speculating is not necessarily bad, so long as the speculator knows the consequences of his actions and is in control of his emotions. Speculating becomes a danger when he begins to lose rational control over his activities or does not thoroughly understand the consequences of his actions.

The third notion to dissipate is that everyone is either a speculator or a businessman. Most people are a combination. For example, many speculators (at least those that survive) will, at some point, take their profits instead of trying for even higher profits. Conversely, most businessmen will take a look at potential future price movements before deciding whether or not to price grain.

The following statements may help you to determine whether you are a speculator or a businessman. Read through them and find the ones that represent you.

Speculator	Businessman
—major goal is selling at the high price of the year	—major goal is making a profit
—focuses attention on day-to-day price movements	—focuses attention on survival and growth of the business
—calculates how much money he lost by not selling at the high price	—calculates what price he needs to cover costs
—planning horizon is short term profits	—planning horizon is long term growth of the business
—looks upon marketing as separate from the business	—integrates marketing as a part of the business
—is often heard saying, "When I sell the price goes up, if I don't sell the price goes down."	—is often heard saying, "I sold at a profitable level."

Emotion control. The Achilles' heel of many producers in their marketing decisions is their inability to control emotions. At any price level, some market information will indicate a price rise while other information will indicate a price decline. Strong emotional feelings may tip the decision making scale one way while logic may indicate the opposite action.

Figure 3-3. Fear and Greed Marketing.

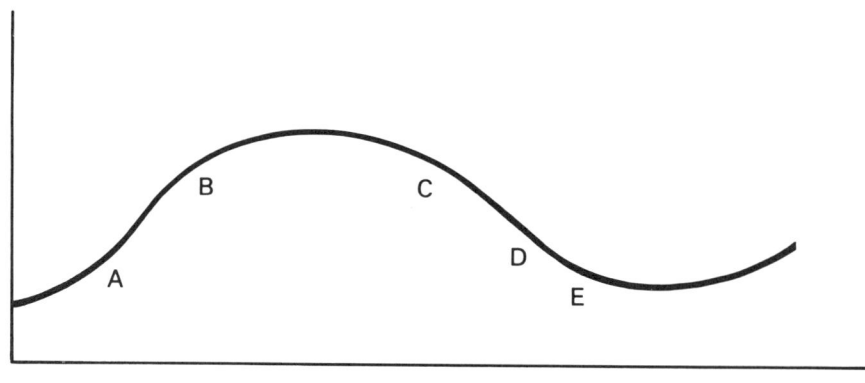

The two most common emotions in marketing grain are fear and greed. Greed carries with it confidence in a price rise. Fear reflects feelings of a price drop. Consequently, greed often results in holding grain for later sale while fear results in selling now. Unfortunately, greed often occurs when prices are high and rising and fear tends to occur when prices are low and falling.

A diagrammatical example of how fear and greed can dictate a marketing program is shown in Figure 3-3. The curved line represents the price trend over a period of time. Obviously, we don't know when the price will rise or how high it will rise. Also, we do not know when the price will fall or how far it will fall. But we do know that over time the price will rise and fall.

At point "A" price is rising and greed is the dominant emotion; it tells us to hold for higher prices. The statement often heard at this point is, "Why sell when price is going higher?" Greed becomes stronger at point "B" and there's a greater urge to hold for higher prices. The producer feels the "sky is the limit" on potential price rises. The first crack in the producer's confidence appears at point "C," but greed is still dominant. He considers the decline as a "temporary setback" and that "price will turn around." At point "D" fear grows stronger and greed begins to wane, with the realization that a good pricing opportunity has been missed. Fear completely dominates at point "E" and no remnants of greed remain. The disillusioned producer decides to sell before he takes a "real beating." And often this happens just before price begins to rise again.

Financial Conditions

Three financial considerations are important as you develop a marketing plan. They are the price needed to cover cash expenditures, the price needed to maintain net worth, and the risk-bearing ability of your business.

Risk bearing ability. The yardstick indicating the financial ability to bear risk is the net worth statement. This statement is a complete financial inventory of the business. A comprehensive listing of the value of all the assets makes up a large portion of the net worth statement. Assets on a cash-grain operation include cash on hand, stored grain, machinery, land, etc. The net worth statement of a typical 400 acre cash-grain farm is presented in Table 3-1.

Another portion of the net worth statement is a listing of financial liabilities. Liabilities are financial claims against the assets of the business. A typical liability of a cash-grain farm may include a long term mortgage and note used to purchase a parcel of land. The outstanding debt on land in Table 3-1 is about $270,000.

The last part of a net worth statement is the net worth. It is commonly computed by subtracting liabilities from assets. Net worth, by definition, is your claim against the assets of the business. It is a residual claim after all other claims (liabilities) have been satisfied.

The debt to asset ratio is an important indicator of risk-bearing ability. The ratio is computed by dividing total liabilities by total

Table 3-1.

NET WORTH STATEMENT

ASSETS			LIABILITIES	
Current			**Current**	
Cash	$	15,000	Machinery payment	$ 10,800
Corn		81,600	Land payment	35,000
Soybeans		51,800	Land rent	11,500
			Land taxes	3,600
			Income & SS taxes	2,150
Total	$	148,400	Total	$ 63,050
Intermediate			**Intermediate**	
Machinery	$	70,000	Machinery loan	$ 24,000
Long Term			**Long Term**	
Land	$	840,000	Land	$271,138
TOTAL ASSETS		$1,058,400	TOTAL LIABILITIES	$358,188
NET WORTH $700,212			DEBT TO ASSET RATIO	.34

assets. It provides an indication of the portion of the assets required to satisfy the liabilities. The ratio of .34 shown in Table 3-1 indicates that 34% of the assets are needed to satisfy claims of the creditors. The remaining portion (66%) is the farmer's claim (Net Worth).

The larger the portion of the business belonging to the farmer, the greater the financial ability to bear risk. The claims of creditors (liabilities) have the first claim against business assets. Consequently, in the event of a financial loss (decline in assets), the farmer's net worth bears the burden. If net worth is large, a substantial loss can be absorbed without bankrupting the business. If net worth is small, a major loss cannot be absorbed without jeopardizing the claims of the creditors.

Determining Your Grain Marketing Objectives 27

Cash-flow breakeven. Another financial factor to consider in marketing is the grain price needed to cover cash expenditure. A positive cash-flow requires that enough cash must flow into the business from the sale of grain to meet cash expenditures. The grain price needed to cover cash expenditures is computed by dividing expenditures by the amount of grain produced.

The first type of cash expenditure for most cash-grain operations is production expenses. These include seed, pesticides, fertilizer, insurance, fuel, repairs, etc. Production expenses for the 200 acres of corn in Table 3-2 are about $26,000. For 200 acres of soybeans the total is about $18,000. Assuming yields of 125 bushels per acre for corn and 38 bushels per acre for soybeans, the production expense is $1.05 per bushel for corn and $2.42 per bushel for soybeans.

Table 3-2.

PRICE NEEDED TO COVER CASH EXPENDITURES AND MAINTAIN NET WORTH.

		Corn		Soybeans	
Production expense:	Total	Per Acre	Per Bushel	Per Acre	Per Bushel
corn	$26,154	$130.77	$1.05	$	$
soybeans	18,364			91.82	2.42
Machinery payment	10,800	27.00	.22	27.00	.71
Land expenditure	50,100	125.25	1.00	125.25	3.30
Family living & taxes	17,150	42.88	.34	42.88	1.13
TOTAL (Cash expenditures)		$325.90	$2.61	$286.95	$7.56
Depreciation	12,000	30.00	.24	30.00	.79
Principal payment	(10,662)	(26.66)	(.21)	(26.66)	(.70)
TOTAL (Net worth)		$329.24	$2.64	$290.29	$7.65

Another cash expenditure is the annual payment on an intermediate machinery loan. The annual payment usually includes interest and a portion of the unpaid principal. The annual machinery loan payment in Table 3-2 is $10,800. This payment amounts to $.22 per bushel for corn and $.71 per bushel for soybeans.

The third type of cash expenditure includes any expenditure for the control of land. Land expenditures include cash rent payments, real estate taxes and payments on land indebtedness. For the 400 acre farm in Table 3-2, 200 acres are owned free of indebtedness, 100 acres are cash rented, and 100 acres were recently purchased with 100%

financing. The land expenditure includes cash rent on 100 acres, the principal and interest payment on the 100 acres recently purchased and real estate taxes on 300 acres. The total expenditure amounts to more than $50,000 annually. When spread evenly over all 400 acres the expenditure is $125.25 per acre or $1.00 per bushel for corn and $3.30 for soybeans.

The last cash expenditure incurred is for family living needs. The expenditure also includes income and self-employment taxes. This represents more than $17,000 for the cash-grain operation presented in Table 3-2.

Total cash expenditures are $325 per acre of corn; $287 per acre of soybeans. After dividing by yield, the per acre totals translate into cash expenditures per bushel of $2.61 for corn and $7.56 for soybeans. Consequently, the grain prices needed to cover cash expenditures are $2.61 for corn and $7.56 for soybeans.

If the farmer sells his grain at the price levels indicated above, cash in-flow will exactly meet cash out-flow. If the selling price exceeds these levels, cash in-flow will exceed cash out-flow. The excess can be used to increase cash reserves, retire existing debt, expand the operation or increase living expenditures. If the grain is sold at prices below these levels, cash out-flow will exceed cash in-flow. The cash deficit will be covered by reducing cash reserves, increasing indebtedness, decreasing family living expenditures or selling production assets.

The timing of the sale will have an effect on the cash-flow breakeven levels. If grain is sold after the cash payments are due, money will need to be borrowed to meet the payments and interest will accrue from the time the payment is made until the time the grain is sold. The accrued interest will raise the breakeven level. If grain is sold before the payment is due, the money can be invested and interest income accrued from the time the grain is sold until payment is due. The interest income will reduce the breakeven levels. Commercial storage charges may also affect the breakeven level.

Net worth breakeven. The grain price needed to maintain the farmer's net worth at its present level is the third financial factor. The net worth breakeven is computed in a manner similar to the cash-flow breakeven. Almost all of the cash expenditures indicated in the previous section decrease net worth. Consequently, income from the sale of grain must be large enough to cover these expenditures. The one exception is principal payments. Principal payments on loans decrease the amount of outstanding liability. Reduced liabilities increase net worth. As a result, income need not cover principal payments.

To maintain net worth, income must also be large enough to cover certain non-cash costs such as depreciation. Depreciation reduces the value of assets and consequently reduces net worth. Cash income must be large enough to compensate for this decline. The income needed to maintain the farmer's net worth must be large enough to cover all cash expenditures except principal payments plus the non-cash cost of depreciation.

For our purposes, assume land values remain constant and machinery and facilities values decrease by an amount equal to depreciation. As a result, the effect of inflation has been removed and the breakeven levels reflect the producer's earned net worth.

To compute the grain price needed to maintain net worth, we simply add depreciation and subtract principal payments from the cash-flow breakeven levels. Depreciation on machinery and equipment is $12,000 for the cash-grain farm in Table 3-2. Principal payments are $10,662. The corn price needed to maintain earned net worth is $2.64 compared to $2.61 for cash-flow requirements. The price needed for soybeans is $7.65 compared to $7.56 for cash flow.

If the farmer sells grain at prices above these breakeven levels, earned net worth will increase. Conversely, if grain is sold for less, earned net worth will decline.

Table 3-3.

NET WORTH STATEMENT

ASSETS			LIABILITIES	
Current			**Current**	
Cash	$ 15,000		Machinery payment	$ 10,800
Corn	81,600		Land taxes	4,800
Soybeans	51,800		Income & SS taxes	9,200
Total	$148,400			$ 24,800
Intermediate			**Intermediate**	
Machinery	$ 70,000		Machinery loan	$ 24,000
Long Term			**Long Term**	
Land	$1,120,000		Land	— —
TOTAL ASSETS	$1,338,400		TOTAL LIABILITIES	$ 48,800
NET WORTH $1,289,600			DEBT TO ASSET RATIO	.04

Cash flow and net worth price breakeven levels, including risk-bearing ability, vary greatly from farmer to farmer. The following three examples are similar to the one shown previously. All are 400 acre cash-grain operations with a corn/soybean rotation. The farms all have identical soil types, storage and drying facilities, and machinery and equipment lines. The farmers also have similar management skills and use the same amount and kind of production inputs. In fact, all four farmers have identical yields (125 bushels corn and 38 bushels soybeans).

The only major difference among the four farm situations is how the land resource is controlled. In the farm situation previously discussed, one-half of the land (200 acres) is owned free of indebtedness. Another 100 acre parcel is cash rented for $115 per acre. The remaining 100 acres were recently purchased for $2,800 per acre and all of the money was borrowed.

The following farm situation is identical except that all 400 acres are owned free of indebtedness. As indicated in Table 3-3, business assets are over a million dollars and only 4% of these assets are needed to satisfy creditors' claims. The grain prices needed to cover cash expenditures are $1.85 per bushel for corn and $5.04 for soybeans, as shown in Table 3-4. The grain prices needed to maintain earned net worth are $1.97 for corn and $5.44 for soybeans. In this situation, breakeven price levels are low and the financial ability to bear risk is good.

Table 3-4.

GRAIN PRICE NEEDED TO COVER CASH EXPENDITURES AND MAINTAIN NET WORTH.

		Corn		Soybeans	
Production expense:	Total	Per Acre	Per Bushel	Per Acre	Per Bushel
corn	$26,154	$130.77	$ 1.05		
soybeans	18,364			$ 91.82	$2.42
Machinery payment	10,800	27.00	.22	27.00	.71
Land expenditure	4,800	12.00	.10	12.00	.32
Family living & taxes	24,200	60.50	.48	60.50	1.59
TOTAL (Expenditures)		$230.27	$ 1.85	$191.32	$5.04
Depreciation	12,000	30.00	.24	30.00	.79
Principal payment	(6,000)	(15.00)	(.12)	(15.00)	(.39)
TOTAL (Net worth)		$245.27	$ 1.97	$206.32	$5.44

Determining Your Grain Marketing Objectives

The next situations (Tables 3-5 and 3-6) represent a cash-rented operation.

Table 3-5.

NET WORTH STATEMENT

ASSETS			LIABILITIES	
Current			**Current**	
Cash	$ 15,000		Machinery payment	$10,800
Corn	81,600		Land rent	46,000
Soybeans	51,800		Income & SS taxes	1,030
Total	$148,400		Total	$57,830
Intermediate			**Intermediate**	
Machinery	$ 70,000		Machinery loan	$24,000
Long Term			**Long Term**	
Land	— —		Land	— —
TOTAL ASSETS	$218,400		TOTAL LIABILITIES	$81,830
NET WORTH $136,570			DEBT TO ASSET RATIO	.37

Table 3-6.

GRAIN PRICE NEEDED TO COVER CASH EXPENDITURES AND MAINTAIN NET WORTH.

		Corn		Soybeans	
Production expense:	Total	Per Acre	Per Bushel	Per Acre	Per Bushel
corn	$26,154	$130.77	$ 1.05		
soybeans	18,364			$ 91.82	$2.42
Machinery payment	10,800	27.00	.22	27.00	.71
Land expenditure	46,000	115.00	.92	115.00	3.03
Family living & taxes	16,030	40.08	.32	40.08	1.06
TOTAL (Cash expenditures)		$312.85	$ 2.51	$273.90	$7.22
Depreciation	10,000	25.00	.20	25.00	.66
Principal payment	(6,000)	(15.00)	(.12)	(15.00)	(.39)
TOTAL (Net worth)		$322.85	$ 2.59	$283.90	$7.49

All 400 acres are rented for $115 per acre. Total assets amount to less than $220,000. Creditors' claims require 37% of the assets, leaving a net worth of about $136,000. The financial ability to bear risk is quite limited. Grain prices needed to cover cash expenditures and maintain net worth are similar to those needed in the first situation.

The last situation represents a farmer who owns all of his land. One-half (200 acres) is owned free of indebtedness. The other one-half was recently purchased for $2,800 per acre and required 100% financing. The total amount of business assets is over one million dollars as indicated in Table 3-7. However, half of the assets are required to satisfy creditors' claims. The farmer's equity is limited to the other half. The grain prices needed to cover cash expenditures are $3.07 for corn and $9.04 for soybeans as indicated in Table 3-8. The high breakeven levels are due to the large land payment. The net worth breakeven levels are $3.00 and $8.82 for corn and soybeans, respectively. These levels are lower than the cash-flow levels because the large principal payments on land and machinery indebtedness are not included.

Table 3-7.

NET WORTH STATEMENT

ASSETS		LIABILITIES	
Current		**Current**	
Cash	$ 15,000	Machinery payment	$ 10,800
Corn	81,600	Land payment	70,000
Soybeans	51,800	Land taxes	4,800
Total	$148,400	Total	$ 85,600
Intermediate		**Intermediate**	
Machinery	$ 70,000	Machinery loan	$ 24,000
Long Term		**Long Term**	
Land	$1,120,000	Land	$542,276
TOTAL ASSETS	$1,338,400	TOTAL LIABILITIES	$651,876
NET WORTH $686,524		DEBT TO ASSET RATIO	.49

As illustrated by the examples above, the financial situation can vary greatly from one farmer to the next. Consequently, it is imperative that you compute price breakeven levels for your situation. The procedure is relatively simple because you have all of the information readily available.

Knowing the price breakeven levels and risk-bearing ability of the business does not provide an automatic solution to your marketing problems. For producers with relatively high price breakeven levels, the market may not provide a profit regardless of when grain is priced during the year. For producers with low price breakeven levels, the market may provide a profit throughout the entire year. However, the price breakeven levels do indicate the financial consequences of a pricing decision—an important factor to consider.

Table 3-8.

GRAIN PRICE NEEDED TO COVER CASH EXPENDITURES AND MAINTAIN NET WORTH.

Production expense:	Total	Corn Per Acre	Corn Per Bushel	Soybeans Per Acre	Soybeans Per Bushel
corn	$26,154	$130.77	$ 1.05		
soybeans	18,364			$91.82	$2.42
Machinery payments	10,800	27.00	.22	27.00	.71
Land expenditures	74,800	187.00	1.50	187.00	4.92
Family living & taxes	15,000	37.50	.30	37.50	.99
TOTAL (Cash expenditures)		$382.27	$ 3.07	$343.32	$9.04
Depreciation	12,000	30.00	.24	30.00	.79
Principal payment	(15,324)	(38.31)	(.31)	(38.31)	(1.01)
TOTAL (Net worth)		$373.96	$ 3.00	$335.01	$8.82

Seasonal Price Patterns

Many commodity markets appear to reflect no discernible seasonal pattern. However, seasonal patterns often appear when several years of prices are combined to find an average.

Seasonal price patterns do not provide a definitive guide for pricing grain. These patterns are only one of several factors needed in developing a marketing plan. A discussion of seasonal price patterns for grains is included in Chapter 4.

Price Outlook

The outlook for future price movements is the fourth factor to consider in developing a marketing plan. Price outlook is probably the overriding force in shaping most marketing plans. However, its importance is frequently exaggerated.

Two approaches to analyzing future price movements have developed. The fundamental approach reflects the traditional supply and demand factors. The technical approach is synonymous with charting, moving averages and similar methods of predicting price movements. The fundamental approach is discussed in Chapter 7. Information on the technical approach is presented in Chapter 13.

MARKETING TOOLS

The marketing plans presented in the previous section are plans of when to price grain. Price can be established before, during or after harvest.

Grain marketing also involves decisions relative to delivering grain and receiving payment. These decisions, along with pricing decisions, can be implemented with the use of marketing tools. Marketing tools allow you to design the payment and delivery aspects of marketing to meet the financial needs of the business. For example, the time for receiving payment can be separated from the time of pricing to meet cash-flow needs or income tax objectives. The time of delivery can be separated from the time of pricing to take advantage of storage returns due to changing basis patterns.

Marketing tools range from physical tools such as storage facilities to intangible tools such as elevator contracts and futures markets. Some elevator contracts allow you to price your grain now but delay delivery and payment until later. These are commonly referred to as forward contracts.

Other elevator contracts allow you to deliver your grain but delay pricing until later. These are commonly referred to as deferred pricing contracts or basis contracts. A similar outcome can be achieved by selling grain and buying futures contracts for later sale. A more complete description of some of the elevator contracts used in marketing is presented in Chapter 5. Futures contracts and futures markets are discussed in Chapter 6.

Below are ways marketing tools are used to determine when grain is priced, when it is delivered and when payment is received.

Harvest Pricing

The most traditional marketing plan is harvest pricing and the most

Determining Your Grain Marketing Objectives

traditional marketing tool used to implement this plan is the cash sale. As indicated below, grain is priced at harvest, delivered at harvest, and payment is received at harvest.

	Pre-Harvest	**Harvest**	**Post-Harvest**
Pricing		X	
Delivery		X	
Payment		X	

Although grain is priced at harvest, delivery and payment can be deferred until after harvest as shown below. This is done with either a forward contract with an elevator or a hedge using the futures market.

	Pre-Harvest	**Harvest**	**Post-Harvest**
Pricing		X	
Delivery			X
Payment			X

Storage must be used in combination with these methods to hold the grain until delivery. Post-harvest delivery and payment are used when the market is providing a storage return due to a wide basis and money is not needed for cash-flow needs. It may also be used to defer income for tax purposes.

Post-Harvest Pricing

Other marketing plans involve pricing after harvest. Grain is priced after harvest with delivery and payment occurring at the same time. This is done by storing grain unpriced for a period after harvest and selling by means of a cash sale. Income is received for cash-flow needs when pricing occurs.

	Pre-Harvest	**Harvest**	**Post-Harvest**
Pricing			X
Delivery			X
Payment			X

Delivery and payment need not occur at the time of pricing. They can occur after pricing. Delaying delivery and payment is done with either a forward contract or a hedge. These tools are used when the market is providing a storage return due to a wide basis.

Grain can be delivered at harvest with pricing and payment occurring after harvest as shown below. The marketing tool used is either a deferred price contract with an elevator or a futures contract.

	Pre-Harvest	**Harvest**	**Post-Harvest**
Pricing			X
Delivery		X	
Payment		(X)	X

With a deferred price contract, grain is delivered at harvest but price is determined after harvest at your discretion. A partial payment may or may not be received at the time of pricing. When the futures market is used, grain is sold and delivered at harvest. Futures contracts are purchased at the time of the grain sale for approximately the same number of bushels. The futures contracts are later sold to establish price.

With these tools pricing can occur after harvest if storage facilities are not available. They also allow you to take advantage of a narrow basis while deferring pricing until later.

As an alternative, delivery can take place after harvest with pricing occurring even later. Grain is stored unpriced until the basis narrows.

Pre-Harvest Pricing

Pre-harvest pricing involves establishing the price for a crop that has not been produced. Delivery is made and payment received when the crop is harvested. The tool used in pre-harvest pricing is either a forward contract with an elevator or a hedge using the futures market.

	Pre-Harvest	**Harvest**	**Post-Harvest**
Pricing	X		
Delivery		X	(X)
Payment		X	(X)

A variation involves pre-harvest pricing with delivery and payment occurring after harvest. Marketing tools involved are either a forward contract or a hedge plus the use of storage. This approach is used to earn storage returns due to a wide basis or defer income for tax purposes.

So there are a number of pricing and marketing options that you can use. The grain marketing alternatives are outlined graphically in Figure 3-4.

Determining Your Grain Marketing Objectives 37

Figure 3-4. Grain Marketing Alternatives.

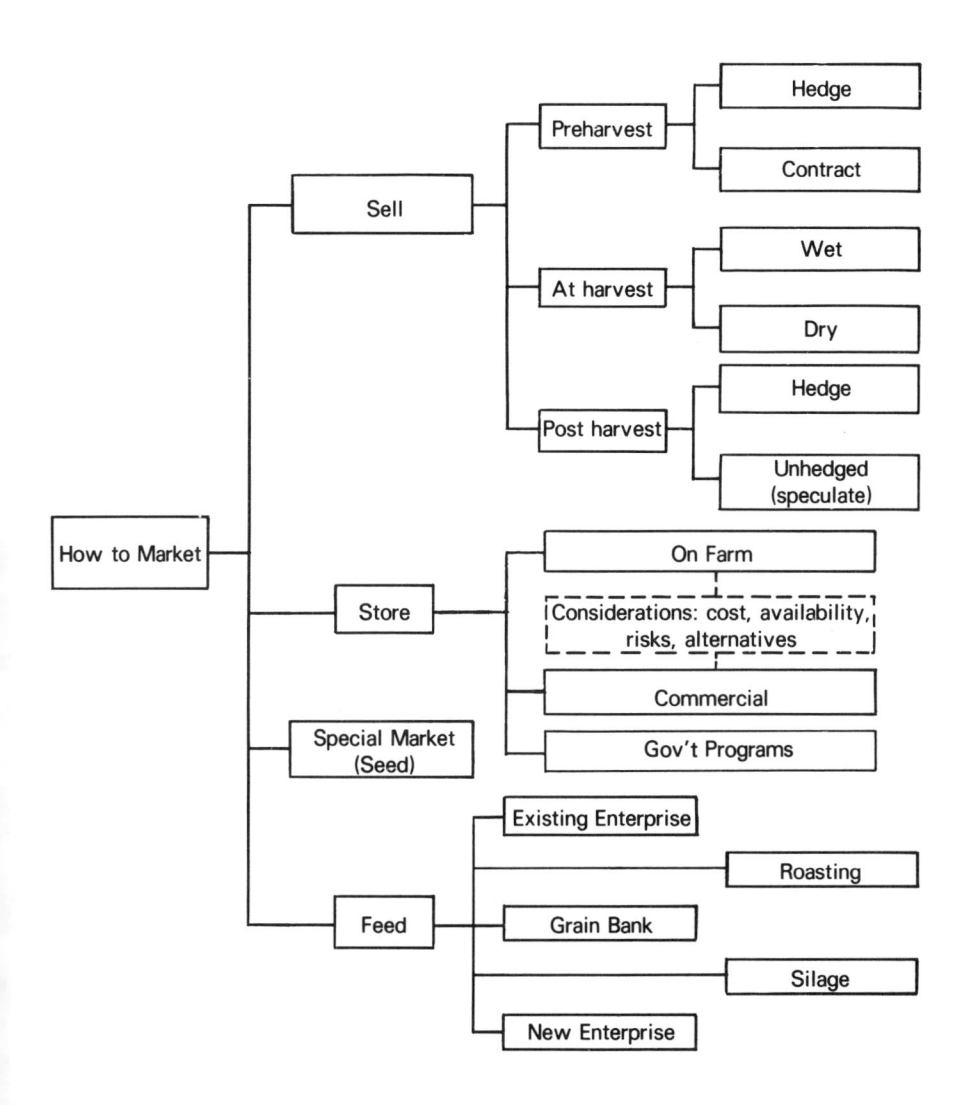

```
                                              ┌── Hedge
                              ┌── Preharvest ──┤
                              │                └── Contract
                              │
                              │                ┌── Wet
                  ┌── Sell ───┼── At harvest ──┤
                  │           │                └── Dry
                  │           │
                  │           │                ┌── Hedge
                  │           └── Post harvest ┤
                  │                            └── Unhedged
                  │                                (speculate)
                  │
                  │           ┌── On Farm
                  │           │   ┌─ Considerations: cost, availability, ─┐
                  │           │   │           risks, alternatives         │
How to Market ────┼── Store ──┤   └─────────────────────────────────────┘
                  │           ├── Commercial
                  │           │
                  │           └── Gov't Programs
                  │
                  ├── Special Market
                  │   (Seed)
                  │
                  │           ┌── Existing Enterprise
                  │           │
                  │           │                    ┌── Roasting
                  └── Feed ───┼── Grain Bank
                              │
                              │                    ┌── Silage
                              └── New Enterprise
```

CHAPTER **4**

Grain Storage as a Marketing Strategy

In 1973, changes in crop prices, moisture discounts, storage charges, interest rates and the basis at harvest time put a new light on consideration of storage of grain. Heavy demand relative to supplies changed the traditional situation of markets automatically moving to carrying charge levels to one in which the highest net price for a commodity may often occur at harvest, when crop supplies are tight relative to demand. This situation has endured, more or less, for the better part of a decade. It is not necessarily permanent, but it would take two back-to-back bumper world crops to turn it around.

Rate of return on investment, availability of commercial storage, and tenancy situation are factors which may change the situation from farm to farm. Still, farmers who store grain can earn money on their storage every year—even when grain prices decline. In some years they may decide to store grain without hedging. In other years, they may wish to hedge by selling futures contracts to offset grain in storage. When the basis (difference between the cash price and futures contract) narrows, the person storing grain earns a storage income.

As farmers gain experience in using the futures markets as a tool in their farm business, they can do selective hedging. An example would be to store corn unhedged until the price rises to an acceptable level or markets begin to top out, then hedge the stored corn by selling futures contracts if the basis is wide. In this case, they could guarantee a price within a few cents and continue to earn a return on storage.

There are, of course, advantages and disadvantages to on farm storage.

Advantages:
1. Avoids selling grain when basis is widest (at harvest).
2. Avoids waiting lines at elevator.
3. Physical life of storage structure normally is much longer than depreciation period.
4. Allows storage for all year at the same facility cost.
5. Allows quality control of grain for livestock feeding.
6. Increases the marketing period.
7. Allows management of income for tax purposes.
8. Allows control over harvesting operation.

Disadvantages:
1. Requires extra handling of grain.
2. Demands extra attention to marketing.
3. Danger of grain going out of condition, pilferage, etc.
4. Added investment and tax, whether facilities are used or idle.
5. Landlord must furnish all storage and receives benefit for only one-half of the storage.

The above lists are not exhaustive, but cover the major considerations for most people.

Drying and Conditioning Grain for Storage

The reason for drying and conditioning grain is to prevent damage from occurring during storage. Prevention is the key; drying and conditioning will have little or no effect once the damage has occurred. If you plan to store grain over the spring and summer months, and will not be maintaining a close check on the grain, then it's usually good advice to dry the grain to 13.5% to 14% moisture content. You may lose 5¢ due to overdrying, but this may save you 25¢ to 50¢ per bushel discount if the grain is allowed to go out of condition.

When corn is sold at harvest, there is usually no marketing incentive to dry, condition, or clean grain to a quality higher than necessary to meet No. 2 grade standards, and also, conditioning will result in fewer bushels to sell. Whether it pays to raise the grain to No. 2 by drying and conditioning before selling will depend upon the market discounts and the costs of conditioning the grain. This must be calculated for individual situations.

When you plan to store grain, it's an entirely different situation. The objective here is to maintain the grain quality during the storage period in order to avoid damage discounts. Drying corn below the maximum amounts of moisture allowed in the No. 2 grade and aeration to prevent damage from moisture migration are cases in point.

When storing corn or other grains for long periods, you should be concerned with the costs of drying and conditioning in comparison to the damage discounts avoided by doing so. You should not be concerned with the effect of drying and conditioning on the immediate market value of the grain. In deciding whether to sell corn at harvest, or dry and store, you will have to determine whether the seasonal price rise, or the change in basis if you decide to hedge, is likely to be large enough to cover the additional risks incurred.

When to Sell?

The answer to this question depends upon the availability of storage, the costs of storage, the current price, and the anticipated seasonal price rise. Years ago when ear corn was stored, part of the income from storage was actually derived from avoiding moisture discounts. You sold a higher quality product after the corn dried during the winter and spring months. When high moisture shelled corn is dried to the point that little or no discounts are involved, the income from storage must come from a seasonal price increase.

The price increase necessary to cover drying and storage costs can serve as a guide to decide which marketing alternative to choose. An example of costs of six alternative methods of marketing corn is shown in Table 4-1. The following assumptions are made:

> The average moisture of the corn at harvest is 22½%. No. 2 corn price at harvest time is $2.80 per bushel. If the corn is marketed from the field, the discount will be 39.2¢ per bushel (1% of the price per bushel for each ½% of moisture above 15½%). The corn that is dried before marketing is reduced to a No. 2 grade. The corn that is stored on the farm is dried to 15% moisture for April sales and 14% moisture for July sales. Commercial storage and drying are available at a cost of 1½¢ per month (with a 12¢ per bushel minimum charge) plus 14¢ per bushel for drying. The commercial firm will issue a warehouse receipt for corn with 14.5% moisture.

In this example, price increases of about 35¢ and 48¢ are needed to offset the total costs of storing corn on the farm from October to April and to July, respectively, as compared to selling at harvest when the price of No. 2 corn is $2.80 per bushel. Price increases of 40¢ and 53¢

Table 4-1. COSTS OF ALTERNATIVE METHODS OF MARKETING CORN.

	Marketing Direct		Commercial Drying & Storage*		Farm Drying & Storage	
	Sold "wet" at harvest	Dried on farm sold at harvest	April 1	July 1	April 1	July 1
Percent moisture content	22½	15½	14½	14½	15	14
Bushels of corn sold	1,000	912.16	896.00	896.00	906.76	896.16
Value of corn	$2408.00	$2408.00	$2408.00	$2408.00	$2408.00	$2408.00
Interest at 12%	XXX	XXX	144.48	216.72	144.48	216.72
Storage cost	XXX	XXX	147.84	192.64	136.01	134.42
Drying cost	XXX	120.00	140.00	140.00	125.00	135.00
Taxes	XXX	XXX	22.40	22.40	22.67	22.40
Extra handling	XXX	XXX	XXX	XXX	22.67	22.40
Total value	$2408.00	$2528.00	$2862.72	$2979.76	$2858.83	$2938.94
Value per bushel with moisture discount	$2.41	—	—	—	—	—
Breakeven price per bushel	—	$2.77	$3.20	$3.33	$3.15	$3.28

*Note: Calculate shrink using a 1.3% reduction in weight for each 1% excess moisture.

are needed to cover costs using commercial storage and drying for similar time periods.

When marketing corn directly from the field (in the above example), you made a profit of 3¢ per bushel on a dry-weight basis (or $27.36) by drying before selling rather than taking the moisture discount at harvest time. In some states, selling corn before personal property taxes are assessed (March 1) would reduce the storage costs about 2¢ per bushel.

Drying to guarantee safe storage costs 3½¢ to 4¢ per bushel. Additional costs may be incurred in on-farm storage if the grain quality is allowed to deteriorate. Costs of storing grain at the elevator increase by the monthly storage fees and interest charges on the grain. Most of the costs of on-farm storage are fixed. Once the initial investment is made, the cost of additional storage time is largely interest charges. When stored on the farm, the farmer is responsible for quality. In commercial storage the elevator is.

Seasonality of Grain Prices

As earlier noted, the potential for profit from grain storage depends, in part, upon a seasonal rise in prices following harvest, assuming you have not hedged or contracted for future delivery. Improvement in basis is another potential source of return from short or intermediate term storage for hedgers. Long term storage can be profitable if there is a general rise in price level that will cover the costs of storage.

The general tendency is for seasonally low grain prices during the harvest period. A heavy supply and pressure on handling, storage, and transportation facilities cause prices to decline and the basis to widen. This is normally followed by a post-harvest rise in prices, as usage reduces the total supply.

Seasonal indexes of corn and soybean prices, based on the years 1970-79, are shown in Figures 4-1 and 4-2. During this period, corn prices were most often at a low point during October-November, followed by recovery in December. Prices dropped back to a lower level during January-April, then rose to a seasonal high in June-August. Soybean prices generally declined into the harvest season, and on the average, were at a still lower level during January-February, then rose steadily to a June peak.

44   MARKETING FOR FARMERS

**Figure 4-1. Seasonal Price Index for No. 1.
          Soybeans, Chicago, 1970-79 Average.**

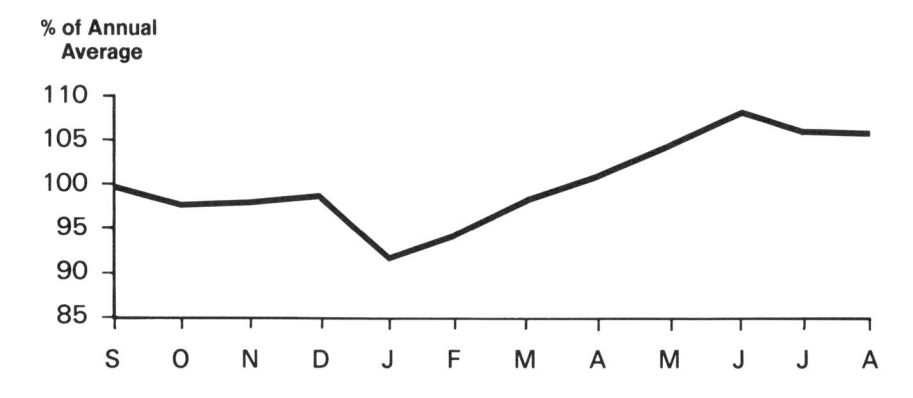

**Figure 4-2. Seasonal Price Index for No. 2 Yellow.
          Corn, Chicago, 1970-79 Average.**

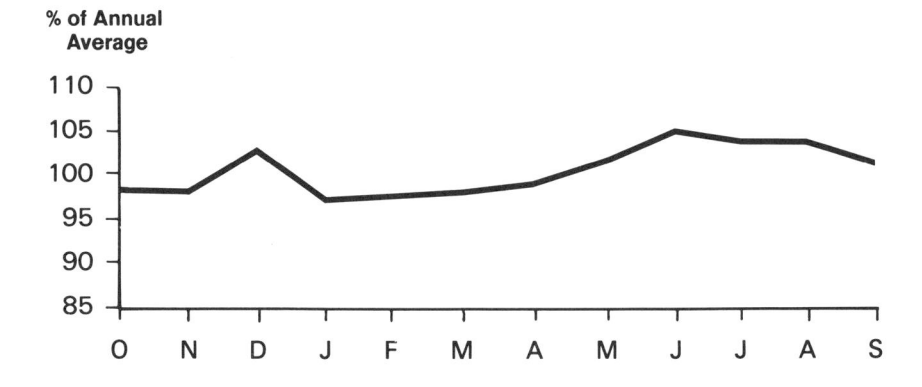

**Figure 4-3. Seasonal Price Index for All Wheat, U.S. Average.
          Farm Price, 1970-79 Average.**

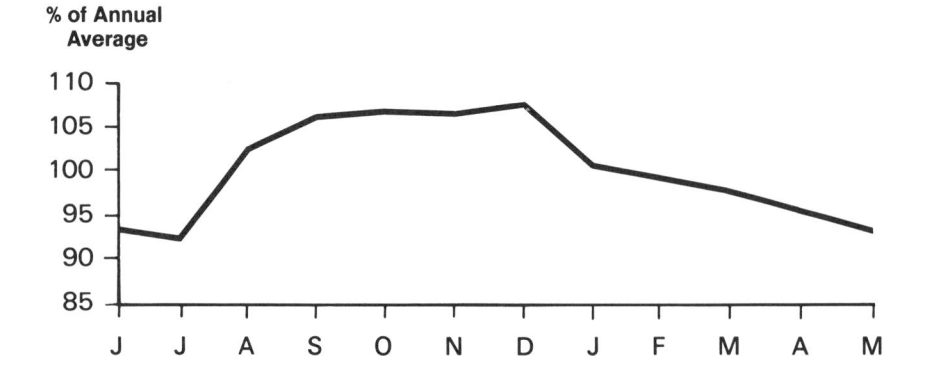

A seasonal index of wheat prices, based on the years 1970-79, is shown in Figure 4-3. Lowest prices during these years were usually in the May-July period, with a fairly strong seasonal rise in August. Prices continued to trend up during the late summer and fall, reaching a peak in December.

Probability of a Storage Return

Table 4-2 shows the results of storing unhedged corn in Iowa for the marketing years from 1959-60 through 1978-79. This is a longer time period than reflected in the seasonal price index in Figure 4-1. All costs of commercial storage have been deducted in computing the storage return, including interest on the stored grain, typical commercial storage charges, and the cost of extra shrinkage and drying to take the moisture 1.5 points below the No. 2 grade.

Short term storage of 2 to 3 months was profitable in 15 of the 20 years, with two years of large losses. Longer term storage into the next summer was profitable only half of the time, with large losses in six of the years. Storage of corn into the next crop year proved profitable in only four years if returns from government storage programs are excluded. Thus, the risk of losses appears to increase as the length of storage is extended. Short term storage is a relatively low risk decision, while storage into summer carries more risk; carrying grain into the next crop year appears to be high risk strategy.

The results from soybean storage were similar, as shown in Table 4-3. Short term storage was profitable in 16 of the 20 years, storage into summer was profitable half of the time, and storage into the next crop year was profitable in only six years.

While this has been the historical record of storage returns on corn and soybeans, individual years have been and will be different. If there are unusual circumstances with respect to crop size or market demands, the normal price pattern may not develop. Seasonal patterns and past storage history can be a guide for developing tentative plans for storage, but you must consider the current year's conditions carefully in making a final decision.

These results can be related to your risk-bearing ability, as discussed in Chapter 3. Short term storage may be an appropriate strategy if you are not in position to risk the large losses that sometime occur from longer term storage. But if you have high equity in your farm and have fairly low cash flow costs, the higher risk alternatives, with a chance of larger returns, may be appropriate.

ECONOMICS OF DRYING CORN

Shrinkage in weight of grain due to the removal of excess moisture is the main economic loss of artificial drying. The amount of shrinkage can be determined mathematically. In addition, account must be taken of a drymatter loss (loss of chaff and other foreign material) which occurs when grain is handled and dried. Handling shrink varies, but is usually estimated to be 0.5%.

Market discounts are usually subtracted from the No. 2 corn price when moisture is above 15.5%. Moisture discounts are designed to (1) adjust for the shrinkage which occurs when excess moisture is removed; (2) cover the costs of drying, handling or conditioning; (3) compensate for risk; and (4) discourage large amounts of high-moisture corn from entering market channels.

Table 4-2. CORN STORAGE RESULTS, 1959-78 CROPS (IOWA). *

	Years Profitable	Average Profit, All Years	Years of Large Loss
Short term storage	15	4.3¢/bu.	2
Storage into summer	10	6.3¢/bu.	6
Storage into next crop year	4	—	5

Table 4-3. SOYBEAN STORAGE RESULTS, 1959-78 CROPS (IOWA). *

	Years Profitable	Average Profit, All Years	Years of Large Loss
Short term storage	16	9.0¢/bu.	2
Storage into summer	10	47.8¢/bu.	6
Storage into next crop year	6	—	4

*Includes loss years.

Grain Storage as a Marketing Strategy

Computing Shrink

The mathematics of shrinkage caused by removal of excess moisture are the same for corn as for other grains. A bushel of No. 2 corn weighing 56 pounds can contain no more than 15.5% moisture or 8.68 pounds of water. Since a bushel of corn at any moisture content weighs 56 pounds, the higher the percentage of moisture contained, the less valuable drymatter present in a bushel. In addition, excess moisture must be removed for safe storage.

The following formula is used to compute total shrink:

$$\left(1 - \frac{100\% - \text{Initial \% Moisture}}{100\% - \text{Final \% Moisture}}\right) + \text{Percentage of Drymatter Loss}$$

To illustrate, consider a lot of corn at 20% moisture. The apparent moisture reduction is 4.5% in order to obtain 15.5%. Using the formula for moisture shrink alone:

$$1 - \frac{100-20}{100-15.5} = 1 - \frac{80}{84.5} = 1 - 0.946746 = 0.05324$$

which is 5.324% actual shrink. The percentage change is weight due to moisture evaporation. The 5.324% reduction in weight is greater than the 4.5% change in moisture content from 20% to 15.5% corn because the percentages are of different figures.

To further illustrate, consider 1,000 bushels of corn (or 56,000 pounds) to be dried from 20% moisture to 15.5%. The beginning and ending drymatter and water components by weight of the 1,000 bushels are as follows:

	Original 1,000 Bushels at 20% Moisture	Remainder of 1,000 Bushels at 15.5% Moisture
Drymatter	44,800 lbs.	44,800 lbs.
Water	11,200 lbs.	8,218 lbs.
Total	56,000 lbs.	53,018 lbs.

Assuming no drymatter loss occurs, the 15.5% moisture corn will consist of the same 44,800 pounds of drymatter which is 84.5% of "1,000 bushels at 15.5%" weighing 53,018 pounds (44,800 ÷ 0.845).

This leaves 8,218 pounds of water (53,018 x 0.155). From these numbers the moisture shrink can be calculated as:

$$1 - \frac{53,018}{56,000} = 0.05324 \text{ or } 5.324\%$$

which is the same result as obtained from the moisture shrink formula given above.

When account is taken of a 0.5% drymatter loss, the total loss due to shrinkage becomes 5.825% (5.325 + 0.5), leaving a remainder of 94.175% of the original 1,000 bushels of 20% corn or 941.75 bushels (shown in column 4 of "returns to drying" tables for the 20% moisture level).

Moisture Discounts

Grain dealers and corn processors buy corn at the standard weight of 56 pounds per bushel and discount from the bid price to compensate for excess moisture (above 15.5% for No. 2 corn). At a given time and location discount rates vary, but a widely used discount is to deduct 1% of the No. 2 bid price for each 0.5% moisture above 15.5%.

To evaluate moisture discounts and to relate them to drying and handling charges, it is helpful to think of the moisture discount as having two parts:

(1) Value of shrinkage and
(2) Imputed or implied drying and handling charge (amount left as "returns to drying").

Item (2) is often referred to as the penalty for selling wet corn.

While the actual shrinkage depends upon the starting and ending levels of moisture plus the amount of drymatter loss (calculated by the formula used above), value of shrinkage (No. 2 price x bushels of shrinkage) varies with the No. 2 price of corn. "Returns to Drying" (discount minus value of shrinkage) varies with both the discount and the No. 2 price of corn. "Returns to Drying" are left to cover drying costs. The net profit from drying corn would be what's left after subtracting drying costs from the "Returns to Drying."

Table 4-4.   **GRAIN SHRINKAGE: When Grain Is Dried to Levels of 13% to 19% Moisture.***

Initial moisture percent	13.0	13.5	14.0	14.5	15.0	15.5	16.0	16.5	17.0	17.5	18.0	18.5	19.0
					percentage of shrinkage								
15.5	3.37	2.81	2.24	1.67	1.09	--	--	--	--	--	--	--	--
16.0	3.95	3.39	2.83	2.25	1.68	1.09	--	--	--	--	--	--	--
16.5	4.52	3.97	3.41	2.84	2.26	1.68	1.10	--	--	--	--	--	--
17.0	5.10	4.55	3.99	3.42	2.85	2.28	1.70	1.10	--	--	--	--	--
17.5	5.67	5.12	4.57	4.01	3.44	2.87	2.29	1.70	1.11	--	--	--	--
18.0	6.25	5.70	5.15	4.59	4.03	3.46	2.88	2.30	1.71	1.11	--	--	--
18.5	6.82	6.28	5.73	5.18	4.62	4.05	3.48	2.90	2.31	1.72	1.11	--	--
19.0	7.40	6.86	6.31	5.76	5.21	4.64	4.08	3.50	2.91	2.32	1.72	1.12	--
19.5	7.97	7.44	6.90	6.35	5.79	5.23	4.67	4.10	3.52	2.93	2.33	1.73	1.12
20.0	8.55	8.01	7.48	6.93	6.38	5.83	5.27	4.70	4.12	3.54	2.94	2.35	1.74
20.5	9.12	8.59	8.06	7.52	6.97	6.42	5.86	5.30	4.72	4.14	3.55	2.96	2.36
21.0	9.70	9.17	8.64	8.10	7.56	7.01	6.46	5.89	5.32	4.75	4.16	3.57	2.97
21.5	10.27	9.75	9.22	8.69	8.15	7.60	7.05	6.49	5.93	5.35	4.77	4.19	3.59
22.0	10.84	10.33	9.80	9.27	8.74	8.19	7.65	7.09	6.53	5.96	5.38	4.80	4.21
22.5	11.42	10.90	10.38	9.86	9.32	8.78	8.24	7.69	7.13	6.57	5.99	5.40	4.83
23.0	11.99	11.48	10.97	10.44	9.91	9.38	8.84	8.29	7.73	7.17	6.60	6.03	5.44
23.5	12.57	12.06	11.55	11.03	10.50	9.97	9.43	8.89	8.34	7.78	7.21	6.64	6.06
24.0	13.14	12.64	12.13	11.61	11.09	10.56	10.03	9.49	8.94	8.38	7.82	7.25	6.68
24.5	13.72	13.22	12.71	12.20	11.68	11.15	10.62	10.09	9.54	8.99	8.43	7.87	7.30
25.0	14.29	13.79	13.29	12.78	12.26	11.74	11.22	10.68	10.14	9.60	9.04	8.48	7.91
25.5	14.87	14.37	13.87	13.37	12.85	12.33	11.81	11.28	10.75	10.20	9.65	9.09	8.53
26.0	15.44	14.95	14.45	13.95	13.44	12.93	12.41	11.88	11.35	10.81	10.26	9.71	9.15
26.5	16.02	15.53	15.03	14.54	14.03	13.52	13.00	12.48	11.95	11.41	10.87	10.32	9.76
27.0	16.60	16.11	15.62	15.12	14.62	14.11	13.60	13.08	12.55	12.02	11.48	10.93	10.38
27.5	17.17	16.69	16.20	15.71	15.21	14.71	14.20	13.68	13.16	12.63	12.09	11.55	11.00
28.0	17.74	17.26	16.78	16.29	15.79	15.29	14.79	14.27	13.75	13.23	12.70	12.16	11.61
28.5	18.32	17.84	17.36	16.87	16.38	15.88	15.38	14.87	14.36	13.83	13.30	12.77	12.23
29.0	18.89	18.42	17.94	17.46	16.97	16.48	15.98	15.47	14.96	14.44	13.92	13.38	12.85

*This table applies to all grains. It includes the moisture shrink and one half of one percent for the dry matter shrink.

Formulas: (1) Shrinkage 100.0% − $\dfrac{(\% \text{ dry matter in wet grain})}{(\% \text{ dry matter in dry grain})}$ × 100) + 0.5% handling shrink.

(2) Value of shrink = price basis grade × shrinkage.
(3) Returns to drying = discount − value of shrinkage.

Illustration of "Returns to Drying" Tables

The tables for "Return to Drying" in the following several pages are for corn prices ranging from $1.90 to $4.30 No. 2 basis grade at 40¢ cost intervals with moisture levels up to 33%. A moisture discount of 1% of price for each ½% of moisture removed is used in all tables. To illustrate:

(1) 1,000 bushels of corn containing 20% moisture (shrinkage discussed above).
(2) No. 2 price of $3.10, Table 4-8.

From Table 4-8 the following results are available for two marketing alternatives:

(1) Sell 941.75 bushels at 15.5% moisture (col. 4): $2,919.41 (col. 5).
(2) Sell 1,000 bushels at 20% moisture: $2,821.00 (col. 3).
Subtracting (2) from (1) gives: $98.41 (col. 6), Total Returns to Drying or the penalty for selling wet corn.

Column 7 of Table 4-8 gives the Returns to Drying per bushel of wet corn of 09.84¢ (98.41 ÷ 1000). Column 8 gives the Returns to Drying per bushel of dry corn of 10.45¢ ($98.41 ÷ 941.75). In either case, there is only $98.41 available to cover drying charges on this 1,000 bushel lot of grain containing 20% moisture.

Drying Costs

Returns to drying can be compared directly to drying costs per bushel on either a wet or dry grain basis. The return per bushel wet may be viewed by the farmer as a breakeven charge by a custom dryer since a charge will be made for each wet bushel dried. If drying and handling services can be obtained at less than the returns to drying per wet bushel, then the owner or producer of the "wet" corn can profitably employ drying services and sell the dried corn.

"Returns to drying per bushel dry" is the relevant number for the owner of the grain who has to cover the costs of drying on a lesser quantity of corn. These returns are higher in each case than for returns to drying per bushel wet because the returns are spread over fewer bushels. Similarly, dryer costs must be spread over the dry bushels of grain sold.

Grain Storage as a Marketing Strategy

Table 4-5. RETURNS TO DRYING (Corn). PRICE $1.90 Per Bushel.

THE VALUE OF 1,000 BUSHELS OF CORN AT VARIOUS MOISTURE LEVELS WHEN THE DISCOUNT RATE AND PRICE OF 15.5% MOISTURE CORN ARE 1.9c PER ONE-HALF POINT OF MOISTURE

(1)	(2)	(3)	(4)	(5)	(6)	(7)	(8)
	Discount		Bushels			Returns To Drying***	
Moist-	Per Bu.	Receipts	Dry At 15.5	Receipts		Per Bu.	Per Bu.
ure	*	Sold Wet	**	Sold Dry	Total	Wet	Dry
(%)	(c)	($)	(Bushels)	($)	($)	(c)	(c)
16.0	1.9	1881.00	989.08	1879.26	-1.74	-.17	-.18
16.5	3.8	1862.00	983.17	1868.01	6.01	.60	.61
17.0	5.7	1843.00	977.25	1856.77	13.77	1.38	1.41
17.5	7.6	1824.00	971.33	1845.53	21.53	2.15	2.22
18.0	9.5	1805.00	965.41	1834.29	29.29	2.93	3.03
18.5	11.4	1786.00	959.50	1823.04	37.04	3.70	3.86
19.0	13.3	1767.00	953.58	1811.80	44.80	4.48	4.70
19.5	15.2	1748.00	947.66	1800.56	52.56	5.26	5.55
20.0	17.1	1729.00	941.75	1788.32	60.32	6.03	6.40
20.5	19.0	1710.00	935.83	1778.07	68.07	6.81	7.27
21.0	20.9	1691.00	929.91	1766.83	75.83	7.58	8.15
21.5	22.8	1672.00	923.99	1755.59	83.59	8.36	9.05
22.0	24.7	1653.00	918.08	1744.35	91.35	9.13	9.95
22.5	26.6	1634.00	912.16	1733.10	99.10	9.91	10.86
23.0	28.5	1615.00	906.24	1721.86	106.86	10.69	11.79
23.5	30.4	1596.00	900.33	1710.62	114.62	11.46	12.73
24.0	32.3	1577.00	894.41	1699.38	122.38	12.24	13.68
24.5	34.2	1558.00	888.49	1688.13	130.13	13.01	14.65
25.0	36.1	1539.00	882.57	1676.89	137.89	13.79	15.62
25.5	38.0	1520.00	876.66	1665.65	145.65	14.56	16.61
26.0	39.9	1501.00	870.74	1654.41	153.41	15.34	17.62
26.5	41.8	1482.00	864.82	1643.16	161.16	16.12	18.64
27.0	43.7	1463.00	858.91	1631.92	168.92	16.83	19.67
27.5	45.6	1444.00	852.99	1620.68	176.68	17.67	20.71
28.0	47.5	1425.00	847.07	1609.43	164.43	18.44	21.77
28.5	49.4	1406.00	841.15	1598.19	192.19	19.22	22.85
29.0	51.3	1387.00	835.24	1586.95	199.95	19.99	23.94
29.5	53.2	1368.00	829.32	1575.71	207.71	20.77	25.05
30.0	55.1	1349.00	823.40	1564.46	215.46	21.55	26.17
30.5	57.0	1330.00	817.49	1553.22	223.22	22.32	27.31
31.0	58.9	1311.00	811.57	1541.98	230.98	23.10	28.46
31.5	60.8	1292.00	805.65	1530.74	238.74	23.87	29.63
32.0	62.7	1273.00	799.73	1519.49	246.49	24.65	30.82
32.5	64.6	1254.00	793.82	1503.25	254.25	25.43	32.03
33.0	66.5	1235.00	787.90	1497.01	262.01	26.20	33.25

*Computed on the basis of the discount for each 1/2% moisture above 15.5%.
**The weight loss through drying includes 1/2% invisible shrink.
***Column (6) is calculated by subtracting column (3) from column (5).
  Column (7) is calculated by dividing column (6) by 1000 bu. and then times 100.
  Column (8) is calculated by dividing column (6) by column (4) and then times 100.

Table 4-6. RETURNS TO DRYING (Corn).   PRICE $2.30 Per Bushel.

THE VALUE OF 1,000 BUSHELS OF CORN AT VARIOUS MOISTURE LEVELS WHEN THE DISCOUNT RATE AND PRICE OF 15.5% MOISTURE CORN ARE 2.3c PER ONE-HALF POINT OF MOISTURE

(1)	(2)	(3)	(4)	(5)	(6)	(7)	(8)
	Discount		Bushels			Returns To Drying***	
Moist-	Per Bu.	Receipts	Dry At 15.5	Receipts		Per Bu.	Per Bu.
ure	*	Sold Wet	**	Sold Dry	Total	Wet	Dry
(%)	(c)	($)	(Bushels)	($)	($)	(c)	(c)
16.0	2.3	2277.00	989.08	2274.89	-2.11	-.21	-.21
16.5	4.6	2254.00	983.17	2261.28	7.28	.73	.74
17.0	6.9	2231.00	977.25	2247.67	16.67	1.67	1.71
17.5	9.2	2208.00	971.33	2234.06	26.06	2.61	2.68
18.0	11.5	2185.00	965.41	2220.45	35.45	3.55	3.67
18.5	13.8	2162.00	959.50	2206.84	44.84	4.48	4.67
19.0	16.1	2139.00	953.58	2193.23	54.23	5.42	5.69
19.5	18.4	2116.00	947.66	2179.62	63.62	6.36	6.71
20.0	20.7	2093.00	941.75	2166.01	73.01	7.30	7.75
20.5	23.0	2070.00	935.83	2152.41	82.41	8.24	8.81
21.0	25.3	2047.00	929.91	2138.80	91.80	9.18	9.87
21.5	27.6	2024.00	923.99	2125.19	101.19	10.12	10.95
22.0	29.9	2001.00	918.08	2111.58	110.58	11.06	12.04
22.5	32.2	1978.00	912.16	2097.97	119.97	12.00	13.15
23.0	34.5	1955.00	906.24	2084.36	129.36	12.94	14.27
23.5	36.8	1932.00	900.33	2070.75	138.75	13.87	15.41
24.0	39.1	1909.00	894.41	2057.14	148.14	14.81	16.56
24.5	41.4	1886.00	888.49	2043.53	157.53	15.75	17.73
25.0	43.7	1863.00	882.57	2029.92	166.92	16.69	18.91
25.5	46.0	1840.00	876.66	2016.31	176.31	17.63	20.11
26.0	48.3	1817.00	870.74	2002.70	185.70	18.57	21.33
26.5	50.6	1794.00	864.82	1989.09	195.09	19.51	22.56
27.0	52.9	1771.00	858.91	1975.48	204.48	20.45	23.81
27.5	55.2	1748.00	852.99	1961.87	213.87	21.39	25.07
28.0	57.5	1725.00	847.07	1943.25	223.26	22.33	26.36
28.5	59.8	1702.00	841.15	1934.65	232.65	23.27	27.66
29.0	62.1	1679.00	835.24	1921.04	242.04	24.20	28.98
29.5	64.4	1656.00	829.32	1907.43	251.43	25.14	30.32
30.0	66.7	1633.00	823.40	1893.83	260.83	26.08	31.68
30.5	69.0	1610.00	817.49	1880.22	270.22	27.02	33.05
31.0	71.3	1587.00	811.57	1866.61	279.61	27.96	34.45
31.5	73.6	1564.00	805.65	1853.00	289.00	28.90	35.87
32.0	75.9	1541.00	799.73	1839.39	298.39	29.84	37.31
32.5	78.2	1518.00	793.82	1825.78	307.78	30.78	38.77
33.0	80.5	1495.00	787.90	1812.17	317.17	31.72	40.25

*Computed on the basis of the discount for each 1/2% moisture above 15.5%.
**The weight loss through drying includes 1/2% invisible shrink.
***Column (6) is calculated by subtracting column (3) from column (5).
   Column (7) is calculated by dividing column (6) by 1000 bu. and then times 100.
   Column (8) is calculated by dividing column (6) by column (4) and then times 100.

Grain Storage as a Marketing Strategy

Table 4-7. RETURNS TO DRYING (Corn). PRICE $2.70 Per Bushel.

THE VALUE OF 1,000 BUSHELS OF CORN AT VARIOUS MOISTURE LEVELS WHEN THE DISCOUNT RATE AND PRICE OF 15.5% MOISTURE CORN ARE 2.7c PER ONE-HALF POINT OF MOISTURE

(1)	(2)	(3)	(4)	(5)	(6)	(7)	(8)
	Discount		Bushels		\multicolumn{3}{c}{Returns To Drying***}
Moist-	Per Bu.	Receipts	Dry At 15.5	Receipts		Per Bu.	Per Bu.
ure	*	Sold Wet	**	Sold Dry	Total	Wet	Dry
(%)	(c)	($)	(Bushels)	($)	($)	(c)	(c)
16.0	2.7	2673.00	989.08	2670.52	-2.48	-.25	-.25
16.5	5.4	2646.00	983.17	2654.55	8.55	.85	.87
17.0	8.1	2619.00	977.25	2638.57	19.57	1.96	2.00
17.5	10.8	2592.00	971.33	2622.59	30.59	3.06	3.15
18.0	13.5	2565.00	965.41	2606.62	41.62	4.16	4.31
18.5	16.2	2538.00	959.50	2590.64	52.64	5.26	5.49
19.0	18.9	2511.00	953.58	2574.67	63.67	6.37	6.68
19.5	21.6	2484.00	947.66	2553.63	74.69	7.47	7.88
20.0	24.3	2457.00	941.75	2542.71	85.71	8.57	9.10
20.5	27.0	2430.00	935.83	2526.74	96.74	9.67	10.34
21.0	29.7	2403.00	929.91	2510.76	107.76	10.78	11.59
21.5	32.4	2376.00	923.99	2494.78	118.78	11.88	12.86
22.0	35.1	2349.00	918.08	2478.81	129.81	12.99	14.14
22.5	37.8	2322.00	912.16	2462.83	140.83	14.08	15.44
23.0	40.5	2295.00	906.24	2446.86	151.86	15.19	16.76
23.5	43.2	2268.00	900.33	2430.88	162.88	16.29	18.09
24.0	45.9	2241.00	894.41	2414.80	173.90	17.39	19.44
24.5	48.6	2214.00	888.49	2398.93	184.93	18.49	20.81
25.0	51.3	2187.00	882.57	2382.95	195.95	19.59	22.20
25.5	54.0	2160.00	876.66	2366.97	206.97	20.70	23.61
26.0	56.7	2133.00	870.74	2351.00	218.00	21.80	25.04
26.5	59.4	2106.00	864.82	2335.02	229.02	22.90	26.48
27.0	62.1	2079.00	858.91	2319.04	240.04	24.00	27.95
27.5	64.8	2052.00	852.99	2303.07	251.07	25.11	29.43
28.0	67.5	2025.00	847.07	2287.09	262.09	26.21	30.94
28.5	70.2	1998.00	841.15	2271.12	273.12	27.31	32.47
29.0	72.9	1971.00	835.24	2255.14	284.14	28.41	34.02
29.5	75.6	1944.00	829.32	2239.16	295.16	29.52	35.59
30.0	78.3	1917.00	823.40	2223.19	306.19	30.82	37.19
30.5	81.0	1890.00	817.49	2207.21	317.21	31.72	38.80
31.0	83.7	1863.00	811.57	2191.23	328.23	32.82	40.44
31.5	86.4	1836.00	805.65	2175.26	339.26	33.93	42.11
32.0	89.1	1809.00	799.73	2159.28	350.28	35.03	43.80
32.5	91.8	1782.00	793.82	2143.30	361.30	36.13	45.51
33.0	94.5	1755.00	787.90	2127.33	372.33	37.23	47.26

*Computed on the basis of the discount for each 1/2% moisture above 15.5%.
**The weight loss through drying includes 1/2% invisible shrink.
***Column (6) is calculated by subtracting column (3) from column (5).
 Column (7) is calculated by dividing column (6) by 1000 bu. and then times 100.
 Column (8) is calculated by dividing column (6) by column (4) and then times 100.

Table 4-8. RETURNS TO DRYING (Corn).   **PRICE $3.10 Per Bushel.**

THE VALUE OF 1,000 BUSHELS OF CORN AT VARIOUS MOISTURE LEVELS WHEN THE DISCOUNT RATE AND PRICE OF 15.5% MOISTURE CORN ARE 3.1c PER ONE-HALF POINT OF MOISTURE

(1) Moisture (%)	(2) Discount Per Bu.* (c)	(3) Receipts Sold Wet ($)	(4) Bushels Dry At 15.5** (Bushels)	(5) Receipts Sold Dry ($)	(6) Total ($)	(7) Per Bu. Wet (c)	(8) Per Bu. Dry (c)
16.0	3.1	3069.00	989.08	3066.16	-2.84	-.28	-.29
16.5	6.2	3038.00	983.17	3047.81	9.81	.98	1.00
17.0	9.3	3007.00	977.25	3029.47	22.47	2.25	2.30
17.5	12.4	2976.00	971.33	3011.13	35.13	3.51	3.62
18.0	15.5	2945.00	965.41	2892.78	47.78	4.78	4.95
18.5	18.6	2914.00	959.50	2974.44	60.44	6.04	6.30
19.0	21.7	2883.00	953.58	2956.10	73.10	7.31	7.67
19.5	24.8	2852.00	947.66	2937.75	85.75	8.58	9.05
20.0	27.9	2821.00	941.75	2919.41	98.41	9.84	10.45
20.5	31.0	2790.00	935.83	2901.07	111.07	11.11	11.87
21.0	34.1	2759.00	929.91	2882.72	123.72	12.37	13.31
21.5	37.2	2728.00	923.99	2864.38	136.38	13.64	14.76
22.0	40.3	2697.00	918.08	2846.84	149.04	14.90	16.23
22.5	43.4	2666.00	912.16	2827.70	161.70	16.17	17.73
23.0	46.5	2635.00	906.24	2809.35	174.35	17.44	19.24
23.5	49.6	2604.00	900.33	2791.01	187.01	18.70	20.77
24.0	52.7	2573.00	894.41	2772.67	199.67	19.97	22.32
24.5	55.8	2542.00	888.49	2754.32	212.32	21.23	23.90
25.0	58.9	2511.00	882.57	2735.98	224.93	22.50	25.49
25.5	62.0	2480.00	876.66	2717.64	237.64	23.76	27.11
26.0	65.1	2449.00	870.74	2699.29	250.29	25.03	28.74
26.5	68.2	2418.00	864.82	2680.95	262.95	26.29	30.41
27.0	71.3	2387.00	858.91	2662.61	275.61	27.56	32.09
27.5	74.4	2356.00	852.99	2644.26	288.26	28.83	33.79
28.0	77.5	2325.00	847.07	2625.92	300.92	30.09	35.52
28.5	80.6	2294.00	841.15	2607.58	313.58	31.36	37.28
29.0	83.7	2263.00	835.24	2589.23	326.23	32.62	39.06
29.5	86.8	2232.00	829.32	2570.89	338.89	33.89	40.86
30.0	89.9	2201.00	823.40	2552.55	351.55	35.15	42.69
30.5	93.0	2170.00	817.43	2534.20	364.20	36.42	44.55
31.0	96.1	2139.00	811.57	2515.86	376.86	37.69	46.44
31.5	99.2	2108.00	805.63	2497.52	389.52	38.95	48.35
32.0	102.3	2077.00	799.73	2479.17	402.17	40.22	50.29
32.5	105.4	2046.00	793.82	2460.83	414.83	41.48	52.26
33.0	108.5	2015.00	787.90	2442.49	427.49	42.75	54.26

*Computed on the basis of the discount (cents) for each 1/2% moisture above 15.5.
**The weight loss through drying includes 1/2% invisible shrink.
***Column (6) is calculated by subtracting column (3) from column (5).
 Column (7) is calculated by dividing column (6) by 1,000 Bu. and then times 100.
 Column (8) is calculated by dividing column (6) by column (4) and then times 100.

Grain Storage as a Marketing Strategy

Table 4-9. RETURNS TO DRYING (Corn).   **PRICE $3.50 Per Bushel.**

THE VALUE OF 1,000 BUSHELS OF CORN AT VARIOUS MOISTURE LEVELS WHEN THE DISCOUNT RATE AND PRICE OF 15.5% MOISTURE CORN ARE 3.5c PER ONE-HALF POINT OF MOISTURE

(1)	(2)	(3)	(4)	(5)	(6)	(7)	(8)
	Discount		Bushels			Returns To Drying***	
Moist-	Per Bu.	Receipts	Dry At 15.5	Receipts		Per Bu.	Per Bu.
ure	*	Sold Wet	**	Sold Dry	Total	Wet	Dry
(%)	(c)	($)	(Bushels)	($)	($)	(c)	(c)
16.0	3.5	3465.00	989.08	3461.79	-3.21	-.32	-.32
16.5	7.0	3430.00	983.17	3441.08	11.08	1.11	1.13
17.0	10.5	3395.00	977.25	3420.37	25.37	2.54	2.60
17.5	14.0	3360.00	971.33	3399.66	39.66	3.97	4.08
18.0	17.5	3325.00	965.41	3378.95	53.95	5.39	5.59
18.5	21.0	3290.00	959.50	3358.24	68.24	6.82	7.11
19.0	24.5	3255.00	953.58	3337.53	82.53	8.25	8.65
19.5	28.0	3220.00	947.66	3316.82	96.82	9.68	10.22
20.0	31.5	3185.00	941.75	3296.11	111.11	11.11	11.80
20.5	35.0	3150.00	935.83	3275.40	125.40	12.54	13.40
21.0	38.5	3115.00	929.91	3254.69	139.69	13.97	15.02
21.5	42.0	3080.00	923.99	3233.98	153.98	15.40	16.66
22.0	45.5	3045.00	918.08	3213.27	168.27	16.83	18.33
22.5	49.0	3010.00	912.16	3192.56	182.56	18.26	20.01
23.0	52.5	2975.00	906.24	3171.85	196.85	19.68	21.72
23.5	56.0	2940.00	900.33	3151.14	211.14	21.11	23.45
24.0	59.5	2905.00	894.41	3130.43	225.43	22.54	25.20
24.5	63.0	2870.00	888.49	3109.72	239.72	23.97	26.98
25.0	66.5	2835.00	882.57	3089.01	254.01	25.40	28.78
25.5	70.0	2800.00	876.66	3068.30	268.30	26.83	30.60
26.0	73.5	2765.00	870.74	3047.59	282.59	28.26	32.45
26.5	77.0	2730.00	864.82	3026.88	296.88	29.69	34.33
27.0	80.5	2695.00	858.91	3006.17	311.17	31.12	36.23
27.5	84.0	2660.00	852.99	2985.46	325.46	32.55	38.16
28.0	87.5	2625.00	847.07	2964.75	339.75	33.97	40.11
28.5	91.0	2590.00	841.15	2944.04	354.04	35.40	42.09
29.0	94.5	2555.00	835.24	2923.33	368.33	36.83	44.10
29.5	98.0	2520.00	829.32	2902.62	382.62	38.26	46.14
30.0	101.5	2485.00	823.40	2881.91	396.91	39.69	48.20
30.5	105.0	2450.00	817.49	2861.20	411.20	41.12	50.30
31.0	108.5	2415.00	811.57	2840.49	425.49	42.55	52.43
31.5	112.0	2380.00	805.65	2819.78	439.78	43.98	54.59
32.0	115.5	2345.00	799.73	2799.07	454.07	45.41	56.78
32.5	119.0	2310.00	793.82	2778.36	468.36	46.84	59.00
33.0	122.5	2275.00	787.90	2757.65	482.65	48.26	61.26

*Computed on the basis of the discount (cents) for each 1/2% moisture above 15.5.
**The weight loss through drying includes 1/2% invisible shrink.
***Column (6) is calculated by subtracting column (3) from column (5).
  Column (7) is calculated by dividing column (6) by 1,000 Bu. and then times 100.
  Column (8) is calculated by dividing column (6) by column (4) and then times 100.

Table 4-10. RETURNS TO DRYING (Corn). PRICE $3.90 Per Bushel.

THE VALUE OF 1,000 BUSHELS OF CORN AT VARIOUS MOISTURE LEVELS WHEN THE DISCOUNT RATE AND PRICE OF 15.5% MOISTURE CORN ARE 3.9c PER ONE-HALF POINT OF MOISTURE

(1) Moisture (%)	(2) Discount Per Bu.* (c)	(3) Receipts Sold Wet ($)	(4) Bushels Dry At 15.5** (Bushels)	(5) Receipts Sold Dry ($)	(6) Total ($)	(7) Returns To Drying*** Per Bu. Wet (c)	(8) Per Bu. Dry (c)
16.0	3.9	3861.00	989.08	3857.42	-3.58	-.36	-.36
16.5	7.8	3822.00	983.17	3834.35	12.35	1.23	1.26
17.0	11.7	3783.00	977.25	3811.27	28.27	2.83	2.89
17.5	15.6	3744.00	971.33	3788.19	44.19	4.42	4.55
18.0	19.5	3705.00	965.41	3765.12	60.12	6.01	6.23
18.5	23.4	3666.00	959.50	3742.04	76.04	7.60	7.92
19.0	27.3	3627.00	953.58	3718.96	91.96	9.20	9.64
19.5	31.2	3588.00	947.66	3695.88	107.88	10.79	11.38
20.0	35.1	3549.00	941.75	3672.81	123.81	12.38	13.15
20.5	39.0	3510.00	935.83	3649.73	139.73	13.97	14.93
21.0	42.9	3471.00	929.91	3626.65	155.65	15.57	16.74
21.5	46.8	3432.00	923.99	3603.58	171.58	17.16	18.57
22.0	50.7	3393.00	918.08	3580.50	187.50	18.75	20.42
22.5	54.6	3354.00	912.16	3557.42	203.42	20.34	22.30
23.0	58.5	3315.00	906.24	3534.35	219.35	21.93	24.20
23.5	62.4	3276.00	900.33	3511.27	235.27	23.53	26.13
24.0	66.3	3237.00	894.41	3488.19	251.19	25.12	28.08
24.5	70.2	3198.00	888.49	3465.12	267.12	26.71	30.06
25.0	74.1	3159.00	882.57	3442.04	283.04	28.30	32.07
25.5	78.0	3120.00	876.66	3418.96	298.96	29.90	34.10
26.0	81.9	3081.00	870.74	3395.88	314.88	31.49	36.16
26.5	85.8	3042.00	864.82	3372.81	330.81	33.08	38.25
27.0	89.7	3003.00	858.91	3349.73	346.73	34.67	40.37
27.5	93.6	2964.00	852.99	3326.65	362.65	36.27	42.52
28.0	97.5	2925.00	847.07	3303.58	378.58	37.86	44.69
28.5	101.4	2886.00	841.15	3280.50	394.50	39.45	46.90
29.0	105.3	2847.00	835.24	3257.42	410.42	41.04	49.14
29.5	109.2	2808.00	829.32	3234.35	426.35	42.63	51.41
30.0	113.1	2769.00	823.40	3211.27	442.27	44.23	53.71
30.5	117.0	2730.00	817.49	3188.19	458.19	45.82	56.05
31.0	120.9	2691.00	811.57	3165.12	474.12	47.41	58.42
31.5	124.8	2652.00	805.63	3142.04	490.04	49.00	60.83
32.0	128.7	2613.00	799.73	3118.96	505.96	50.60	63.27
32.5	132.6	2574.00	793.82	3095.88	521.88	52.19	65.74
33.0	136.5	2535.00	787.90	3072.81	537.81	53.78	68.26

*Computed on the basis of the discount (cents) for each 1/2% moisture above 15.5.
**The weight loss through drying includes 1/2% invisible shrink.
***Column (6) is calculated by subtracting column (3) from column (5).
  Column (7) is calculated by dividing column (6) by 1,000 Bu. and then times 100.
  Column (8) is calculated by dividing column (6) by column (4) and then times 100.

Grain Storage as a Marketing Strategy

Table 4-11. RETURNS TO DRYING (Corn).   **PRICE $4.30 Per Bushel.**

THE VALUE OF 1,000 BUSHELS OF CORN AT VARIOUS MOISTURE LEVELS WHEN THE DISCOUNT RATE AND PRICE OF 15.5% MOISTURE CORN ARE 4.3c PER ONE-HALF POINT OF MOISTURE

(1)	(2)	(3)	(4)	(5)	(6)	(7)	(8)
	Discount		Bushels			Returns To Drying***	
Moist-	Per Bu.	Receipts	Dry At 15.5	Receipts		Per Bu.	Per Bu.
ure	*	Sold Wet	**	Sold Dry	Total	Wet	Dry
(%)	(c)	($)	(Bushels)	($)	($)	(c)	(c)
16.0	4.3	4257.00	989.08	4253.06	-3.94	-.39	-.40
16.5	8.6	4214.00	983.17	4227.61	13.61	1.36	1.38
17.0	12.9	4171.00	977.25	4202.17	31.17	3.12	3.19
17.5	17.2	4128.00	971.33	4176.72	48.72	4.87	5.02
18.0	21.5	4085.00	965.41	4151.28	66.28	6.63	6.87
18.5	25.8	4042.00	959.50	4125.84	83.84	8.38	8.74
19.0	30.1	3999.00	953.58	4100.39	101.39	10.14	10.63
19.5	34.4	3956.00	947.66	4074.95	118.95	11.89	12.55
20.0	38.7	3913.00	941.75	4049.51	136.51	13.65	14.49
20.5	43.0	3870.00	935.83	4024.06	154.06	15.41	16.46
21.0	47.3	3827.00	929.91	3998.62	171.62	17.16	18.46
21.5	51.6	3784.00	923.99	3973.17	189.17	18.92	20.47
22.0	55.9	3741.00	918.08	3947.73	206.73	20.67	22.52
22.5	60.2	3698.00	912.16	3922.29	224.29	22.43	24.59
23.0	64.5	3655.00	906.24	3896.84	241.84	24.18	26.69
23.5	68.8	3612.00	900.33	3871.40	259.40	25.94	28.81
24.0	73.1	3569.00	894.41	3845.96	276.96	27.70	30.97
24.5	77.4	3526.00	888.49	3820.51	294.51	29.45	33.15
25.0	81.7	3483.00	882.57	3795.07	312.07	31.21	35.36
25.5	86.0	3440.00	876.66	3769.62	329.62	32.96	37.60
26.0	90.3	3397.00	870.74	3744.18	347.18	34.72	39.87
26.5	94.6	3354.00	864.82	3718.74	364.74	36.47	42.17
27.0	98.9	3311.00	858.91	3693.29	382.29	38.23	44.51
27.5	103.2	3268.00	852.99	3667.85	399.85	39.98	46.88
28.0	107.5	3225.00	847.07	3642.41	417.41	41.74	49.28
28.5	111.8	3182.00	841.15	3616.96	434.96	43.50	51.71
29.0	116.1	3139.00	835.24	3591.52	452.52	45.25	54.18
29.5	120.4	3096.00	829.32	3566.07	470.07	47.01	56.68
30.0	124.7	3053.00	823.40	3540.63	487.63	48.76	59.22
30.5	129.0	3010.00	817.49	3515.19	505.19	50.52	61.80
31.0	133.3	2967.00	811.57	3489.74	522.74	52.27	64.41
31.5	137.6	2924.00	805.65	3464.30	540.30	54.03	67.06
32.0	141.9	2881.00	799.73	3438.86	557.86	55.79	69.76
32.5	146.2	2838.00	793.82	3413.41	575.41	57.54	72.49
33.0	150.5	2795.00	787.90	3387.97	592.97	59.30	75.26

*Computed on the basis of the discount (cents) for each 1/2% moisture above 15.5.
**The weight loss through drying includes 1/2% invisible shrink.
***Column (6) is calculated by subtracting column (3) from column (5).
  Column (7) is calculated by dividing column (6) by 1,000 Bu. and then times 100.
  Column (8) is calculated by dividing column (6) by column (4) and then times 100.

Drying costs will vary widely for each situation, but 1¢ or so per point of moisture removed per bushel should cover operating costs of most systems. Depending upon the total volume of grain dried, most drying systems will incur a total drying cost of about 2¢ per point of moisture removed.

In the above example, corn was dried from 20% to 15.5%, thus 4.5 points of moisture were removed. With returns of about 10¢ per bushel on both wet and dry basis, total drying costs of perhaps 9¢ leave a small per bushel return for the management decision. In certain cases, only the operating cost of the otherwise unused dryer need be charged against the grain dried to obtain management returns to drying.

Tables 4-5 through 4-11 reveal that returns to drying increase both with moisture level and price of corn. The trade also appears to be saying it can handle high moisture corn only with an incentive. From the point of view of a penalty, some increase in returns to drying with moisture level and price increases may be justified due to greater risk. Check with your elevator for other possible discounts for low quality or damaged corn. On-farm drying can facilitate harvest delivery.

However, for the low moisture levels of corn, the returns to drying may be below the actual costs of drying and handling including risk. On the other hand, the returns to drying appear to be underestimated at the lower levels of moisture removal. This is due to the possible overestimate of actual shrinkage from drymatter loss. In each of the tables, the results show negative returns for removing the first one-half point of moisture above 15.5%.

ECONOMICS OF DRYING SOYBEANS

Wet harvesting seasons, considerations for decreasing field losses with timeliness of harvest, and expanding production have stimulated interest in and the need for drying soybeans. With proper management, on-the-farm or elevator drying is quite feasible with existing grain drying equipment.

Market discounts are usually subtracted from the No. 1 soybean price when moisture is above 13%.

Shrinkage Loss from Drying

Shrinkage of grain from the removal of excess moisture is the main economic loss due to artificial drying. The amount of shrinkage caused by the removal of excess moisture can be determined mathematically. We must take account of a drymatter loss (loss of chaff and other foreign material) which occurs when grain is handled and dried. This invisible shrink or handling shrink varies but is usually estimated to be 0.5%.

The mathematics of shrinkage due to removal of excess moisture is the same for soybeans as for other grains. A bushel of No. 1 soybeans weighing 60 pounds can contain no more than 13% moisture or 7.8 pounds of water. Since a bushel of soybeans at any moisture content weighs 60 pounds, the higher the percentage of moisture contained, the less valuable drymatter present in a bushel. In addition, excess moisture must be removed for safe storage. For long term safe storage, soybeans should be dried to 11% moisture. However, with proper storage management, it is possible to maintain soybeans at higher moisture levels.

The following formula is used to compute total shrink:

$$\left(1 - \frac{100\% - \text{Initial \% Moisture}}{100\% - \text{Final \% Moisture}}\right) + \text{Percentage of Drymatter Loss}$$

To illustrate, suppose we have soybeans at 16% moisture. The apparent reduction is 3% in order to obtain 13% soybeans. Using the formula for moisture shrink alone:

$$1 - \frac{100-16}{100-13} = 1 - \frac{84}{87} = 1 - 0.965517 = 0.034483$$

which is 3.4483% actual shrink. The percentage change in weight due to moisture shrinkage, 3.45, is greater than the percentage change in moisture content from 16% to 13% soybeans (3%) because the percentages are of different figures. In one case, you are comparing the percentage moisture in grain before and after drying; in the other case, you are subtracting the moisture content after drying from the moisture content before drying.

For example, consider 1,000 bushels of soybeans to be taken from 16% moisture to 13%. The beginning and ending drymatter and water components of the 1,000 bushels are as follows:

	Original 1,000 Bushels at 16% Moisture	Remainder of 1,000 Bushels at 13% Moisture
Drymatter	50,400 lbs.	50,400 lbs.
Water	9,600 lbs.	7,531 lbs.
Total	60,000 lbs.	57,931 lbs.

Assuming no drymatter loss occurs, the 13% moisture soybeans will consist of the same 50,400 pounds of drymatter which is 87% of "1,000 bushels of 13%" weighing 57,931 pounds (50,400 ÷ 0.87). We must have 7,531 pounds of water (57,931 x 0.13). From these numbers our moisture shrink can be calculated as:

$$1 - \frac{57,931}{60,000} = 0.034483 \text{ or } 3.45\%$$

which is the same result as obtained from the moisture shrink formula given above.

When we take into account a 0.5% drymatter loss, the total loss due to shrinkage becomes 3.9483% (3.4483 + 0.5), leaving a remainder of 96.052% of the original 1,000 bushels of 16% soybeans or 960.52 bushels (shown in column 4 of the tables for the 16% moisture level).

Moisture Discounts

Grain dealers and soybean processors buy soybeans at the standard weight of 60 pounds per bushel and discount from the bid price to compensate for excess moisture (above 13% for No. 1 soybeans). At a given time and location discount rates vary, but a widely used discount is to deduct 1% of the No. 1 bid price for each 0.5% moisture above 13.

To evaluate moisture discounts and to relate them to drying and handling charges, it is helpful to think of the moisture discount as having two parts:

(1) Value of shrinkage and
(2) Imputed or implied drying and handling charge (amount left as "returns to drying").

Item (2) is often referred to as the penalty for selling wet soybeans.

Grain Storage as a Marketing Strategy

While the actual shrinkage depends upon the starting and ending levels of moisture plus the amount of drymatter loss (calculated by the preceding formula), value of shrinkage (No. 1 price x bushels of shrinkage) varies with the No. 1 price of soybeans. "Returns to drying" (discount-value of shrinkage) vary with both the discount and the No. 1 price of soybeans. "Returns to drying" are left to cover drying costs. The net profit from drying soybeans would be what is left after subtracting drying cost from the "returns to drying."

Illustration of "Returns to Drying" Tables

The tables for "Returns to Drying" listed on the next several pages are for soybeans ranging from $5 to $8 No. 1 basis grade at 50¢ intervals with moisture levels up to 22%. A moisture discount of 1% of price for each ½% of moisture removed is used in all tables. To illustrate:

(1) 1,000 bushels of soybeans containing 16% moisture (shrinkage discussed above).

(2) No. 1 price of $5.50, Table 4-13.

From Table 4-13 the following results are available for two marketing alternatives:

(1) Sell 960.52 bushels (col. 4) at 13% moisture: $5,282.84 (col. 5)
(2) Sell 1,000 bushels at 16% moisture: $5,170 (col. 3)

Subtracting (2) from (1) gives: $112.84 (col. 6), Total Returns to Drying or the penalty for selling wet soybeans.

Column 7 of Table 4-13 gives the returns to drying per bushel of wet soybeans of 11.28¢ ($112.84 ÷ 1000). Column 8 gives the returns to drying per bushel of dry soybeans of 11.75¢ ($112.84 ÷ 960.52).

Drying Costs

Returns to drying can be compared directly to drying costs per bushel on either a wet or dry basis. The return per bushel wet may be viewed by the farmer as a breakeven charge by a custom dryer since a charge will be made for each wet bushel dried. If drying and handling services can be obtained at less than the returns to drying per wet bushel, then the owner or producer of the wet soybeans can profitably employ drying service and sell the dried soybeans.

"Returns to drying per bushel dry" is the relevant number for the owner of the grain who has to cover costs of his dryer with a shrunken quantity of soybeans. These returns are higher in each case than for returns to drying per bushel wet, because the returns are spread over fewer bushels. Similarly, dryer costs must be spread over the dry bushels of grain sold.

Drying costs will vary widely for each situation, but 1¢ or so per point of moisture removed per bushel should cover operating costs of most systems. Depending upon the total volume of grain dried, most drying systems will incur a total drying cost of about 2¢ per point of moisture removed.

In the example above, soybeans were dried from 16% to 13%, thus 3 points of moisture were removed. With returns of more than 11¢ per bushel on both wet and dry basis, total drying costs of perhaps 6¢ leave a sizable return for the management decision. In certain cases only the operating cost of the otherwise unused dryer needs to be charged against the grain dried to obtain management returns to drying.

Tables 4-12 through 4-22 reveal that returns to drying rise both with moisture level and price of soybeans. The trade also appears to be saying it can handle high moisture soybeans only at a very great incentive. Also, as moisture level increases, some increase in returns to drying may be justified because of greater risk. Unless somewhat restrictive practices are adhered to, soybean drying may cause cracking and splitting of beans, for which additional price discounts may be incurred. Check with your elevator for other possible discounts for low quality or damaged beans. Hazards, such as overheating and fire, must be guarded against. These considerations may contribute to the high penalty currently prevailing for selling wet soybeans.

However, for the low moisture levels of soybeans, the returns to drying may be in line with actual costs of drying and handling, including risk. On the other hand, the returns to drying appear to be underestimated at the lower levels of moisture removal. This is due to the possible overestimate of actual shrinkage from drymatter loss. In each of the tables, the results show negative returns for removing the first one-half point of moisture above 13%.

For example in Table 4-13, if a five bushel drymatter shrink is added back to column 4 of the first line, receipts sold dry would increase by $27.50, making returns to drying positive. Similarly, the returns to drying for soybeans with low levels of excess moisture are probably underestimated because of the overestimate of drymatter loss.

Grain Storage as a Marketing Strategy 63

Table 4-12. RETURNS TO DRYING (Beans).

PRICE $5.00 Per Bushel.

THE VALUE OF 1,000 BUSHELS OF BEANS AT VARIOUS MOISTURE LEVELS WHEN THE DISCOUNT RATE AND PRICE OF 13.0% MOISTURE BEANS ARE 5.0c PER ONE-HALF POINT OF MOISTURE

(1) Moisture (%)	(2) Discount Per Bu.* (c)	(3) Receipts Sold Wet ($)	(4) Bushels Dry At 13.0** (Bushels)	(5) Receipts Sold Dry ($)	(6) Total ($)	(7) Returns To Drying*** Per Bu. Wet (c)	(8) Per Bu. Dry (c)
13.5	5.0	4950.00	989.25	4946.26	-3.74	-.37	-.38
14.0	10.0	4900.00	983.51	4917.53	17.53	1.75	1.78
14.5	15.0	4850.00	977.76	4888.79	38.79	3.88	3.97
15.0	20.0	4800.00	972.01	4860.06	60.06	6.01	6.18
15.5	25.0	4750.00	966.26	4831.32	81.32	8.13	8.42
16.0	30.0	4700.00	960.52	4802.59	102.59	10.26	10.68
16.5	35.0	4650.00	954.77	4773.85	123.85	12.39	12.97
17.0	40.0	4600.00	949.02	4745.11	145.11	14.51	15.29
17.5	45.0	4550.00	943.28	4716.38	166.38	16.64	17.64
18.0	50.0	4500.00	937.53	4687.64	187.64	18.76	20.01
18.5	55.0	4450.00	931.78	4658.91	208.91	20.89	22.42
19.0	60.0	4400.00	926.03	4630.17	230.17	23.02	24.86
19.5	65.0	4350.00	920.29	4601.44	251.44	25.14	27.32
20.0	70.0	4300.00	914.54	4572.70	272.70	27.27	29.82
20.5	75.0	4250.00	908.79	4543.97	293.97	29.40	32.35
21.0	80.0	4200.00	903.05	4515.23	315.23	31.52	34.91
21.5	85.0	4150.00	897.30	4486.49	336.49	33.65	37.50
22.0	90.0	4100.00	891.55	4457.76	357.76	35.78	40.13

*Market discount is computed on the basis of the discount (cents) for each 1/2% moisture above 13.0.
**The weight loss through drying includes 1/2% invisible shrink for all drying combinations.
***Column (6), total returns to drying, is calculated by subtracting column (3) from column (5).
Column (7) is calculated by dividing column (6) by 1,000 Bu. and then times 100 to get cents per bushel wet.
Column (8) is calculated by dividing column (6) by column (4) and then times 100 to get cents per bushel dry.

Table 4-13. RETURNS TO DRYING (Beans).

PRICE $5.50 Per Bushel.

THE VALUE OF 1,000 BUSHELS OF BEANS AT VARIOUS MOISTURE LEVELS WHEN THE DISCOUNT RATE AND PRICE OF 13.0% MOISTURE BEANS ARE 5.5¢ PER ONE-HALF POINT OF MOISTURE

(1) Moisture (%)	(2) Discount Per Bu.* (¢)	(3) Receipts Sold Wet ($)	(4) Bushels Dry At 13.0** (Bushels)	(5) Receipts Sold Dry ($)	(6) Total ($)	(7) Returns To Drying*** Per Bu. Wet (¢)	(8) Per Bu. Dry (¢)
13.5	5.5	5445.00	989.25	5440.89	4.11	-.41	-.42
14.0	11.0	5390.00	983.51	5409.28	19.28	1.93	1.96
14.5	16.5	5335.00	977.76	5377.67	42.67	4.27	4.36
15.0	22.0	5280.00	972.01	5346.06	66.06	6.61	6.80
15.5	27.5	5225.00	966.26	5314.45	89.45	8.95	9.26
16.0	33.0	5170.00	960.52	5282.84	112.84	11.28	11.75
16.5	38.5	5115.00	954.77	5251.24	136.24	13.62	14.27
17.0	44.0	5060.00	949.02	5219.63	159.63	15.96	16.82
17.5	49.5	5005.00	943.28	5188.02	183.02	18.30	19.40
18.0	55.0	4950.00	937.53	5156.41	206.41	20.64	22.02
18.5	60.5	4895.00	931.78	5124.80	229.80	22.98	24.66
19.0	66.0	4840.00	926.03	5093.19	253.19	25.32	27.34
19.5	71.5	4785.00	920.29	5061.58	276.58	27.66	30.05
20.0	77.0	4730.00	914.54	5029.97	299.97	30.00	32.80
20.5	82.5	4675.00	908.79	4998.36	323.36	32.34	35.58
21.0	88.0	4620.00	903.05	4966.75	346.75	34.68	38.40
21.5	93.5	4565.00	897.30	4935.14	370.14	37.01	41.25
22.0	99.0	4510.00	891.55	4903.53	393.53	39.35	44.14

*Market discount is computed on the basis of the discount (cents) for each 1/2% moisture above 13.0.
**The weight loss through drying includes 1/2% invisible shrink for all drying combinations.
***Column (6), total returns to drying, is calculated by subtracting column (3) from column (5).
Column (7) is calculated by dividing column (6) by 1,000 Bu. and then times 100 to get cents per bushel wet.
Column (8) is calculated by dividing column (6) by column (4) and then times 100 to get cents per bushel dry.

Grain Storage as a Marketing Strategy

Table 4-14. RETURNS TO DRYING (Beans).

PRICE $6.00 Per Bushel.

THE VALUE OF 1,000 BUSHELS OF BEANS AT VARIOUS MOISTURE LEVELS WHEN THE DISCOUNT RATE AND PRICE OF 13.0% MOISTURE BEANS ARE 6.0c PER ONE-HALF POINT OF MOISTURE

(1) Moisture (%)	(2) Discount Per Bu.* (c)	(3) Receipts Sold Wet ($)	(4) Bushels Dry At 13.0** (Bushels)	(5) Receipts Sold Dry ($)	(6) Total ($)	(7) Returns To Drying*** Per Bu. Wet (c)	(8) Per Bu. Dry (c)
13.5	6.0	5940.00	989.25	5935.52	-4.48	-.45	-.45
14.0	12.0	5880.00	983.51	5901.03	21.03	2.10	2.14
14.5	18.0	5820.00	977.76	5866.55	46.55	4.66	4.76
15.0	24.0	5760.00	972.01	5832.07	72.07	7.21	7.41
15.5	30.0	5700.00	966.26	5797.59	97.59	9.76	10.10
16.0	36.0	5640.00	960.52	5763.10	123.10	12.31	12.82
16.5	42.0	5580.00	954.77	5728.62	148.62	14.86	15.57
17.0	48.0	5520.00	949.02	5694.14	174.14	17.41	18.35
17.5	54.0	5460.00	943.28	5659.66	199.66	19.97	21.17
18.0	60.0	5400.00	937.53	5625.17	225.17	22.52	24.02
18.5	66.0	5340.00	931.78	5590.69	250.69	25.07	26.90
19.0	72.0	5280.00	926.03	5556.21	276.21	27.62	29.83
19.5	78.0	5220.00	920.29	5521.72	301.72	30.17	32.79
20.0	84.0	5160.00	914.54	5487.24	327.24	32.72	35.78
20.5	90.0	5100.00	908.79	5452.76	352.76	35.28	38.82
21.0	96.0	5040.00	903.05	5418.28	378.28	37.83	41.89
21.5	102.0	4980.00	897.30	5383.79	403.79	40.38	45.00
22.0	108.0	4920.00	891.55	5349.31	429.31	42.93	48.15

*Market discount is computed on the basis of the discount (cents) for each 1/2% moisture above 13.0.
**The weight loss through drying includes 1/2% invisible shrink for all drying combinations.
***Column (6), total returns to drying, is calculated by subtracting column (3) from column (5).
Column (7) is calculated by dividing column (6) by 1,000 Bu. and then times 100 to get cents per bushel wet.
Column (8) is calculated by dividing column (6) by column (4) and then times 100 to get cents per bushel dry.

Table 4-15. RETURNS TO DRYING (Beans).

PRICE $6.50 Per Bushel.

THE VALUE OF 1,000 BUSHELS OF BEANS AT VARIOUS MOISTURE LEVELS WHEN THE DISCOUNT RATE AND PRICE OF 13.0% MOISTURE BEANS ARE 6.5c PER ONE-HALF POINT OF MOISTURE

(1) Moisture (%)	(2) Discount Per Bu.* (c)	(3) Receipts Sold Wet ($)	(4) Bushels Dry At 13.0** (Bushels)	(5) Receipts Sold Dry ($)	(6) Total ($)	(7) Returns To Drying*** Per Bu. Wet (c)	(8) Per Bu. Dry (c)
13.5	6.5	6435.00	989.25	6430.14	-4.86	-.49	-.49
14.0	13.0	6370.00	983.51	6392.79	22.79	2.28	2.32
14.5	19.5	6305.00	977.76	6355.43	50.43	5.04	5.16
15.0	26.0	6240.00	972.01	6318.07	78.07	7.81	8.03
15.5	32.5	6175.00	966.26	6280.72	105.72	10.57	10.94
16.0	39.0	6110.00	960.52	6243.36	133.36	13.34	13.88
16.5	45.5	6045.00	954.77	6206.01	161.01	16.10	16.86
17.0	52.0	5980.00	949.02	6168.65	188.65	18.86	19.88
17.5	58.5	5915.00	943.28	6131.29	216.29	21.63	22.93
18.0	65.0	5850.00	937.53	6093.94	243.94	24.39	26.02
18.5	71.5	5785.00	931.78	6056.58	271.58	27.16	29.15
19.0	78.0	5720.00	926.03	6019.22	299.22	29.92	32.31
19.5	84.5	5655.00	920.29	5981.87	326.87	32.69	35.52
20.0	91.0	5590.00	914.54	5944.51	354.51	35.45	38.76
20.5	97.5	5525.00	908.79	5907.16	382.16	38.22	42.05
21.0	104.0	5460.00	903.05	5869.80	409.80	40.98	45.38
21.5	110.5	5395.00	897.30	5832.44	437.44	43.74	48.75
22.0	117.0	5330.00	891.55	5795.09	465.09	46.51	52.17

*Market discount is computed on the basis of the discount (cents) for each 1/2% moisture above 13.0.
**The weight loss through drying includes 1/2% invisible shrink for all drying combinations.
***Column (6), total returns to drying, is calculated by subtracting column (3) from column (5).
Column (7) is calculated by dividing column (6) by 1,000 Bu. and then times 100 to get cents per bushel wet.
Column (8) is calculated by dividing column (6) by column (4) and then times 100 to get cents per bushel dry.

Table 4-16. RETURNS TO DRYING (Beans).   Price $7.00 Per Bushel.

THE VALUE OF 1,000 BUSHELS OF BEANS AT VARIOUS MOISTURE LEVELS WHEN THE DISCOUNT RATE AND PRICE OF 13.0% MOISTURE BEANS ARE 7.0¢ PER ONE-HALF POINT OF MOISTURE

(1) Moisture (%)	(2) Discount Per Bu.* (¢)	(3) Receipts Sold Wet ($)	(4) Bushels Dry At 13.0** (Bushels)	(5) Receipts Sold Dry ($)	(6) Total ($)	(7) Returns To Drying*** Per Bu. Wet (¢)	(8) Returns To Drying*** Per Bu. Dry (¢)
13.5	7.0	6930.00	989.25	6924.77	-5.23	-.52	-.53
14.0	14.0	6860.00	983.51	6884.54	24.54	2.45	2.50
14.5	21.0	6790.00	977.76	6844.31	54.31	5.43	5.55
15.0	28.0	6720.00	972.01	6804.08	84.08	8.41	8.65
15.5	35.0	6650.00	966.26	6763.85	113.85	11.39	11.78
16.0	42.0	6580.00	960.52	6723.62	143.62	14.36	14.95
16.5	49.0	6510.00	954.77	6683.39	173.39	17.34	18.16
17.0	56.0	6440.00	949.02	6643.16	203.16	20.32	21.41
17.5	63.0	6370.00	943.28	6602.93	232.93	23.29	24.69
18.0	70.0	6300.00	937.53	6562.70	262.70	26.27	28.02
18.5	77.0	6230.00	931.78	6522.47	292.47	29.25	31.39
19.0	84.0	6160.00	926.03	6482.24	322.24	32.22	34.80
19.5	91.0	6090.00	920.29	6442.01	352.01	35.20	38.25
20.0	98.0	6020.00	914.54	6401.78	381.78	38.18	41.75
20.5	105.0	5950.00	908.79	6361.55	411.55	41.16	45.29
21.0	112.0	5880.00	903.05	6321.32	441.32	44.13	48.87
21.5	119.0	5810.00	897.30	6281.09	471.09	47.11	52.50
22.0	126.0	5740.00	891.55	6240.86	500.86	50.09	56.18

*Market discount is computed on the basis of the discount (cents) for each 1/2% moisture above 13.0.
**The weight loss through drying includes 1/2% invisible shrink for all drying combinations.
***Column (6), total returns to drying, is calculated by subtracting column (3) from column (5).
Column (7) is calculated by dividing column (6) by 1,000 Bu. and then times 100 to get cents per bushel wet.
Column (8) is calculated by dividing column (6) by column (4) and then times 100 to get cents per bushel dry.

Table 4-17. RETURNS TO DRYING (Beans).

PRICE $7.50 Per Bushel.

THE VALUE OF 1,000 BUSHELS OF BEANS AT VARIOUS MOISTURE
LEVELS WHEN THE DISCOUNT RATE AND PRICE OF 13.0% MOISTURE BEANS ARE
7.5¢ PER ONE-HALF POINT OF MOISTURE

(1) Moist-ure (%)	(2) Discount Per Bu. * (c)	(3) Receipts Sold Wet ($)	(4) Bushels Dry At 13.0 ** (Bushels)	(5) Receipts Sold Dry ($)	(6) Total ($)	(7) Returns To Drying*** Per Bu. Wet (c)	(8) Per Bu. Dry (c)
13.5	7.5	7425.00	989.25	7419.40	-5.60	-.56	-.57
14.0	15.0	7350.00	983.51	7376.29	26.29	2.63	2.67
14.5	22.5	7275.00	977.76	7333.19	56.19	5.82	5.95
15.0	30.0	7200.00	972.01	7290.09	90.09	9.01	9.27
15.5	37.5	7125.00	966.26	7246.98	121.98	12.20	12.62
16.0	45.0	7050.00	960.52	7203.88	153.88	15.39	16.02
16.5	52.5	6975.00	954.77	7160.78	185.78	18.58	19.46
17.0	60.0	6900.00	949.02	7117.67	217.67	21.77	22.94
17.5	67.5	6825.00	943.28	7074.57	249.57	24.96	26.46
18.0	75.0	6750.00	937.53	7031.47	281.47	28.15	30.02
18.5	82.5	6675.00	931.78	6988.36	313.36	31.34	33.63
19.0	90.0	6600.00	926.03	6945.26	345.26	34.53	37.28
19.5	97.5	6525.00	920.29	6902.16	377.16	37.72	40.98
20.0	105.0	6450.00	914.54	6859.05	409.05	40.91	44.73
20.5	112.5	6375.00	908.79	6815.95	440.95	44.09	48.52
21.0	120.0	6300.00	903.05	6772.84	472.84	47.28	52.36
21.5	127.5	6225.00	897.30	6729.74	504.74	50.47	56.25
22.0	135.0	6150.00	891.55	6686.64	536.64	53.66	60.19

*Market discount is computed on the basis of the discount (cents) for each 1/2% moisture above 13.0.
**The weight loss through drying includes 1/2% invisible shrink for all drying combinations.
***Column (6), total returns to drying, is calculated by subtracting column (3) from column (5).
Column (7) is calculated by dividing column (6) by 1,000 Bu. and then times 100 to get cents per bushel wet.
Column (8) is calculated by dividing column (6) by column (4) and then times 100 to get cents per bushel dry.

Grain Storage as a Marketing Strategy

Table 4-18. RETURNS TO DRYING (Beans).

PRICE $8.00 Per Bushel.

THE VALUE OF 1,000 BUSHELS OF BEANS AT VARIOUS MOISTURE
LEVELS WHEN THE DISCOUNT RATE AND PRICE OF 13.0% MOISTURE BEANS ARE
8.0c PER ONE-HALF POINT OF MOISTURE

(1)	(2)	(3)	(4)	(5)	(6)	(7)	(8)
Moist-ure (%)	Discount Per Bu.* (c)	Receipts Sold Wet ($)	Bushels Dry At 13.0** (Bushels)	Receipts Sold Dry ($)	Total ($)	Returns To Drying*** Per Bu. Wet (c)	Per Bu. Dry (c)
13.5	8.0	7920.00	989.25	7914.02	-5.98	-.60	-.60
14.0	16.0	7840.00	983.51	7868.05	28.05	2.80	2.85
14.5	24.0	7760.00	977.76	7822.07	62.07	6.21	6.35
15.0	32.0	7680.00	972.01	7776.09	96.09	9.61	9.89
15.5	40.0	7600.00	966.26	7730.11	130.11	13.01	13.47
16.0	48.0	7520.00	960.52	7684.14	164.14	16.41	17.09
16.5	56.0	7440.00	954.77	7638.16	198.16	19.82	20.75
17.0	64.0	7360.00	949.02	7592.18	232.18	23.22	24.47
17.5	72.0	7280.00	943.28	7546.21	266.21	26.62	28.22
18.0	80.0	7200.00	937.53	7500.23	300.23	30.02	32.02
18.5	88.0	7120.00	931.78	7454.25	334.25	33.43	35.87
19.0	96.0	7040.00	926.03	7408.28	368.28	36.83	39.77
19.5	104.0	6960.00	920.29	7362.30	402.30	40.23	43.71
20.0	112.0	6880.00	914.54	7316.32	436.32	43.63	47.71
20.5	120.0	6800.00	908.79	7270.34	470.34	47.03	51.75
21.0	128.0	6720.00	903.05	7224.37	504.37	50.44	55.85
21.5	136.0	6640.00	897.30	7178.39	538.39	53.84	60.00
22.0	144.0	6560.00	891.55	7132.41	572.41	57.24	64.20

*Market discount is computed on the basis of the discount (cents) for each 1/2% moisture above 13.0.
**The weight loss through drying includes 1/2% invisible shrink for all drying combinations.
***Column (6), total returns to drying, is calculated by subtracting column (3) from column (5).
Column (7) is calculated by dividing column (6) by 1,000 Bu. and then times 100 to get cents per bushel wet.
Column (8) is calculated by dividing column (6) by column (4) and then times 100 to get cents per bushel dry.

Table 4-19. RETURNS TO DRYING (Beans).

PRICE $8.50 Per Bushel.

THE VALUE OF 1,000 BUSHELS OF BEANS AT VARIOUS MOISTURE
LEVELS WHEN THE DISCOUNT RATE AND PRICE OF 13.0% MOISTURE BEANS ARE
8.5¢ PER ONE-HALF POINT OF MOISTURE

(1) Moisture (%)	(2) Discount Per Bu.* (¢)	(3) Receipts Sold Wet ($)	(4) Bushels Dry At 13.0** (Bushels)	(5) Receipts Sold Dry ($)	(6) Total ($)	(7) Returns To Drying*** Per Bu. Wet (¢)	(8) Per Bu. Dry (¢)
13.5	8.5	8415.00	989.25	8408.65	-6.35	-.64	-.64
14.0	17.0	8330.00	983.51	8359.80	29.80	2.98	3.03
14.5	25.5	8245.00	977.76	8310.95	65.95	6.59	6.74
15.0	34.0	8160.00	972.01	8262.10	102.10	10.21	10.50
15.5	42.5	8075.00	966.26	8213.25	138.25	13.82	14.31
16.0	51.0	7990.00	960.52	8164.40	174.40	17.44	18.16
16.5	59.5	7905.00	954.77	8115.55	210.55	21.05	22.05
17.0	68.0	7820.00	949.02	8066.70	246.70	24.67	25.99
17.5	76.5	7735.00	943.28	8017.84	282.84	28.28	29.99
18.0	85.0	7650.00	937.53	7968.99	318.99	31.90	34.03
18.5	93.5	7565.00	931.78	7920.14	355.14	35.51	38.11
19.0	102.0	7480.00	926.03	7871.29	391.29	39.13	42.25
19.5	110.5	7395.00	920.29	7822.44	427.44	42.74	46.45
20.0	119.0	7310.00	914.54	7773.59	463.59	46.36	50.69
20.5	127.5	7225.00	908.79	7724.74	499.74	49.97	54.99
21.0	136.0	7140.00	903.05	7675.89	535.89	53.59	59.34
21.5	144.5	7055.00	897.30	7627.04	572.04	57.20	63.75
22.0	153.0	6970.00	891.55	7578.19	608.19	60.82	68.22

*Market discount is computed on the basis of the discount (cents) for each 1/2% moisture above 13.0.
**The weight loss through drying includes 1/2% invisible shrink for all drying combinations.
****Column (6), total returns to drying, is calculated by subtracting column (3) from column (5).
Column (7) is calculated by dividing column (6) by 1,000 Bu. and then times 100 to get cents per bushel wet.
Column (8) is calculated by dividing column (6) by column (4) and then times 100 to get cents per bushel dry.

Table 4-20. RETURNS TO DRYING (Beans).

PRICE $9.00 Per Bushel.

THE VALUE OF 1,000 BUSHELS OF BEANS AT VARIOUS MOISTURE LEVELS WHEN THE DISCOUNT RATE AND PRICE OF 13.0% MOISTURE BEANS ARE 9.0¢ PER ONE-HALF POINT OF MOISTURE

(1) Moisture (%)	(2) Discount Per Bu.* (c)	(3) Receipts Sold Wet ($)	(4) Bushels Dry At 13.0** (Bushels)	(5) Receipts Sold Dry ($)	(6) Total ($)	(7) Returns To Drying*** Per Bu. Wet (c)	(8) Per Bu. Dry (c)
13.5	9.0	8910.00	989.25	8903.28	-6.72	-.67	-.68
14.0	18.0	8820.00	983.51	8851.55	31.55	3.16	3.21
14.5	27.0	8730.00	977.76	8799.83	69.83	6.98	7.14
15.0	36.0	8640.00	972.01	8748.10	108.10	10.81	11.12
15.5	45.0	8550.00	966.26	8696.38	146.38	14.64	15.15
16.0	54.0	8460.00	960.52	8644.66	184.66	18.47	19.22
16.5	63.0	8370.00	954.77	8592.93	222.93	22.29	23.35
17.0	72.0	8280.00	949.02	8541.21	261.21	26.12	27.52
17.5	81.0	8190.00	943.28	8489.48	299.48	29.95	31.75
18.0	90.0	8100.00	937.53	8437.76	337.76	33.78	36.03
18.5	99.0	8010.00	931.78	8386.03	376.03	37.60	40.36
19.0	108.0	7920.00	926.03	8334.31	414.31	41.43	44.74
19.5	117.0	7830.00	920.29	8282.59	452.59	45.26	49.18
20.0	126.0	7740.00	914.54	8230.86	490.86	49.09	53.67
20.5	135.0	7650.00	908.79	8179.14	529.14	52.91	58.22
21.0	144.0	7560.00	903.05	8127.41	567.41	56.74	62.83
21.5	153.0	7470.00	897.30	8075.69	605.69	60.57	67.50
22.0	162.0	7380.00	891.55	8023.97	643.97	64.40	72.23

*Market discount is computed on the basis of the discount (cents) for each 1/2% moisture above 13.0.
**The weight loss through drying includes 1/2% invisible shrink for all drying combinations.
***Column (6), total returns to drying, is calculated by subtracting column (3) from column (5).
Column (7) is calculated by dividing column (6) by 1,000 Bu. and then times 100 to get cents per bushel wet.
Column (8) is calculated by dividing column (6) by column (4) and then times 100 to get cents per bushel dry.

Table 4-21. RETURNS TO DRYING (Beans).

PRICE $9.50 Per Bushel.

THE VALUE OF 1,000 BUSHELS OF BEANS AT VARIOUS MOISTURE LEVELS WHEN THE DISCOUNT RATE AND PRICE OF 13.0% MOISTURE BEANS ARE 9.5c PER ONE-HALF POINT OF MOISTURE

(1) Moisture (%)	(2) Discount Per Bu.* (c)	(3) Receipts Sold Wet ($)	(4) Bushels Dry At 13.0** (Bushels)	(5) Receipts Sold Dry ($)	(6) Total ($)	(7) Returns To Drying*** Per Bu. Wet (c)	(8) Per Bu. Dry (c)
13.5	9.5	9405.00	989.25	9397.90	-7.10	-.71	-.72
14.0	19.0	9310.00	983.51	9343.30	33.30	3.33	3.39
14.5	28.5	9215.00	977.76	9288.71	73.71	7.37	7.54
15.0	38.0	9120.00	972.01	9234.11	114.11	11.41	11.74
15.5	47.5	9025.00	966.26	9179.51	154.51	15.45	15.99
16.0	57.0	8930.00	960.52	9124.91	194.91	19.49	20.29
16.5	66.5	8835.00	954.77	9070.32	235.32	23.53	24.65
17.0	76.0	8740.00	949.02	9015.72	275.72	27.57	29.05
17.5	85.5	8645.00	943.28	8961.12	316.12	31.61	33.51
18.0	95.0	8550.00	937.53	8906.52	356.52	35.65	38.03
18.5	104.5	8455.00	931.78	8851.93	396.93	39.69	42.60
19.0	114.0	8360.00	926.03	8797.33	437.33	43.73	47.23
19.5	123.5	8265.00	920.29	8742.73	477.73	47.77	51.91
20.0	133.0	8170.00	914.54	8688.13	518.13	51.81	56.65
20.5	142.5	8075.00	908.79	8633.53	558.53	55.85	61.46
21.0	152.0	7980.00	903.05	8578.94	598.94	59.89	66.32
21.5	161.5	7885.00	897.30	8524.34	639.34	63.93	71.25
22.0	171.0	7790.00	891.55	8469.74	679.74	67.97	76.24

*Market discount is computed on the basis of the discount (cents) for each 1/2% moisture above 13.0.
**The weight loss through drying includes 1/2% invisible shrink for all drying combinations.
***Column (6), total returns to drying, is calculated by subtracting column (3) from column (5).
Column (7) is calculated by dividing column (6) by 1,000 Bu. and then times 100 to get cents per bushel wet.
Column (8) is calculated by dividing column (6) by column (4) and then times 100 to get cents per bushel dry.

Grain Storage as a Marketing Strategy

Table 4-22. RETURNS TO DRYING (Beans).

PRICE $10.00 Per Bushel.

THE VALUE OF 1,000 BUSHELS OF BEANS AT VARIOUS MOISTURE LEVELS WHEN THE DISCOUNT RATE AND PRICE OF 13.0% MOISTURE BEANS ARE 10.0¢ PER ONE-HALF POINT OF MOISTURE

(1) Moisture (%)	(2) Discount Per Bu.* (c)	(3) Receipts Sold Wet ($)	(4) Bushels Dry At 13.0** (Bushels)	(5) Receipts Sold Dry ($)	(6) Total ($)	(7) Returns To Drying*** Per Bu. Wet (c)	(8) Per Bu. Dry (c)
13.5	10.0	9900.00	989.25	9892.53	-7.47	-.75	-.76
14.0	20.0	9800.00	983.51	9835.06	35.06	3.51	3.56
14.5	30.0	9700.00	977.76	9777.59	77.59	7.76	7.94
15.0	40.0	9600.00	972.01	9720.11	120.11	12.01	12.36
15.5	50.0	9500.00	966.26	9662.64	162.64	16.26	16.83
16.0	60.0	9400.00	960.52	9605.17	205.17	20.52	21.36
16.5	70.0	9300.00	954.77	9547.70	247.70	24.77	25.94
17.0	80.0	9200.00	949.02	9490.23	290.23	29.02	30.58
17.5	90.0	9100.00	943.28	9432.76	332.76	33.28	35.28
18.0	100.0	9000.00	937.53	9375.29	375.29	37.53	40.03
18.5	110.0	8900.00	931.78	9317.82	417.82	41.78	44.84
19.0	120.0	8800.00	926.03	9260.34	460.34	46.03	49.71
19.5	130.0	8700.00	920.29	9202.87	502.87	50.29	54.64
20.0	140.0	8600.00	914.54	9145.40	545.40	54.54	59.64
20.5	150.0	8500.00	908.79	9087.93	587.93	58.79	64.69
21.0	160.0	8400.00	903.05	9030.46	630.46	63.05	69.81
21.5	170.0	8300.00	897.30	8972.99	672.99	67.30	75.00
22.0	180.0	8200.00	891.55	8915.52	715.52	71.55	80.26

*Market discount is computed on the basis of the discount (cents) for each 1/2% moisture above 13.0.
**The weight loss through drying includes 1/2% invisible shrink for all drying combinations.
***Column (6), total returns to drying, is calculated by subtracting column (3) from column (5).
Column (7) is calculated by dividing column (6) by 1,000 Bu. and then times 100 to get cents per bushel wet.
Column (8) is calculated by dividing column (6) by column (4) and then times 100 to get cents per bushel dry.

CHAPTER **5**

Selling through Cash Contracts

The 1970's were the start of a major change in grain marketing. Unlike the previous decade, price variability was extreme. In several marketing years corn prices varied as much as $1.00 per bushel. Wheat prices were also subject to wide variations. Soybeans exhibited extreme market contortions. The causes for this price variability are complex, but the result is clear—increasing price risk throughout the grain marketing system.

The grain industry had to relearn lessons it had forgotten during the decades when government price supports acted as the price setter. The industry faced an increasing need to reduce price risk. Many grain farms had been using commodity futures to hedge risks; others found that forward contracts were more suitable to their needs. Grain processors and elevators had always used a combination of forward contracts and hedges on the futures market to reduce their risks. Country elevators had sometimes contracted with farmers, but it was not a very organized or regularized process. Farmers were often not interested in contracting. And, in many cases, farmers who contracted were unwilling to honor contract terms when the market went up after the contract was signed.

Forward contract sales have become more regularized in recent years. Most contracts follow a similar pattern of terms. Farmers and elevators have both learned to live up to the terms—or to seek legal remedies when the other party does not.

Why Cash Forward Contracts?

There are several reasons to use cash forward contracts as a part of your marketing plan. The objective of cash forward sales usually lies in one of the following areas:

1. To capture pricing opportunities through the marketing year.
2. To fix a price and reduce price risk.
3. To guarantee a market outlet.
4. To increase the availability of capital.

Capturing pricing opportunities. One of the main reasons to sell through cash forward contracts is that they allow you to price grain when good price opportunities are available. Compared with a harvest sale, forward contracting often gives you a chance to capture better prices. It also allows you to market several times during the year and possibly improve your average price.

Reducing price risk. With increasing price variability comes increasing risk. This is especially true if you are highly leveraged with borrowed funds—you have a high proportion of total production costs which must be paid in cash during the marketing year. Your breakeven price is higher than that of a farmer with greater equity in his operation. Cash forward sales reduce the risk of price decline.

Assuring a market. If you don't have sufficient on-farm storage to handle all your crop at harvest, the cash forward contract can guarantee a market for your grain. You might also want a market guarantee if you are growing a crop new to your area. As sunflowers expanded across the upper Midwest, some seed companies offered forward contracts to encourage production. Farmers were thus assured that they would have a buyer for their crops.

Capital availability. Grain producers who are short of capital sometimes use forward contracts to improve their ability to borrow. Bankers and other lenders have, in some cases, insisted that grain be priced in advance to assure the soundness of loans. Bankers are naturally risk avoiders. Any plan which increases the certainty of your making a profit is bound to increase your standing in a lender's eyes.

CONTRACTING ALTERNATIVES

When you sell grain through a contract, you and the buyer are agreeing to a plan covering several terms of the transaction. Usually the contract will spell out these terms in detail. In fact, the main reason to use a contract is to specify the terms in advance. In the past, most grain was sold on a spot basis. Farmers delivered grain to the local elevator. The grain was weighed and graded and the farmer was paid the elevator's posted price less any discounts for moisture or other quality factors.

In recent years, elevators and farmers have discovered that they would often be better off to arrange the terms of sale in advance of the delivery of the grain. This is a forward contract. With it, both you and the elevator can more accurately plan your future business. You can plan your cash-flows from grain sales. Elevators can estimate their transportation and storage needs more accurately and arrange for financing of grain purchases.

While contract terms can be extremely varied, there are three main contract types: cash forward sales contracts; delayed or deferred pricing contracts; and deferred or delayed payment contracts.

Cash Forward Sale Contracts

Cash forward sale contracts are the most common of the three. They usually specify a fixed price, subject to appropriate discounts for moisture and quality factors. Cash forward sale contracts are often available as much as a full year prior to delivery, although most are entered into for much shorter periods of time. An example cash forward sales contract is shown in Figure 5-1.

Common contract terms include specification of the quantity, quality, timing of delivery, grading procedures and terms for dispute settlement. Contracts are often presented on printed forms with the blanks filled in by the buyer. Read the contract before you sign, and try to evaluate what circumstances might arise that could cause trouble. Ask for written clarification of any language you don't understand. Don't be reluctant to ask that particular terms be changed to fit your situation. For example, cash forward contracts often give the buyer some discretion about the exact delivery date. If you are making the contract to insure the availability of a market at a particular time, a delay in delivery could be costly.

Figure 5-1.

GRAIN SALES CONTRACT

                                             CONTRACT NO. _____

THIS AGREEMENT, made and entered into this_____day of, _____ 19____, by and between_____ of (city and state)____(hereinafter called Seller), and____of (city and state)____(hereinafter called Buyer), wherein each of the parties agree to the following terms and conditions of the sale of Seller's____(hereinafter called Grain).

    1. Seller agrees to sell and deliver to Buyer at Buyer's elevator or to Buyer's designated recipient for Buyer's account on or before the____day of_____, 19___, _____bushels of_____, Grade No._____, said grain to be clean, sound and merchantable according to the established grading standards of the USDA, and subject to Buyer's discounts applicable at the day of delivery, for the agreed on price of _____DOLLARS ($____) per bushel, less any pre-payment, discount or dockage arising from the condition of the grain. All grain to meet Pure Food and Drug Act Requirements.

    2. Seller agrees that in event Buyer or its designated recipient is incapable of receiving all or part of said grain on the date it is offered for delivery by Seller, Seller will hold all or so much of the grain as cannot be received and deliver it to Buyer or its designated recipient upon receipt of notice that the grain can be delivered.

    3. Seller and Buyer agree that the selling price quotation for the grain herein is binding upon both parties and that market fluctuations after the date of this contract shall have no effect on either party's obligation hereunder and will not excuse non-performance of this contract by either party.

    4. Seller and Buyer agree that this is a contract for delivery of Seller's grain and is not a futures contract which can be purchased back by Seller. Seller's failure or inability to deliver said grain in no way relieves him of his obligation of delivery of said grain, and Seller agrees Buyer may enforce this contract by an action for specific performance, except should delivery of grain be made impossible solely because of a natural disaster, Buyer agrees that upon proper notification from Seller, prior to the delivery date or within the extended delivery period, if Buyer exercises his option to extend the contract, to permit Seller to reimburse Buyer for any and all losses Buyer may suffer from Seller's partial performance or non-performance of this contract in lieu of delivery of all or part of said grain.

    5. In the event of default by either party all sums due shall be payable without relief from valuation and appraisement laws and with reasonable attorney fees, and with interest at the rate of eight per cent (8%) per year, calculated monthly from the date of default.

    6. Seller agrees that Buyer may extend the due date for delivery of the grain beyond the aforementioned date at Buyer's sole option on written notification of such extension to Seller mailed to Seller's address as shown on this contract.

    7. Seller agrees that Buyer or its designated recipient shall have the sole option of accepting or rejecting any grain in excess of the contract amount and if accepted, it is agreed Buyer will pay Seller Buyer's closing market price on the date of delivery if delivered to Buyer's elevator and Buyer's closing market price on the date of receipt of notification of such excess delivery from either Seller and Buyer's designated recipient if delivered to designated recipient.

    8. Seller warrants all grain delivered to Buyer will be free and clear of all liens and encumbrances, and that Seller has and will pass merchantable title.

    9. The word "bushels" as used herein means the equivalent number of pounds of said grain as established by the Bureau of Weights and Measures.

    10. This Agreement constitutes the entire understanding of the parties, and may be modified only by a signed writing of both parties, excepting Buyer's right to extend this contract, and is binding on the heirs, assigns and successors of the parties.

SELLER:_____   BUYER:_____
                  NAME

_____   BY:_____
              ADDRESS   TITLE

Some contracts include provisions to cover situations where buyers are unable to accept delivery because of the unavailability of rail cars, facility breakdowns, or other reasons. Provisions to adjust the price for changes in freight rates are also included in some contracts. Similarly, allowance is sometimes made for situations in which factors beyond the control of sellers, such as weather-related harvesting delays, make it impossible to deliver grain on schedule.

Delayed or Deferred Pricing Contracts

Delayed or deferred pricing contracts allow setting the price sometime after delivery. Thus, the agreement may cover delivery terms similar to the cash forward contract, while the terms for setting the price will differ. A delayed pricing contract permits the farmer to deliver grain and continue to speculate on the price. Usually it will contain a price formula which allows the seller to fix the price at a later date. There are two common types of pricing formulas being used by country elevators, the fixed basis contract and the service charge contract (Figures 5-2 and 5-3).

Fixed basis contracts. These contracts base the pricing formula on the commodity futures price. When the grain is delivered title passes to the elevator. The seller agrees to a formula which relates price paid to the commodity futures market, usually the futures price less the basis on the day of delivery. The seller has up to several months to choose when the price will be set. Whenever the seller chooses to price, he is paid the futures price minus the basis on the day he delivered the grain. Thus, he is "fixing" the basis when he delivers the grain.

Under fixed basis contracts the elevator normally sells the grain immediately after delivery; at the same time, the elevator buys futures contracts to protect the obligation to the seller. Later, when the seller prices the grain, the elevator sells the futures contracts. Because the elevator sells the grain soon after delivery and does not need all of the proceeds to cover its futures position, the seller usually gets a partial payment at delivery. The remaining payment is made when the grain is priced.

Service charge contracts. These contracts base the pricing formula on the local cash price. The elevator charges a service fee for each month the seller chooses to delay pricing. When the seller chooses to price, he is paid the current local price minus the accumulated service charges. As with fixed basis contracts, sellers also have an extended period to choose the price under service charge contracts. The elevator also takes title when the grain is delivered and may move

Figure 5-2.

PRICE LATER CONTRACT

(Not Storage)

DOE GRAIN COMPANY
RAE, ILLINOIS 61849

Seller as identified below agrees that Buyer does hereby purchase from Seller and Seller does hereby sell to Buyer _____ bushels of _____ ,
                             (quantity)   (Type and Grade)
subject to market discounts applicable to Buyer at time of (cross out one): (delivery/pricing) under following terms and conditions:

    1. The fixing of the price of the Grain is deferred, and may be established by Seller at any time, but not later than _____ , 19_____, and upon demand by the Seller, the Buyer is obligated to pay his regular bid price upon the date of demand for the commodities being priced by the Seller. If no such notice is given by the Seller by the date established in the preceding sentence, the Buyer's offered price on that date shall control, and Buyer shall promptly give Seller written notice of that price, unless a renewal has been written prior to the above expiration date covering the same Grain covered by this contract and agreed to by both Buyer and Seller. The following statements are made a part of this agreement pursuant to applicable regulations:

(a) Title to the Grain described in this contract passed to Buyer upon delivery of the Grain to him.
(b) The duration of this contract shall not exceed 12 months from the date delivery is completed.
(c) The buyer is required to maintain liquid assets equal to ninety percent of price later obligations by Illinois law.

    2. Buyer may deduct from the purchase price applicable charges on grain ticket or the specific following charges:

Deferment Charge: (specify) _____

Other Charges: (specify)   _____

    3. THE GRAIN COVERED BY THIS CONTRACT IS SOLD (NOT STORAGE) AND AS SUCH IS COVERED BY A GRAIN DEALER'S BOND FOR A PERIOD OF 160 DAYS FROM THE DATE OF DELIVERY OR PRICING, WHICHEVER IS LATER, MAXIMUM 270 DAYS.

_____   _____
Seller(s) Signature   Date   Representing Buyer   Date

_____   _____
            Address   Address

Selling through Cash Contracts

Figure 5-3.

BASIS PURCHASE CONTRACT

DATE _____   **CONTRACT NO.** _____

UNDERSIGNED SELLER hereby sells _____ bushels of _____
                                                         grade and grain
to BUYER subject to the following terms and conditions:

    1. SELLER has, as of the date of this contract, delivered to BUYER the quantity and type of grain indicated above. The delivery of grain is documented on scale tickets at buyer's scale.

Title and all other rights of ownership and control over the grain under this contract are transferred to BUYER.

    2. BUYER hereby grants the SELLER option to establish final cash price in accordance with the following terms and conditions:

(a) Basis portion of final cash price is hereby established at _____¢ under the _____ Future Option on the Chicago Board of Trade.
(b) SELLER may price grain between 9:40 a.m. and 1:00 p.m. on any day the Chicago Board of Trade is open between today and the _____ day of _____ .
(c) SELLER may, at his option and expense, spread to a basis to another Chicago Board of Trade contract on or prior to date in section "b" above.
(d) If SELLER does not establish final cash price on or before above date, the BUYER will establish price based on the closing range of the first trading day following the above date on the Chicago Board of Trade.
(e) All bushels shall be priced or spread forward at one time.

    3. Final price shall be subject to grade discounts at market scale of BUYER at time of delivery. Shrinkage, drying, and any other charges that may be applicable, shall be deducted before determining the final quantity and price of grain sold under this contract.

    4. The BUYER agrees to pay the SELLER _____ dollars per bushel at the time this contract is entered into between the buyer and seller, and to pay the final remaining balance on the day this contract is priced as outlined in Item 2, part (b).

    5. SELLER hereby warrants that title to the above grain is free from encumbrance of any nature whatsoever, and the SELLER has good and merchantable title, with the right to dispose of same. It is further agreed by and between the BUYER and SELLER that this contract shall be binding upon the heirs, administrators and executors of the respective parties and that this contract cannot be assigned without given consent of the other party.

_____ By _____
              Seller   Representing Buyer

_____   _____
       Phone Number   Dated

the grain immediately. The elevator will then buy futures to protect its obligation to the seller. In general, the elevator should set the service charge high enough to compensate for expected narrowing of the basis. As in the basis contract the elevator normally makes a partial payment at delivery, with the remainder paid when the grain is priced.

Either type of delayed pricing contract offers the opportunity to speculate on grain price after delivery. This may be an advantage if you don't have on-farm storage or access to commercial storage and think that prices will rise. The partial payment at delivery gives an immediate return of a substantial part of your investment in the grain. You should recognize that similar benefits may be realized by selling cash grain and purchasing a similar quantity of futures yourself.

The fixed basis contract should be used only when you think the current basis is narrow. If you lock yourself into a wide basis you are foregoing the opportunity to capture gains available by hedging stored grain when the basis is expected to narrow. You also need to be aware of the possibility that even if prices rise after delivery, the futures price may not rise as much as the cash price. Thus, shifting speculation from cash grain to futures may mean less potential price gain than holding stored grain for later sale.

The service charge contract should be compared closely to the cost of the commercial storage. If the service charge is equal to commercial storage costs, you may be better off to hold the grain in commercial storage. You would then have the opportunity to speculate without losing title to the grain.

You should consider very carefully the potential results of delayed pricing. Many sellers have assumed that they would receive no less than the delivery time price. This is not the case. If prices decline after delivery you will receive a lower price. You should also be aware that the security offered by a delayed pricing contract is not as great as that offered by warehouse receipts for stored grain. If the elevator should have financial problems, the law generally gives warehouse receipt holders priority when settling financial claims against the elevator.

Delayed or Deferred Payment Contracts

Farmers continue to use cash accounting as the normal method. This means that it sometimes pays, taxwise, to defer income until the next accounting year. The deferred payment contract allows the delivery and pricing of grain, with payment deferred to a later date. Deferring payment had been treated as a legitimate tax avoidance practice by the IRS. In recent years the IRS has treated deferred payment contracts with some suspicion. They have argued that under those contracts where farmers could use the contract as security for a loan, farmers had constructive receipt of the money. Thus, the IRS treated the income as taxable when the contract was made. Recently, the IRS has reevaluated its position and has issued rules which will permit farmers using cash accounting to use deferred payment contracts as an income management device. You should consult your tax advisor on the latest ruling if you plan to use deferred payment contracts.

Potential tax savings from deferred payment should be compared with earnings from investing grain receipts if received in the current accounting year. You should also carefully evaluate the financial position of the buyer offering the deferred payment contract. You could find yourself on the short end if the elevator has financial difficulties between the time you deliver grain and the time you are to receive payment. Figure 5-4 provides an example of a deferred payment contract.

CONTRACTING GUIDELINES

There are several general rules which will help you evaluate cash contracts as compared to other ways of marketing grain. First, always remember that using cash contracts commits you to a legal obligation. You need to understand the obligation and its consequences. Second, cash contracts can reduce price risk, but risk of loss from weather, fire, or other damage remains. Insurance and good storage practices are an important part of the marketing process. Third, sales methods help you meet your marketing goals and objectives. The use of cash contracts complements plans for spacing sales through the season, scale up selling and other marketing plans. Fourth, cash contract sales are one method for accomplishing your marketing objectives. They should always be compared with hedging on futures, storage of grain for later sale, sale of grain and purchase of futures and other selling methods.

Finally, keep in mind that specific legal requirements for grain contracts vary among states. Make sure the provisions of a contract are compatible with laws in your state.

CASH CONTRACTS VERSUS HEDGING WITH FUTURES

Cash contracts and hedging with futures are both methods for forward pricing. There are several differences between the two methods. Cash contracts may be negotiated for any quantity agreeable to buyer and seller. Futures, on the other hand, trade in 5,000 or 1,000 bushel units. Cash contracts do not require the payment of commission fees or margin deposits, which are required to trade futures contracts. It may be more difficult to withdraw from cash contracts because they require specific renegotiation between buyer and seller.

In general, cash contracts require less knowledge of the marketing system beyond the local market level. Hedging with the futures markets does require some understanding of, and attention to, the workings of the commodity futures exchanges. This might include an understanding of both fundamental and technical factors which cause futures prices to behave in particular ways. You need to have a knowledge of historic cash-futures price relationship (basis) patterns if you're going to use the the futures market. Hedging through futures "fixes" the price only to the extent that you can forecast the basis. While basis patterns are more predictable than price level changes, there is some risk of basis change.

If you have not used forward pricing before, you will probably want to start with cash contracts. As you become accustomed to this method and learn more about hedging with futures, you may discover that you want to try this, too. As your experience increases, you will find that both cash contracts and hedging have their place in your marketing plan.

Selling through Cash Contracts

Figure 5-4.

DEFERRED SALES CONTRACT

a partnership
John Doe Grain Co., Anytown, Nebraska, a corporation, hereinafter known as Buyer, and
an association
_____, hereinafter known as Seller, covenant and agree as follows:

Buyer agrees to purchase from Seller approximately_____bushels of _____ at the agreed price of $_____ per bushel under the following terms and conditions to wit:

Seller shall deliver the above described grain within_____days to Buyer's elevator in Anytown, Nebraska.

Seller hereby warrants that title to the above grain is free from encumbrance of any nature whatsoever and that Seller has good and merchantable title, with the right to dispose of the same. Seller hereby authorizes the Buyer to contract for the sale or disposition of said grain for its own account either before or after delivery to the elevator above designated without further authorization from Seller except this contract and buyer shall not be required to account for or pay the balance of said purchase price until the _____day of _____, 19_____.

Seller hereby acknowledges receipt of the sum of $_____ to apply on this contract and the balance shall not be due until the_____day of _____, 19_____, it being the intent of all parties hereto that said sale shall not be completed until final payment by the Buyer to the Seller and it is specifically agreed that Seller shall, under no circumstances be entitled to the balance due herein until the _____day of _____, 19_____.

Buyer agrees that it will pay the balance due without interest on the due date as fixed herein to the Seller.

It is further agreed by and between the Buyer and Seller that this contract shall be binding upon the heirs, administrators, executors of the respective parties and that this contract can not be assigned.

Dates this _____day of _____, 19_____.

JOHN DOE GRAIN COMPANY

_____   By _____
Witness   Buyer

_____   _____
Witness   Seller

CHAPTER **6**

Futures Markets for Grain

Assume it's March 1981 and new crop soybean futures are trading at $9.20, basis November. That is considerably above the variable cost of production. It surely looks attractive—but, the soybean loan is only $5.05 per bushel and if everyone plants a big soybean acreage, the price may fall by harvest time. What can you do? You can sell new crop soybean futures and put on a production hedge—let the speculator take the risk that overproduction will drive prices lower.

Futures markets are now being used by an increasing number of producers who recognize the vital role they perform in protecting buyers and sellers alike. But to many farmers the futures market is still a strange and mysterious institution, conducted by and for speculators, most of whom are wheeler-dealers and manipulators who somehow get rich by selling something they don't have and buying something they don't want. Or, it is thought to be too complicated to be understood by ordinary farmers.

Futures trading is complicated. But then, if you don't know anything about them, so are planting and successfully growing a crop of corn or feeding out a bunch of steers. To be sure, there are a good many wheeler-dealer types in commodity futures. But futures trading is also populated by people with deeper stakes in agriculture—processors, packers, elevator operators and farmers. The futures market serves real economic functions. It is a way of transferring risk and is a mechanism of price discovery. These functions are performed because futures contracts have real legal and economic meaning. People often get hung up on "how can you sell something you don't have?" You can't, but you can make a contract to deliver something at a future time and place. That is what happens when you sell commodity futures.

On the other side of the contract, a buyer agrees to accept delivery of the commodity at some future time and place. The two parties, anonymous to each other, are not just buying and selling futures contracts—they are making a new contract to effect physical transfer of the commodity involved according to specifications. For various reasons, physical delivery usually does not take place. For example, the specific place of delivery (say Chicago) may not be convenient to either buyer or seller. To avoid delivery, offsetting contracts are made. It is the function of the commodity exchanges and brokers to provide the facilities and services necessary for contract making.

Farmer Use of Futures

The principal reasons for farmer participation in futures trading is to set a price for crops in advance of harvest and to lock in storage profits. While some of the complexities of the futures market can be avoided through forward cash contracting, there is one major problem. You can't always find a buyer willing to give you a profitable price at the time you want to make a deal. By using the futures market, a farmer producing any commodity traded can sell his crop as much as a year in advance with no searching for a buyer. And if subsequent market developments cause him to have second thoughts, he can get out of the deal honestly and readily by purchasing an offsetting contract. This flexibility is a unique and most valuable feature of the futures market. Use of the futures markets allows farmers to separate the time of pricing from the time of delivery.

COMMODITY EXCHANGES

Commodity futures are traded on more than a dozen exchanges in the United States and Canada, but there are only seven which are directly functional for farmers:

Chicago Board of Trade. Founded in 1865, this is the oldest of the exchanges and is the largest in terms of dollar volume of contracts traded. While there are other commodities traded, those of primary interest to farmers are corn, Soft Red Winter wheat, oats, soybeans, soybean oil, soybean meal and iced broilers.

Chicago Mercantile Exchange. This exchange was founded in 1874 and for many years specialized in butter and eggs, with use primarily by the storage trade. In more recent years, contracts have been introduced in a variety of commodities. Largest volume is in the livestock sector. Futures are traded in live cattle, feeder cattle, live hogs, pork bellies, fresh eggs, Idaho potatoes and grain sorghum.

Kansas City Board of Trade. Situated in the center of the Great Plains Wheat Belt, the exchange has been serving the trade since 1869. Futures trading in various commodities has been offered over the years, but the mainstay has been Hard Red Winter wheat. A growing interest is developing in other contracts, including corn and grain sorghum.

Minneapolis Grain Exchange. Once a thriving center for futures trading activity, this exchange, founded in 1881, is essentially a cash market today. The principal futures commodities traded are Dark Northern Spring wheat and Durum wheat.

New York Mercantile Exchange. Somewhat like its Chicago counterpart, this market also had its origin in serving the butter and egg trade. It was established in 1872. The only contracts of agricultural relevance are Maine potatoes and frozen boneless beef.

New York Cotton Exchange. Founded in 1870, this exchange has undergone numerous changes over the years. Today it offers trading in three agricultural commodities—cotton, wool and frozen concentrated orange juice.

Winnipeg Grain Exchange. While it is functionally difficult, if not impossible, to utilize the facilities on a delivery basis, there is trade in commodities not available on U.S. markets which may offer hedging opportunities. Its origin dates back to 1887, but it was reorganized as the Winnipeg Grain Exchange in 1908. Commodities of interest to producers in the United States include barley, oats, flaxseed, rapeseed, rye and cattle.

In addition to being a meeting place for buyers and sellers of commodities, the futures markets provide a "forum" for international information exchange which is the cornerstone of the commodity pricing system. Price determination in a futures market evolves out of an interpretation of fundamental supply and demand considerations for the commodity in question plus many other variables. A drouth in Argentina, a flood in India, a bumper crop forecast, a change in Common Market policy, or a longshoremen's strike at Gulf ports—all are reflected in the trading pits of the various exchanges. Because the futures markets are clearing houses for these price making forces, a speculator, a central Illinois farmer, a feed manufacturer in West Germany, or an oilseed processor in Japan can be equally informed of the collective assessment of these conditions and, within moments, take a market position based upon their interpretation of the market facts.

FUTURES TRADERS

There are basically two groups of traders in commodity markets—the speculators and the hedgers. Each group has a different purpose for trading.

The speculator attempts to anticipate market price movements. He wants to be "long," or have bought, when the value of a contract is rising or is expected to rise. If prices are declining, he hopes to have a "short" position, or have sold the commodity. He seldom owns any of the commodity he trades, nor does he have any desire to take or make delivery on a contract.

The hedger, on the other hand, is involved in owning or producing the physical commodity he trades on the futures market. A hedger might be a livestock feeder, a crop farmer, a country elevator manager, or a grain or livestock processor. Any of these people could be hedgers by using futures contracts to offset their position in the cash market. In other words, hedgers are people who either use or produce commodities traded on the various futures market exchanges. They buy and sell futures contracts to avoid the risk of unfavorable price movement on the cash market. In order to be hedged, the producer must have a position in the futures market that is opposite to his position in the cash market.

Speculators

The commodity speculator assumes the risk that the commodity hedger seeks to avoid. Without him, the futures market couldn't exist. He is not, in the strict definition of the term, a gambler, who wagers on the basis of chance. A speculator has varying degrees of knowledge and information about the markets.

Who is the average speculator? Contrary to what you may think, he is not normally the older, established, well-to-do businessman looking for a new investment interest in life. While there are some in this category, the majority of speculators are relatively young and well educated.

A "veteran" trader is judged so, not by his age, but by how long he has been trading. He's a veteran because he has taken his lumps and has learned to handle himself in the markets. And he may or may not be rich for his efforts.

The percentage of veteran traders in the commodity markets is low compared to the whole. At any one time, they are greatly outnumbered by novice traders who will give up the battle after the first skirmish. These new traders come into the markets because they've read it's too dry in the Southwest, or there is a drouth in the Midwest, or TGE is running rampant in the nation's farrowing houses, or a myriad of other reasons—most of which seem to imply impending disaster for the farmer. Almost to a man, people coming into the commodity markets for the first time would rather be "bulls" (who think prices are going higher) than "bears" (who think prices are going lower); thus the greatest surge of speculative activity normally is set off by bullish news.

Why? Maybe it's the ingrained optimism of most people, but a more accurate explanation probably is that it's easier to visualize Kansas wheat wilting under a relentless sun and pelted by wind-driven dust than it is to spend tedious hours studying supply-demand prospects and the hundreds of other factors that may indicate larger than needed supplies and probable price declines.

This does not make the speculator your enemy or an adversary who wishes you misfortune. If their success in the markets at times depends on you being the loser, it's not for personal reasons. And besides, if you understand speculators well enough, and your timing is right, they will set up better hedging opportunities than you could ever get without them.

One note of caution. Farmers are not immune to bullish speculation and indeed, every year there are farmers who jump into commodity speculation with the rest of the novice traders, often to their later sorrow. The farmer-speculator will note poor growing conditions in his local area, combine this with similar hearsay about other areas (usually learned from a farmer friend who vacationed several states away), and figure harvest prices will be well above current futures quotes. He goes "long" in the market by buying one or more futures contracts for the month nearest harvest. Put another way, he's buying the commodity now for a price he believes is lower than it will be before the contract expires. As he has no use for the physical commodity, he will sell an offsetting contract before expiration, he hopes for more than the price at which he bought. The difference in price, if indeed the price does rise, is his profit after he deducts brokerage commissions and other expenses of the transaction.

The usual problem is that in his haste to "make a killing," the farmer-speculator neglects to consider possible changes in demand for the commodity, foreign supplies, and export prospects and is inclined to discount USDA crop estimates, if they disagree with his personal assessment.

Even if he's right on price direction, there are hazards and pitfalls along the way. If the market goes against his position (down), he must come up with more margin money. In a downtrending market, he will be tempted to close out his position and buy back in at a lower level so as to either reduce his losses or increase the potential for gain over the long pull. He must worry about the daily, and at times hourly, market fluctuations. As a result, he can compound his mistakes with every move he makes. Unless he has extreme confidence in his original plan, he may be right in his long term analysis, but still lose money because of "in and out" trading due to day-to-day market pressure.

This isn't to say that you should steer clear of the futures markets. But unless you have the considerable market knowledge required and the time to keep abreast of it, stick to hedging commodities you produce with the purpose of reducing the risk of price decline.

Hedgers

As a hedger, you have some advantages over the speculator with equal market knowledge:

1. Your purpose in trading is to set the price of the commodity in advance, or to lock in a return to storage. Also, since you own (or will produce) and at the same time have sold equal amounts of the commodity you are dealing in, you are better protected than the speculator. Losses in a futures market position may be compensated for by an increasing value of the actual product which you also own.

2. You are primarily concerned about the long term market trend. The successful hedger has put enough thought and time into the market to come up with a good long-range plan. Although it's important to keep a close eye on market developments, the primary objective should be to follow that plan.

The problem that many farmers have had with hedging is that they fall victim to the short term pressures and end up not as hedgers but as speculators in their own right. If you change your marketing plan without at least as much thought as you put into the decision to hedge in the first place, you may be joining ranks with the speculator whether you want to or not.

Let's say you hedge soybeans by selling a January contract because you have calculated that at the price reflected (January futures minus the basis at the time you sell) you can make an acceptable return on your production. So you have "locked in" that price. The problem comes when the futures price starts rising. If you lift your hedge (buy back your contract) you will take a loss on the futures trading and also lose your insurance. If the market later declines, you may take a loss in the cash sale also, or at least sell for a price lower than originally locked in through hedging. When you place a hedge, you may gain protection from falling prices, but you also give up the chance to profit from rising prices.

COSTS OF FUTURES TRADING

To trade commodities you must either own a membership in a specific exchange or transact your business through an agent or broker who has such a membership. Fees charged by brokers are negotiable, but for most traders, there is a set amount per contract trade. Table 6-1 lists the main agricultural commodities which are traded and where they are traded. It is not a complete listing of the commodities traded for future delivery through organized exchanges. The table also shows a sample of the brokerage fee or commission charged. However, these are subject to change.

Margins

"Margins" and "margin calls" are words which strike fear into the hearts of many speculators and hedgers—unjustly so, for it is margins and margin calls which insure that futures markets and brokerage firms remain solvent and that only those who can demonstrate fiscal responsibility continue as futures traders. Let's examine the question of margins and margin calls in more detail and clarify the function and mechanics of the subject.

When trading in the futures market by either buying or selling a futures contract, a "margin," or good faith money, deposit is required by the futures exchange. The margin deposit is made for you by the brokerage house, which in turn will require that you deposit offsetting funds with it. For example, to place a storage hedge on 5,000 bushels of corn, you would sell one contract of corn futures on the Chicago Board of Trade. When the order is filled, a margin deposit (usually less than 10% of the actual value of the contract) must be made with the Exchange by the broker. This is called "initial margin."

The broker, in turn, will ask you for a deposit with him of enough margin money to cover his deposit. He may ask for additional margin above that required by the Exchange, depending on the brokerage firm, the commodity being traded, and the volatility of the marketplace. Many brokerage firms require a minimum account deposit of $2,500.

Once deposited, the margin must be kept current if it is to continue to provide about the same degree of protection to the Exchange and the broker. An adverse price movement will bring a call from the Exchange to the brokerage firm (and thus to you) for additional or "maintenance margin" to restore the margin account to the original level. The hedger must be ready to put a check in the mail immediately. If the broker does not receive the money within about two days (although the time varies among brokerage firms), one or more of your contracts will be closed out at the market the following day in order to restore the proper margin balance. Should the price continue to change against your position, you will be called on regularly to bring your margin deposit back up to the required minimum maintenance margin level.

An increase in the futures price, which results in a margin call, is very likely reflected in a similar increase in the cash value of the grain that is being produced or held in storage. Thus, the hedge is still in force and functioning properly. It is only when adequate financial and mental preparation have not been made that a margin call is a matter of concern. If a portion of the futures account is closed out

Table 6-1.

FUTURES CONTRACTS IN AGRICULTURAL PRODUCTS.

Commodity and Exchange	Size of Contract	Commission*
WHEAT		
Chicago Board of Trade	5,000 Bu.	$60
Kansas City Board of Trade	5,000 Bu.	$60
Minneapolis Grain Exchange	5,000 Bu.	$60
Mid-America Commodity Exchange	1,000 Bu.	$25
CORN		
Chicago Board of Trade	5,000 Bu.	$60
Mid-America Commodity Exchange	1,000 Bu.	$25
OATS		
Chicago Board of Trade	5,000 Bu.	$55
Mid-America Commodity Exchange	1,000 Bu.	$25
SOYBEANS		
Chicago Board of Trade	5,000 Bu.	$65
Mid-America Commodity Exchange	1,000 Bu.	$25
SOYBEAN MEAL		
Chicago Board of Trade	100 Tons	$60
SOYBEAN OIL		
Chicago Board of Trade	60,000 Lbs.	$60
SUNFLOWER SEED		
Minneapolis Grain Exchange	100,000 Lbs.	$60
CATTLE		
Chicago Mercantile Exchange	40,000 Lbs.	$60
Mid-America Commodity Exchange	20,000 Lbs.	$40
FEEDER CATTLE		
Chicago Mercantile Exchange	42,000 Lbs.	$60
BONELESS BEEF (Frozen)		
New York Mercantile Exchange	36,000 Lbs.	$55
HOGS		
Chicago Mercantile Exchange	30,000 Lbs.	$55
Mid-America Commodity Exchange	15,000 Lbs.	$30
PORK BELLIES		
Chicago Mercantile Exchange	36,000 Lbs.	$65
EGGS		
Chicago Mercantile Exchange	22,500 Doz.	$60
BROILERS		
Chicago Board of Trade	30,000 Lbs.	$55
Chicago Mercantile Exchange	30,000 Lbs.	$55
POTATOES		
New York Mercantile Exchange	50,000 Lbs.	$55
Chicago Mercantile Exchange	50,000 Lbs.	$57
COTTON		
New York Cotton Exchange	50,000 Lbs.	$75

*Subject to change.

due to a failure to meet margin calls, a true hedge still exists only if you immediately sell a similar amount of cash grain.

To prevent liquidation, make certain that both you and your banker understand this important aspect of commodity futures trading before entering into a hedge so that adequate plans may be made in advance of a possible margin call. You may be able to set up an automatic margin "loan" through your bank to meet this "time crisis" aspect of hedging. Rather than an automatic loan, however, you may wish to use margin calls as review points—a signal that it is time to sit down with both your broker and your banker (preferably together) and review your initial hedging plan to determine if the facts, as stated in your pre-hedge evaluation, are still valid and if the hedge is still desirable.

A further consideration about margin deposits is that they do not bear interest if deposited in cash. Therefore interest should be included as a cost of hedging. It is possible to deposit some types of interest bearing securities (such as U.S. Treasury Bills), rather than cash, for the initial margin money. But you must check this with your broker to find out what is currently acceptable. Also, remember that if you have a short hedge in futures against storage, and the futures price declines, the additional "paper profit" above the initial margin requirement can be withdrawn from the account. If a large surplus of margin money accumulates, this would be advisable. To do this, contact your broker and ask him to mail you a check or to send a check to your bank. Some brokerage firms have established "ready asset" accounts that will pay interest on surplus margin.

BASIS

Probably the most often used and least understood word encountered in hedging is *basis*. Basis is simply the difference between a futures price and a cash price. A Chicago futures price generally reflects the Chicago cash price plus the cost of storage, insurance and interest from today until delivery date of the contract some time ahead.

The *local basis* is the difference between the futures price and your local cash price. This may differ from the basis at the delivery point by roughly the transportation costs from your local market to the delivery point, but is also influenced by supply-demand conditions at various places.

Determine Local Basis

Figure your local grain basis like this:

1. Obtain cash quotes from your local elevator for several years for the time you normally sell grain (perhaps March 30 for corn). Three to four years or longer may be necessary to obtain an accurate figure.
2. Determine the closing price of the futures contract that matures closest to the normal sale time (May Chicago corn in the case of a March 30 sale date). Select a futures and a cash price for the same day.
3. Subtract the cash price from the futures price (cash should be less) for each year and average the basis. This may be referred to as your "normal local basis."

Actual Cash Value

The basis is important to the hedger because he seldom either makes or takes delivery of the physical commodity in Chicago or other delivery points to complete his futures transaction. By subtracting his "normal local basis" from the selected futures price, the hedger is able to closely estimate the actual local cash value that can be locked in through hedging.

Most cash commodity markets show a seasonal pattern of price variation. Grain markets are often lowest at harvest and increase in price as the consumption season progresses.

Basis for Grain

As noted earlier, basis is the difference between the cash price of grain at your local elevator and various futures contracts. It is different in various areas of the country and changes as time passes. It is the voice of the marketplace, indicating the demand for grain. It reflects the supply and demand for storage, and change in basis over a period of time is a gross return to storage. Storage costs must be subtracted to arrive at a net return to storage when hedging.

Five items must be specified to fully describe a specific basis:

1) The commodity
2) The particular futures option
3) The time, i.e., date
4) The location
5) The difference between the cash and futures price

Why is this basis or difference important to you? Keeping a local basis chart will show you the direction of your local cash market and will point out advantageous sale points locally. It is the prerequisite to successful use of the marketing tools of price later contracts, basis contracts, and hedging. You must know your local basis and its traditional trends in order to intelligently use the futures.

Figure 6-1. CORN BASIS—LAFAYETTE, INDIANA 10-2-79.

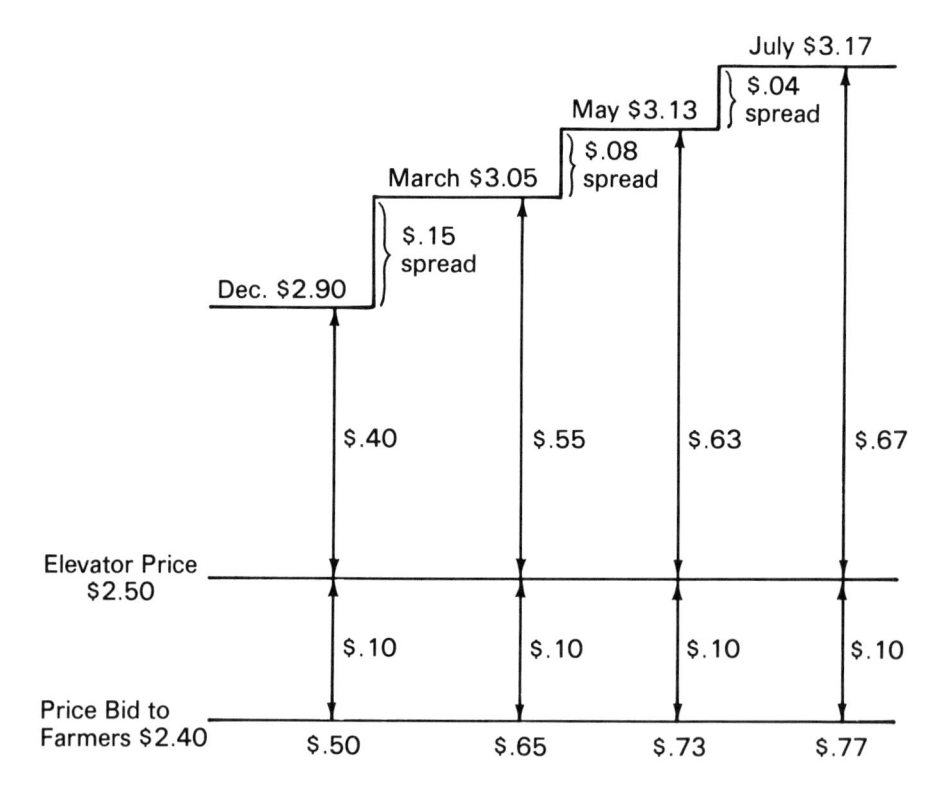

```
                                                              July $3.17
                                                              } $.04
                                              May $3.13       } spread
                                              } $.08
                              March $3.05     } spread
                              } $.15
                              } spread
              Dec. $2.90

              $.40            $.55            $.63            $.67

Elevator Price
    $2.50
              $.10            $.10            $.10            $.10

Price Bid to
Farmers $2.40
              $.50            $.65            $.73            $.77
```

Let's take a look at a one day picture of the basis that existed in the fall of 1979, as shown in Figure 6-1. The futures prices are rounded, an elevator margin of 10¢ is assumed and the farm price of corn is $2.40.

Developing a Basis Chart

Technically, basis is the difference between two prices, the cash price at your elevator and the closing futures prices at the Commodity Exchange, such as the Chicago Board of Trade. Since both of these prices fluctuate, it is easier to visualize if you construct a basis chart. This can be done by either of two methods—by plotting futures price minus cash price or by plotting cash price minus futures price. The method illustrated in Figure 6-2 is to plot cash minus futures by setting the particular futures contract price at zero and plotting the cash price in relation to it. This will show the basis below the futures and that the cash price gains in relation to the futures price as the life of the contract shortens. With this method, a separate chart must be made for each option. Spreads can be kept in table form or charted separately.

You need both historical basis data and current basis data. The historical basis data is used: 1) to determine what an average expected basis is for fall sales, and 2) as a benchmark to judge the current basis.

Elevators typically keep their old records of cash prices paid to farmers. They are usually willing to let you use these records to gather historical price data. For historical data, one price per week is satisfactory and will reduce the workload. Select a midweek day, such as Tuesday, Wednesday, or Thursday, so that the weekend bids do not exert an unreasonable influence on your chart. But use the same day each week. If the day falls on a holiday, select a price on either side of the holiday. A separate columnar page for each grain for each month is recommended. The cash and futures prices are entered on half of the page. On the other half, the relationship of the local cash price to each of the futures prices is entered.

Historical data on futures prices is available from statistical yearbooks published by the Chicago Board of Trade and other exchanges. They can be obtained from the exchanges, libraries in major cities, or from agricultural economics libraries at land grant universities.

100   MARKETING FOR FARMERS

Figure 6-2. WEEKLY NORTH CENTRAL IOWA CORN BASIS (IN CENTS UNDER JULY FUTURES).

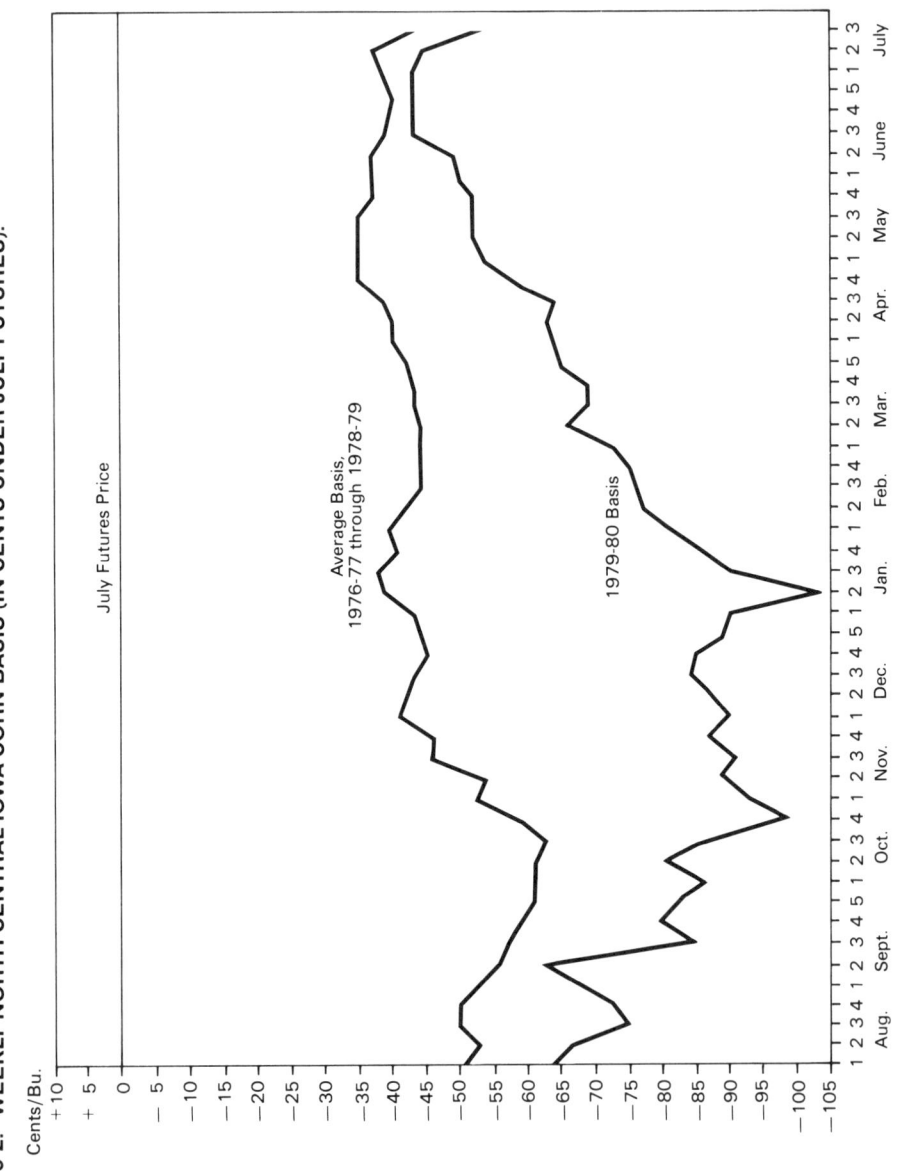

Futures Markets for Grain   101

The next step is to plot the data on graph paper. The price (in cents) is on the vertical axis and the weeks of the month on the horizontal axis. Start your chart a couple months ahead of the marketing year. Since the basis data reflects negative numbers (when plotting cash minus futures), set the zero line (which represents the futures price) near the top of the graph. Plot the data each week, and connect the plots with a line. Figure 6-2 shows data for a three year period where the prices for the various years were averaged together, as well as for an individual year. You may want to plot the individual years on separate graphs.

Interpretation of Basis Charts

A clear understanding of a basis chart is the first and most important step you can take if you're serious about grain marketing.

1. Evaluate the storage returns that can be locked in through hedging. The basis is quite variable at harvest time, but tends to level out as the futures contract approaches maturity. In October 1979, the basis was about 25¢ wider than the average shown in Figure 6-2, reflecting, in part, higher interest rates. Rather than sell corn at $2.32 per bushel ($.85 under the July futures), a producer could hedge and lock in a gross return to storage of $.45 per bushel as the basis narrows to about 40¢ under the July in June 1980.

2. Determine the price that can be locked in through forward pricing by hedging. If you know that the July corn basis narrows to 40¢ under the July by June, all you have to do is to look at the July futures quotation and subtract 40¢.

3. Determine when to use a basis contract, sell grain, or sell grains and buy futures. If the basis rises quickly, early in the marketing year, the voice of the market is telling you to: a) sign a basis contract if you like the basis but don't like the price and think the futures will go higher, or b) sell the cash grain and buy futures if you think the futures will go higher. If you think the futures will go lower, sell the cash grain.

4. Understand why harvest time is the worst time of the year to sell grain. Selling at a wide basis is selling at the biggest discount of the year. If you think the futures price will decline, hedge and continue to earn a return to storage.

5. Understand why elevators have minimum storage charges and service charges on deferred priced grain.

The most favorable time for an elevator to hedge is when the basis is the widest. If elevators did not have a minimum storage charge, a customer could deliver his grain at harvest and sell it 4 to 6 weeks later, after the basis has narrowed about 20¢ per bushel.

On deferred priced grain, the grain is moved on into the marketing channels. The producer is pricing on the current basis. The elevator manager has sold on the wide basis at harvest time. The service charges plus the interest on the money he received from the sale of the grain has to offset the change in basis, or he will lose part of his margin and possibly even have a loss on the deal.

6. Understand why some elevators are not offering storage to farmers. Elevator managers who understand hedging have realized that they can earn a return to storage that is greater than farmers are willing to pay.

7. Evaluate the quality of a bid. To evaluate a local bid, call the elevator for a cash bid quote, and subtract it from the futures price to determine the current basis. Then compare the current basis with the historical basis.

FUTURES PRICE MOVEMENT

The basic working premise behind any hedging operation is that cash and futures prices tend to seek a common level as each futures contract expires. Since the cash and futures contracts in the same crop year are subject to the same basic economic fundamentals, they should respond alike to those fundamentals—all rising in a bullish situation and all falling under a bearish market influence.

In general, this is the case. However, it should be noted that even though the cash and futures contracts in a commodity may move in the same direction, they seldom move to the same degree over any period of time. The farther the contract month is from the current cash period, the looser the relationship.

For example, in a bull (upward) move, the cash and nearby futures contracts will generally rise faster than the distant contracts in the same crop year. Conversely, in a bear (downward) market, the cash and nearby futures will normally fall faster than the distant contracts.

The reason? In a bull market there is often a shortage of the commodity for immediate use in relation to demand. High prices are needed to ration the available supply, and to stimulate greater production. As a result, the cash market and nearby contracts tend to gain on the distant contracts since the shortage is current and, through price rationing, should be eased somewhat by the time the distant contracts are ready to be settled for delivery. In an oversupply situation, the nearby contracts feel the weight of deliveries and the need for values to drop sufficiently to "price" the surplus into consumption.

There are usually scores of such moves between cash and futures contracts during the crop year. However, as the time approaches for a futures contract to expire, you can expect the degree of such fluctuations between that contract and the cash to lessen. At the delivery points (approved warehouses in Chicago, St. Louis, and Toledo), at delivery time (on the first business day of the option month), the cash and futures prices tend to converge.

As a result, the hedger normally puts his hedges in the contract month closest to the time he expects to move the hedged product, unless there is a narrow spread between futures options and he expects the spread to widen. For example, a grain elevator manager who buys corn in November and expects to move it in February will hedge in the March contract because it should be more in line with the cash price than the more distant May or July contract. For the same reason, the soybean grower who plans to sell at harvest will place his hedge in the November contract, or the cotton grower in the December contract.

FUTURES PRICES AS FORECASTS

Futures prices should not be interpreted as specific price forecasts for the delivery month of the contract. A futures market does focus attention on prospective market conditions and it provides a mechanism for registering a price in some future time period.

However, it is unlikely that either speculators or hedgers in an active futures market view price quotations as a price forecast. Speculators buy or sell contracts because they believe prices will change from their current level. This is the only way they could hope to make a profit in the market. Similarly, hedgers want to lock in a price through hedging that appears more favorable than their expectations of later cash prices. Some hedgers may be willing to price at some discount below their actual expectation of cash prices in order to obtain a greater degree of price certainty.

Thus, futures prices may actually reflect a level that none of the participants in the market really expect to continue for very long. Historical data provides evidence that futures prices are not reliable forecasts of cash prices in the future.

TAX TREATMENT OF FUTURES TRANSACTIONS

For federal income tax purposes, commodity futures contracts that are speculative in nature are considered to be capital assets. Speculative transactions therefore result in either capital gains or losses. A contract held for more than six months is given long term capital gain or loss treatment. A speculator, however, is limited to a capital loss (short or long term) deduction of $3,000 per year. Losses greater than $3,000 may be carried over to later years.

Profits from commodity speculation are taxable as capital gains. A net short term gain must be included in full as gross income. But only 40% of a net long term capital gain is includible in gross income.

Futures contracts used solely for hedging purposes are not treated as capital assets. Transactions that are made to reduce speculative risks due to price fluctuations inherent in a taxpayer's business are considered, for income tax purposes, to be a legitimate business insurance. The cost of such operations, including any losses sustained, is deductible as a business expense. Likewise, any profit realized from a hedging operation must be included in the gross income of the taxpayer. The burden of proof rests with the hedger. Even though he has identified the transaction as a hedge, he must be able to prove that he entered the market for price protection. Accurate records should be maintained showing the actual cash position at the time of the hedge.

HOW TO HEDGE

Grain Production Hedge

In the simplest form a grain production hedge involves a sale of futures against the particular grain being produced so that the impact of declining harvest prices can be eliminated, or at least minimized, for grain that must be sold during the harvest season. In recent years, placing a hedge at planting time has often not worked out well. Due to a variety of factors, prices anticipated in the spring were lower than those actually received during harvest. However, there have been some that did work.

The final concern of the farmer is when to lift his hedge, that is, buy an offsetting contract. To maintain price protection for the full period, a grain producer should maintain his short position in the futures market for as long as he owns the cash grain, closing out his futures position the same day he sells the grain. Early lifting of the hedge leaves him susceptible to losses from further declines in the cash market. At the same time, if the hedger stays short in the futures market past the time he sells the cash grain, he stands to lose if the futures price rises.

The fundamental tool of a hedger is a knowledge of the local basis. By deducting the basis from the futures price he can estimate the net value of his grain. If his timing is right, proper hedging will reduce price risk and add to the profits from grain sales.

We can illustrate a production hedge by referring back to the soybean market situation discussed at the beginning of the chapter. It's March 2, 1981, and new crop soybean futures are trading at $9.20, basis the November. It's an attractive price, but because it is so attractive, there's the possibility of a big soybean crop which could drive harvest prices down. You can lock in the high price, though, by selling new crop soybean futures.

Once you have made the decision to plant soybeans and put on a production hedge, you must determine these things:

How much to sell. Refer to the Hedging Matrix on page 115 to select the proper number of contracts. In case weather, disease or insects should prevent you from achieving expected production levels, you may wish to sell only up to 75% of "normal" production (based on average yields for your farm for the last three years). Remember that what you sell you must either produce or buy back in order to fulfill the sales commitment you have made in the form of a production hedge. If you sell more than you eventually grow, you have become a speculator—short soybeans and creating risk—the opposite of your purpose, which is to transfer price risk to someone else.

When to sell. This decision will be based partly on the size of your operation. If you will grow only enough to sell one contract (5,000 bushels), you will obviously have only one opportunity to pick the level at which to place the production hedge (unless you deal through the Mid-America Exchange which has 1,000 bushel contracts). But, say your operation is a large one and you expect to produce up to 30,000 bushels. You plan to hedge 20,000 bushels or four contracts for harvest delivery. In this case, it may be wise to average your sales level by selling one contract ahead of the government's April Planting Intentions Report (usually out about April 15); one in mid-June after your beans are planted and the spring weather risk is behind you; another in early July, just ahead of the government July Actual Plantings Report; and the fourth contract in mid-September/early October, when your crop is pretty well made and you can be reasonably sure of your production level. If your beans are early and the crop has done better than average, you may be able to sell an additional contract just prior to combining, assuming you still like the price level. Be careful at this stage not to overextend yourself, however, as a harvest disaster could still sharply reduce your production and make you a short speculator. If you spread your sales, the price received will differ from the $9.20 price on March 2.

What to do if the fundamentals change. This is a critical part of your pre-hedging plan. You expect a big U.S. crop due to the high price level and think that overproduction will depress prices. What do government and trade economists think? Get copies of the USDA Fats and Oils Situation report and a situation report from your advisory service, commodity broker or University Extension Service. Check these reports and file them for references as the season unfolds. Now watch for your benchmark reports:

January and April acreage intentions—about January 15 and April 15—will give the first indication of farmers' planting intentions. To keep your hedging plan in effect, this report should confirm your expectations of a big crop.

April stocks report—about April 24—is a critical old crop benchmark and will give an indication of usage to date and expected old crop stocks levels. Low usage and high stocks would be a plus to your program. If usage is high, you must reevaluate the level of new crop output that will be considered large enough to depress prices.

June actual plantings report—about June 30—is the key report, since you now have a fix on how many acres were actually planted and can estimate the final crop outturn, given normal weather. Check this level against earlier expectations (yours, government's and trade sources) which were developed in April.

July stocks report—about July 24—is the semi-final old crop check on usage and expected carryout. This should reconfirm your ideas about how much new crop output will be too much.

Weekly weather crop reports—released each Monday afternoon during the growing season. Your broker will have these reports. They should serve as a general guide to the progress of the crop and will alert you to any significant change in growing conditions.

Private information services—such as Doane's Agricultural Report. These professional monitoring and analysis reports will keep you abreast of world events and current trade thinking, as well as price trends in other markets and important legislative actions in Washington, D.C.

Significant changes in the early season expected supply-demand situation may be revealed by any of the above reports and analyses. Changes toward additional supply or less demand may indicate that you should advance the timing of your hedge selling before the new bearish forces push prices lower. Changes toward less supply or more demand may encourage you to delay your hedge selling to take advantage of a firming price trend. Or, they may change so drastically that a production hedge is no longer desirable (an impending crop failure or the appearance of unexpected demand from Russia or China, for example). But unless you have taken the time to make a pre-hedging plan and record the expected supply-demand situation, you will not have the necessary benchmarks against which to judge changes.

When you sell futures you lock in a price between your hedging date and harvest or sale date, if grain is stored. For that reason, and because no one can consistently pick the top of a market, you may want to spread your hedge sales over several weeks. This will allow you to average out your hedging price and give you additional time to assess the emerging new crop supply-demand balance before committing your entire production. However, this can result in a lost opportunity should prices rise. Also with hedging, you must contend with margin requirements and interest lost as a result of margin payments.

But, remember the outlook at the time you initiated your hedging program! Prices were exceptionally good by historical standards at that time and the futures market offered a return you would have been happy to accept. There was also the distinct possibility that a large acreage could send prices down near loan level at harvest.

So, either you must pick some dates to do your hedging, or you must determine a price level that will satisfy you, and when that price is offered, hedge up. Then, unless the fundamentals change, stick with your original hedging program—the one that was decided in the cool of winter when you were objective and not emotionally involved in the market.

Price Protection for Stored Grain

The shift to field shelling of corn has brought some unexpected side effects. To avoid harvest bottlenecks of delivering corn to country elevators, farmers have built drying and storage facilities of their own. They are hoping to increase income by holding grain.

In keeping ownership of corn or any other grain you also leave yourself open to the financial risk involved in storing. Managers of elevators or processing plants who are accustomed to storing grain have utilized the storage hedge for years. You can also use this management tool to advantage. The principles of using the storage hedge are about the same for either of the two situations. The basic requirement is that a solid, known price relationship must exist between local markets and the futures market.

Briefly, the storage hedge works like a production hedge in forward pricing grain. The anticipated sale price is found by deducting the normal basis from the futures contract near the end of the intended storage period. Storage hedgers typically use spring or summer contracts. The target price represents the approximate net price the market is bidding for late season delivery.

The manager who buys grain to put into storage places his hedge when the grain is bought. A farmer interested in hedging the grain he produced and will store would do best to pick the time when he thinks the basis is the widest, and/or the price is about to top out and decline. This affords him the maximum potential for the basis to narrow, and/or highest net price. Typically, the price spread is the broadest when the local market congestion peaks.

Covering Feed Purchases

Hedging feed purchases in the futures market before buying the actual cash grain has several advantages. First, it allows you to save the price of storage until you're ready to use the feed. The typical price pattern is for the cash market to start low at harvest and rise steadily by enough to at least cover storage costs. By the use of a hedge you avoid building storage space yourself and can also avoid paying for commercial storage. However, you will pay for the change in basis from harvest until you purchase the feed.

You have less capital tied up in the feed, too. For example, 5,000 bushels of corn at $3.00 would involve a cash outlay of $15,000. If you bought this grain at harvest for use six months later, interest at 12% for that half year would be $900. If you're right in your market analysis, the hedge could be held with a margin deposit of about $2,250, to be returned when the hedge is lifted.

Additionally, the use of the hedge allows flexibility. Because of low feeding profits, for instance, you might decide to cut back on the size of your feeding operation. In that case, your demand for feed would be less, so your hedge could be lifted by selling an off-setting contract. If you owned the cash grain you would have the task, and possibly the loss, of selling the grain.

Another example: In the fall, at the peak of harvest, a feeder wants to buy corn for use the following summer. He considers the price at that time to be low relative to what he expects it to be in the summer. However, he has neither the bin space, nor the capital needed to store grain. What can he do?

He may be able to use the futures market by buying a deferred contract. The option month bought should call for delivery shortly after the time he plans to buy the cash grain and lift the hedge. In this case he may pick the May contract with plans to buy corn in April.

In mid-October 1980, the May '81 contract was trading about $3.75. Deducting the normal basis or price spread between the feeder's local market and the futures market shows the market was offering to sell corn at a price equivalent to $3.35 the following April. He buys the May contract at $3.75 and plans to wait until April to buy the cash corn and lift his hedge. In April 1981, assume the May future had risen to $4.00 and the local cash corn market was $3.60. The feeder buys cash corn for $3.60 and sells his May contract for $4.00. This gives him a 25¢ gain on his futures position to put against the

$3.60 cash corn, making an effective price of $3.35—his original target price for the corn purchase.

Had the gain on the futures market been less than the gain in cash price, the effective price of the corn would have been higher than his target price by an amount equal to the narrowing of the basis. On the other hand, if the basis had widened, the effective price of the cash corn would have been less than the target by an amount equal to the widening of the basis.

In brief, a good feeding hedge depends on the basis holding a predetermined or normal level or being wider than normal. This is the opposite of the storage hedge, where you hope the basis will hold steady or narrow.

The feed hedge and the storage hedge are exact opposites, and it is unlikely that you would want to use both on the same grain at the same time. However, it is reasonable to put a storage hedge on corn and a feed hedge on soybean meal at the same time. These two commodities do not necessarily follow the same patterns.

Feeding hedges, or hedges against forward purchases, can be and are used for different purposes. The livestock feeder can hedge purchases of corn, oats, sorghum, soybean meal or other commodities actively traded on futures exchanges. However, the size of the contracts (5,000 bushels for most grains and 100 tons for soybean meal) limits the use of the feed hedge at the Chicago Board of Trade. The Mid-America Exchange has contracts that call for 1,000 bushels of grain and 50 tons of soybean meal.

With a feeding hedge or forward purchase hedge, as well as a forward sale hedge, you must remember that you are working to establish a target price when you place the hedge. You must be willing to accept this price and be certain that it will not become more of a financial burden than taking the risk on the cash market. Also, you will miss the target price by an appreciable amount if the basis deviates sharply from the normal pattern.

CHOOSING A BROKER

Perhaps the most critical decision you will make when starting on a futures hedging program is choosing a broker. Next to your banker, your broker will be in closest contact with your farming and financial operation. It is imperative that your broker view your hedging operation in the same perspective as you. You must both have the same goals in mind and have a clear mutual understanding of the hedging plan. He must understand your level of knowledge of futures operations and be committed to helping you learn more about this new aspect of your farm business. He should have a reasonable knowledge about your operation and should be willing to visit with your banker and possibly your wife to answer any questions they may have about the technical aspects of hedging in futures.

Some do's and don'ts in selecting a broker

1. *Don't* pick a broker from the telephone directory. *Do* visit the brokerage office so that you can judge the overall operation of the commission house and evaluate its staff.

2. *Don't* settle for the first broker to reach you when you come through the door. *Do* interview as many brokers as necessary to find the one whose manner, bearing, and personality fit your own.

3. *Don't* insist on the "old pro" of the office. *Do* insist that the office have an "old pro." Often a newer, younger broker who is still building a clientele will be willing and able to spend considerably more time concentrating on your individual account and in acquiring a thorough understanding of your situation and needs. But, it is imperative that the office have a seasoned, veteran broker so that if problems arise your broker can draw on his knowledge and experience. (Keep in mind, however, that he can only give advice—you must give the order.)

4. *Don't* assume that the closest office is the best. *Do* visit brokerage offices out of town and evaluate them against your local agency. A long distance call (and you can normally call collect or on a toll free number) is a small inconvenience to pay for the best service.

5. *Don't* open an account without checking for backup services at the brokerage. *Do* ask for copies of research reports, check on order execution time and efficiency. Ask for samples of profit and loss statements, confirmation notices and other papers to be sure they are professionally done in a manner which is clear to you. Ask about additional services such as "hot lines" to the trading floor. Get the most for your commission dollar—the rate is the same, but the service varies widely between brokerage houses.

6. *Don't* spread your business around. *Do* find the best broker and stay with him. The advantages of having all your hedging eggs in one basket are numerous. Your broker can evaluate your total hedging program only when he knows your total program. Precise record keeping is essential to hedging; and it's difficult if you have more than one account. Also, when you work with only one broker, it is much easier to build the bond of confidence necessary to a successful hedging program.

7. *Don't* assume you have to stick with the first broker you try. *Do* give him a fair chance to work out a successful program with you. If, after a trial period, you do not feel comfortable with him, pick a new broker. Remember Steps 1 and 2 outlined above. They will reduce the likelihood of having to switch horses in midstream.

8. *Don't* accept your gut feeling about the man or the firm. *Do* ask for references of other hedging clients, and check them out.

9. Use your broker for an additional source of information, but only as an order taker.

SAMPLE PROBLEMS

Hedging—with Storage

Grain analysts see a possibility of December 1981 corn futures reaching $4.00. With a 15¢ spread between December '81 and March '82 corn, the March contract would then be the equivalent of $4.15—if this occurred. Assume the corn basis is 20¢ under the March futures on February 1 at your local elevator. Also, the usual harvest basis is 50¢ under the December option.

Use the following T diagram to show how a farmer could price his corn for delivery on February 1, 1982. Assume cash corn price is $3.25 on February 1, 1982.

Date	Cash Transactions	Futures Transactions	Basis
	Expected price _____		
	By (date) _____		

What price could you lock in for delivery at harvest time?

Assume an interest rate of 10% and a commission charge of $50 per 5,000 bushel contract. What spread is needed between the March and May corn to make it profitable to roll the hedge forward?

Pre-Harvest Hedge — No Storage

Facts:

1. Projected harvest date is October 1.
2. The historical basis on October 1 is 40¢ under December futures.
3. Currently the December futures is trading at $3.60.
4. Cash corn prices at harvest time turned out to be $2.80 per bushel.
5. The actual basis turns out to be 45¢ under the December futures.

Use this information to fill in the T diagram below to illustrate the mechanics of hedging.

Date	Cash Transactions	Futures Transactions	Basis
	Expected price _____ By (date) _____		

HEDGING MATRIX

The Hedging Matrix (table 6-2) is a simple set of figures designed to help you pick the number of futures contracts to sell in a grain production hedge. Across the top of the tables are yield figures in bushels per harvested acre and down the extreme left hand column are the number of bushels to be hedged. In the second column from the left are the number of contracts to be sold against anticipated production. To use the matrix, simply locate the yield level, in bushels per harvested acre, that you can *count on* producing year in and year out, excepting the most adverse insect, weather and disease conditions. It doesn't matter whether the crop is wheat, corn or soybeans. Go down the column under your normal yield until you find the approximate number of acres you plan to harvest. Go across that row to the left of the page and determine the *maximum* number of contracts and bushels you should hedge. For example, if you grow 30 bushels per acre wheat and plan to harvest 1,500 acres, you may hedge up to nine contracts (45,000 bushels) of wheat futures.

Futures Markets for Grain

Table 6-2.

HEDGING MATRIX

Bushels	Number of Contracts	Yield per Harvested Acre (Acres)															
		10	20	30	40	50	60	70	80	90	100	110	120	130	140	150
5,000	1	500	250	167	125	100	84	72	63	56	50	46	42	39	36	34
10,000	2	1000	500	334	250	200	167	143	125	112	100	91	84	77	72	67
15,000	3	1500	750	500	375	300	250	215	188	167	150	137	125	116	108	100
20,000	4	2000	1000	667	500	400	334	286	250	223	200	182	167	165	143	134
25,000	5	2500	1250	834	625	500	417	358	313	278	250	228	209	193	179	167
30,000	6	3000	1500	1000	750	600	500	409	375	334	300	273	250	231	215	200
35,000	7	3500	1750	1167	875	700	584	500	438	389	350	319	292	270	250	234
40,000	8	4000	2000	1334	1000	800	667	572	500	445	400	364	334	308	286	267
45,000	9	4500	2250	1500	1125	900	750	643	563	500	450	409	375	347	322	300
50,000	10	5000	2500	1667	1250	1000	834	715	625	556	500	455	417	385	358	334
75,000	15	7500	3750	2500	1875	1500	1250	1071	938	834	750	682	625	577	536	500
100,000	20	10000	5000	3334	2500	2000	1667	1429	1250	1112	1000	910	834	770	715	667

Figure 6-3.

Hedging Record

Date	Futures Transaction	Cash Transaction	Basis
_____	Sold _____ Bu @_____	Bought _____ Bu @___	_____
_____	Bought _____ Bu @_____	Sold _____ Bu @___	_____

(a) futures gain or loss _____   (b) cash gain or loss _____

Total gain or loss
(total of a & b) _____   Basis Change _____

How could this trade have been improved? _____

Date	Futures Transaction	Cash Transaction	Basis
_____	Sold _____ Bu @_____	Bought _____ Bu @___	_____
_____	Bought _____ Bu @_____	Sold _____ Bu @___	_____

(a) futures gain or loss _____   (b) cash gain or loss _____

Total gain or loss
(total of a & b) _____   Basis Change _____

How could this trade have been improved? _____

Date	Futures Transaction	Cash Transaction	Basis
_____	Sold _____ Bu @_____	Bought _____ Bu @___	_____
_____	Bought _____ Bu @_____	Sold _____ Bu @___	_____

(a) futures gain or loss _____   (b) cash gain or loss _____

Total gain or loss
(total of a & b) _____   Basis Change _____

How could this trade have been improved? _____

Figure 6-4.

CORN PRICE AND BASIS RECORD.

Col. 1	Col. 2	Col. 3	Col. 4						Col. 5						Col. 6		
	Cash Price		Option Months and Futures Prices						Basis						Spreads		
Date	Old Crop	New Crop	March	May	July	Sept.	Dec.	March	May	July	Sept.	Dec.	Dec. March	March May	May July

Figure 6-5.

SOYBEAN PRICE AND BASIS RECORD.

Col. 1	Col. 2	Col. 3	Col. 4									Col. 5								Col. 6		
	Cash Price		Option Months and Futures Prices									Basis								Spreads		
Date	Old Crop	New Crop	March	May	July	Aug.	Sept.	Nov.	Jan.	March	May	July	Aug.	Sept.	Nov.	Jan.	Nov. Jan.	March May	May July

Futures Markets for Grain

Figure 6-6.

WHEAT PRICE AND BASIS RECORD.

Col. 1	Col. 2	Col. 3	Col. 4						Col. 5						Col. 6		
	Cash Price		Option Months and Futures Prices						Basis						Spreads		
Date	Old Crop	New Crop	March	May	July	Sept.	Dec.		March	May	July	Sept.	Dec.		July Dec.	Dec. March	March May

CHAPTER 7

Grain Markets: Sources of Information and Market Factors

Volatility in grain prices and rapid changes in market conditions have been key aspects of U.S. agriculture in the recent past. In the years ahead, growing world demand is likely to bring even more rapid and dramatic fluctuations in prices. To effectively market grain in the 1980's, farmers will need to spend more time keeping current on U.S. and world supply-demand conditions and incorporating such information in a marketing plan. In the years ahead, farmers also will need to sharpen their analytical skills and their ability to evaluate how changes in supplies, exports and other market factors will affect prices. In short, they will need to become more business oriented, using the same sources of information that are heavily relied on by the grain trade.

In developing information-gathering skills, farmers need answers to three major questions: (1) what factors will have the greatest influence on prices? (2) where can I get current, timely information about these factors? and (3) how much impact would a specific change in these factors have on prices?

USDA's system for estimating crop production and monitoring world agriculture forms the backbone of our market information network. This system has developed over the years with a major purpose being to provide objective, unbiased information farmers can use in production and market planning. To make our free enterprise economy work effectively, buyers and sellers also need equal access to information on supply-demand conditions. Publicly funded and disseminated agricultural information is intended to help meet this requirement, and to help farmers be as informed as the people who buy their products. The system also provides information needed to guide policy decisions on price support levels, export credit funding, reserve programs and other matters of vital interest to agriculture.

Market information developed by USDA's reporting system is available from a variety of private sources, as well as from Extension Services of most land grant universities. Private sources include market advisory services, market letters from major brokerage firms, radio and television stations, farm organizations and farm magazines. With the exception of radio and television stations, most of these sources also analyze the USDA supply information and indicate what price trends are expected.

THE USDA MARKET INFORMATION SYSTEM

Since the USDA information-gathering system is the basic source of grain market information, let's look at the available information, where it comes from and why it is important. Information from the USDA can be grouped into four categories: (1) estimates of U.S. grain and oilseed supplies, including production and stocks; (2) other U.S. market information, including prices, exports, reserve supplies and related information; (3) foreign crop and demand information; (4) economic analysis of the first three types of information.

Estimates of U.S. Grain and Oilseed Supplies

This part of the USDA system includes estimates of acreage, yield per acre, production and stocks, both for individual states and for the U.S. Accurate supply information is one of the first requirements needed to accurately evaluate the price outlook for farm products. USDA crop estimation work is done by trained professionals who hold civil service positions rather than politically appointed jobs. Civil service appointments are intended to insure that political motivations do not influence estimates of farm production.

Estimates of planted and harvested acreages are developed with the use of scientific sampling procedures, farmer questionnaires, phone contacts and on-farm visits. Initial indications of planted acreage traditionally have been provided in January and April planting intentions surveys. Then in late June, estimates of acreages devoted to spring-planted crops are released. Estimated acreage planted to winter wheat traditionally has been released in December. These acreage reports provide indications of year-to-year shifts from one crop to another, and provide the base for public and private estimates of production.

Monthly crop reports. During the growing season, USDA releases monthly reports showing the current year's potential production of major crops. These reports, as well as most other major crop and livestock reports, are developed in elaborate "lock-up" procedures to prevent premature release of the information. Specialists working on the report enter a locked and guarded room, and stay there until the report has been completed and released to the public. Information for the national report is compiled from individual state data delivered to the "lock-up" room.

The monthly crop reports are based on information from farmer questionnaires, as well as information from objective yield survey techniques. Objective yield survey procedures involve carefully applied measurements of plants and counts of ears or seed pods in precise areas in sample farm fields. At harvest-time, these sample areas are harvested, dried, weighed and converted to equivalent yields per acre. Thus, monthly crop reports reflect both farmers' opinions of their crop prospects and potential yields based on actual plant developments at that point in time.

USDA's monthly crop reports are heavily used by the grain trade as a guide to the price outlook. Over the years, several private crop forecasts have emerged and usually are released to clients a few days ahead of the USDA report. These private crop surveys are much less extensive than USDA procedures and use official USDA acreage data. Often their main purpose is to anticipate what the official report will show. If the USDA crop estimates differ significantly from earlier private forecasts, a price reaction is likely. If official estimates are in line with private reports, little or no market reaction to the USDA report would be anticipated.

While farmers sometimes are critical of crop reports, this source of information is important for several reasons. First, the reports give farmers an objective look at crop conditions outside their own local area. The Corn Belt, for example, covers an area nearly a thousand miles wide and as much as 400 miles from north to south. The wheat and soybean belts cover even larger sections of the United States. In an area of this size, it is impossible to judge national crop prospects by looking only at conditions in your own local area. Second, without official estimates, the grain trade would have more information on crop prospects than farmers. That would put you at a disadvantage in marketing your products. Third, with no official figures on supplies, the markets would be much more subject to rumors than at present.

Grain stocks. In addition to acreage reports and monthly crop forecasts, USDA issues grain stocks reports in January, April, June and October. These reports complete the supply picture by showing stocks on hand from previous crops. In the case of corn and other feedgrains, changes in stocks during the quarter also provide indications of how much grain is being fed domestically. Reported exports and processing use are subtracted from the change in stocks, with the remainder being apparent utilization for livestock feed. These quarterly stocks reports thus provide the only exact indications of how much grain is being used in the domestic livestock sector. For corn, that's still the largest part of our total demand. For that reason, quarterly stocks reports are an important indicator of the outlook for corn prices.

Information from these reports usually is summarized in medium-sized and larger local newspapers, the *Wall Street Journal* and farm radio broadcasts. More detail is available through state extension services, market advisory newsletters and through your state's crop reporting service.

Monitoring week-to-week crop conditions. In evaluating hedging and forward contracting alternatives during the growing season, it often is helpful to watch crop conditions across the Grain Belt on a week-to-week basis. USDA's *Weekly Weather and Crop Bulletin* is an important tool for doing this. This report is published through the cooperation of USDA, state crop reporting services and the National Weather Service. Each issue has a national precipitation map showing how much moisture was received during the previous week. Brief summaries of fieldwork progress by states, crop conditions as a percent of normal, and ratings of crops by percentages that are excellent, good, fair and poor also are included. With this information, you can determine whether crop conditions are improving, deteriorating or holding steady in major producing states.

This same report also contains easy to read maps showing 30-day precipitation and temperature forecasts. In times of drought, it has drought-index maps that can help you pinpoint how severe and how extensive such problems are. During the winter and early spring, snow-cover maps indicate whether the winter wheat crop is being protected from severe cold weather. At times, three-month weather forecasts also are included in the report.

In addition to domestic weather and crop conditions, the *Weekly Weather and Crop Bulletin* has weekly highlights of weather developments in the grain belts of Europe, Australia, South America, China and Russia. Summaries of this information often are broadcast on farm radio programs and published in farm magazines and in market outlook letters. But if you want more complete monitoring of U.S. and world crop conditions, the full report can be obtained from USDA at a very modest cost. In early 1982, it was available at a U.S. subscription price of $13 per year, from NOAA/USDA Joint Agricultural Weather Facility, USDA South Building, Washington, D.C. 20250. Checks should be made payable to U.S. Department of Commerce, NOAA.

Other U.S. market information. In addition to information on grain supplies, USDA and the Census Bureau provide information on export movements and domestic processing of grain. Important details of this information are published from time to time in the *Wall Street Journal* and in a weekly USDA publication called *Grain Market News*, available from the Grain Market News Branch, USDA, 14th and Independence Ave. S.W., Washington, D.C. 20250.

Each week, the USDA reports how much grain has been exported from the United States, along with the amount exported during the same week a year earlier and season-to-date total exports. This series provides a week-by-week barometer of export demand and should be compared with official projections of marketing year total exports. Monthly Census Bureau reports show the amount of soybeans being processed, comparable year-earlier figures, and stocks of soybeans, soybean oil and meal at processing plants at the end of the month. This information can be used to determine whether domestic crushings are up or down from the previous year, and whether product stocks are rising or declining. If crushings are down from last year, a weak demand situation is indicated. A similar indication would be shown if soybean product stocks have been rising for two or more months.

Along with these reports, USDA's monthly cattle on feed and quarterly sow farrowing reports are other indicators of the domestic demand for feedgrains and soybean meal. These reports provide an indication of whether domestic feed demand is increasing, decreasing or remaining static.

In years when a grain reserve program is in effect, weekly movements of grain into and out of reserve stocks can be an important price indicator. Heavy movement of grain into the reserve would indicate potentially higher prices later in the season. Heavy withdrawals from reserve stocks, on the other hand, could be a stabilizing or temporarily depressing influence on prices. Information on reserve stocks is compiled by USDA's Agricultural Stabilization and Conservation Service. It can be obtained from outlook letters of State Extension Services, from market advisory services and from state ASCS offices.

EXPORT DEMAND INDICATORS

Export demand is a key influence on prices for your crops. But keep in mind that a given level of exports will affect prices differently from one year to the next, depending on the size of the U.S. crop. Information about foreign crop prospects is gathered by USDA through its network of Agricultural Consuls located in foreign countries, through world weather data, and through foreign government reports. The USDA also sends out specialists periodically to evaluate conditions in important foreign production and consumption areas. This information is summarized in a brief report entitled *Weekly Roundup of World Production and Trade*. Highlights of this report often are publicized by the farm press, advisory services and in outlook materials from university extension services. The full report—usually 5 to 7 pages—is available from FAS Information Service, U.S. Department of Agriculture, South Building, Washington, D.C. 20250.

World Crop Estimates

In addition to weekly reports on foreign developments, USDA also publishes monthly world crop estimates during the growing season. These reports contain estimates of world grain stocks and production by countries and regions, and by type of grain. Also included are projections of world consumption, exports and imports. These reports are a major input into public and private projections of export demand for U.S. grains and oilseeds. Unless you want the detailed information, major implications of these reports usually can be obtained from university outlook materials, advisory services or market letters of commodity brokerage firms. If you want the full report, it can be obtained from the same address as the *Weekly Roundup of World Production and Trade.*

Crop Information from Russia and China

Inadequate crop information from Russia and China is probably the biggest limitation in evaluating foreign demand for U.S. grains and oilseeds. Unlike most western nations, grain importing in each of these countries is done entirely by a single large government purchasing agency. For competitive reasons, these agencies do not publish advance estimates of their grain crops until most of their purchasing has been completed. USDA crop estimates for these two major grain importers are based on detailed weather analysis, reports from travelers who have visited the grain areas, Soviet and Chinese newspaper accounts and U.S. crop evaluation teams, whenever possible.

In the years ahead, additional efforts probably will be made to improve the advance estimates of Soviet and Chinese crops. Long term grain agreements also will continue to be used to prevent major unexpected disruptions in U.S. grain markets. Such agreements typically require the importing nation to stay within minimum and maximum purchase levels. To exceed maximum levels, advance consultation and approval from the U.S. Administration is required. Because of the nature of Soviet and Chinese purchasing agencies, daily or weekly monitoring of U.S. export sales also is used to alert farmers when these countries are making heavy purchases of U.S. grains.

Key Foreign Countries

Major grain exporting countries are limited in number. That means you need to watch only a few key areas in evaluating potential direct competition for the year ahead. For soybeans, the largest competitors are Brazil, Argentina, Malaysia, and Canada. Since Brazil and Argentina are south of the equator, their planting and harvesting seasons are reversed six months from ours. Soybeans are their main oilseed crop. Malaysia is the major source of palm oil, an important competitor of soybean oil. Rapeseed is Canada's main oilseed crop. It has a high oil content, with somewhat lower quality of protein than soybean meal.

Major feedgrain exporting countries are Argentina, South Africa, Australia, Canada and France. The first three are in the Southern

Hemisphere. Argentina, France and South Africa are substantial producers of corn, while the other two export primarily oats and barley. In the past, Brazil also was a modest exporter of corn. However, growing domestic demand shifted that country to a net corn importer in the late 1970's.

Major wheat exporting countries include Canada, Australia, Argentina and France, in addition to the United States. From time to time, modest exportable supplies of wheat also have been available from Spain, Turkey and other European nations.

Grain importing countries are much more numerous, with local production influencing their levels of grain imports in any given year. In that sense, production in grain importing countries also competes with U.S. grains and oilseeds. Corn, soybean and soybean meal exports go primarily to industrialized nations—Europe, Japan, Russia, Korea, Taiwan and, more recently, Mexico.

Soybean oil exports tend to move to developing nations—India, the Middle East, other Asian countries and Latin America. Wheat exports go to a wide range of developed and developing countries including European countries, Russia, China, Japan, other South Asian nations, the Middle East and Latin America.

ANALYSIS OF GRAIN MARKET INFORMATION

To use these sources of market information effectively, you need some way of determining the net effect on grain supplies and prices. The tool commonly used in doing this for grains and soybeans is the supply-demand balance sheet. A balance sheet is simply a way of comparing available supplies with expected utilization. Its purpose is to determine whether carryover stocks will be increasing or decreasing at the end of the marketing year. If carryover stocks are increasing substantially, grain prices will likely decline unless offset by government policy actions. Declining carryover stocks nearly always place upward pressure on grain or soybean prices.

Grain Balance Sheets

Table 7-1 shows a typical U.S. corn balance sheet. In the hypothetical example, beginning carryover stocks of old-crop corn were 1,250 million bushels in the previous marketing year. Weather was favorable and the crop was large, bringing total supplies to slightly over 9 billion bushels. Total usage of U.S. corn amounted to 7,325 million bushels, leaving ending carryover stocks at 1,726 million bushels. These stocks represent the beginning carryover for the current marketing year. They are unusually large and probably caused depressed prices in the early part of the previous marketing year.

Table 7-1. EXAMPLE CORN BALANCE SHEET, (in Millions of Bushels).

	Previous Year (Oct.-Sept. Mktg. year)	Current Year	Projected for Coming Year
Supplies:			
Beginning carryover, Oct. 1	1,250	1,726	828
Production	7,800	6,500	7,900
Imports	1	2	1
Total	9,051	8,228	8,729
Utilization:			
Livestock feed	4,300	4,100	4,300
Food, industrial & seed	625	700	50
Exports	2,400	2,600	2,650
Total	7,325	7,400	7,700
Ending carryover, Oct. 1	1,726	828	1,029

For the current year, drought has reduced the crop substantially below the previous season. Imports have doubled—primarily from Canada—but still represent an insignificant part of the total supply. Even with large beginning carryover stocks, total U.S. corn supplies are down more than 800 million bushels from the previous year. That's a strong indication average prices for the marketing year will be well above the preceding year.

Projections for the three utilization categories indicate exports will increase, probably due to crop problems in major foreign grain consuming and/or exporting countries and a long term upward trend in foreign livestock feeding. Because of higher feed costs and improved cash-grain alternatives, U.S. livestock feeding is expected to decline. Processing use is expected to continue its long term upward trend. As a result, carryover stocks are projected to decline to about one-half of the previous year's level.

Projections for the coming year are shown as they might appear by midsummer of the current marketing year. At that time, the projections obviously are still tentative and would need to be adjusted from month to month for changing U.S. and world crop conditions. The hypothetical balance sheet indicates U.S. and world crop prospects are favorable at this stage of the growing season. Even with an anticipated upward trend in utilization, the next season's ending carryover stocks are expected to rise modestly. Rising carryover stocks indicate the coming year's average price is likely to be modestly below the current marketing year.

Balance sheets for corn, soybeans, wheat and other grains are published periodically by USDA's Economics and Statistics Service. The branch of USDA which publishes these projections is separate from the one which develops crop estimates and grain stocks data. Its main task is to analyze demand prospects and government programs, and to determine likely prices for major crops. Balance sheets prepared by USDA usually include projections of U.S. average farm prices. To use this information in developing a marketing plan, you first need to know how your local price differs from the U.S. average. That information can be obtained from your own local price records of previous years or from your state's extension service.

There are several ways you might use projected season average prices in your marketing plan. Suppose your goal is to sell your corn crop at 25¢ per bushel above the season average price. In that case, you would want to make substantial sales at times when cash or forward pricing opportunities exceed the projected season average price by at least that amount. If current prices are substantially below the projected season average price, that would be a signal to delay marketings and wait for higher prices. If prices are near the projected season average price, it would be advisable to figure storage costs closely in deciding whether to sell the crop now or wait for a normal seasonal rise in prices.

Another way to use the balance sheet is in analyzing the impact of changing crop conditions. Let's say that during the summer months, serious drought cuts crop projections in table 7-1 by 440 million bushels. That amounts to a 5% reduction in total supplies. As a general rule, each 1% change in total corn supplies—with other market factors being unchanged—would tend to change the season average price by about 2% in the opposite direction. Therefore, a 5% reduction in corn supplies would be expected to boost the coming year's season average price by about 10% above previous projections. For soybeans, each 1% change in total supplies would be expected to change prices by about 2½% if other price-making influences remain unchanged.

These are general rules of thumb. However, you should be alert to other things that can make prices either more or less responsive. For example, if carryover stocks are already near the minimum level needed by the trade, prices will likely respond more sharply to supply changes. For corn and soybeans, minimum stocks needed to meet normal feeding, processing and exporting activities at the end of the marketing year would be about four weeks' supply. In our example balance sheet in table 7-1, that figures out to about 600 million bushels for the coming year.

With a large increase in supplies, government programs may make prices less responsive than these rules would indicate. If prices are near the loan rate, excess supplies may be taken off the market and placed under price support loans. If a reserve program exists, more grain can be attracted into the reserve through adjustments in storage payments and interest charges on reserve loans. Such actions would limit the downward pressure on prices in case of an unusually large crop.

In evaluating price prospects for corn and soybeans, you also need to consider the number of livestock being grain fed and the profitability of livestock and poultry feeding. Domestic feeding is still the largest source of demand for the U.S. corn crop and is a major outlet for soybean meal. If feeding profits are strong, a given reduction in corn supplies would have greater impact on corn prices than when feeding margins are depressed.

To evaluate the impact of large unexpected new export sales, you would first need to convert such sales from metric tons (in which they usually are reported) to bushels. A metric ton (2,205 pounds) contains 36.8 bushels of soybeans or wheat, or 39.4 bushels of corn. When you've determined the total bushels of new sales, then calculate the percent of the total U.S. supply it represents. If other market factors remain unchanged, you can get an idea of the potential price impact by using the rules of thumb we noted earlier. For example, if unexpected new corn export sales equal 5% of the current season's total corn supply, you could expect the season average corn price to be about 10% above previous projections.

Also note that a reserve program can "short-circuit" these rules of thumb in years of short crops. At times when carryover stocks are being sharply reduced and a government reserve program is in existence, reserve release and call prices may be the main determinant of prices. Release and call prices are the levels at which reserve stocks can return to commercial channels. They may sometimes pull prices to a higher level than these general rules would suggest.

You can get on USDA's mailing list for its regularly scheduled updates on grain balance sheets by writing to: Information Staff, ESS, U.S. Department of Agriculture, South Building, 14th and Independence Ave. S.W., Washington, D.C. 20250 and requesting that your name be placed on the mailing list for *Agricultural Supply and Demand Estimates.* USDA also publishes farmer newsletters on wheat, feedgrains and soybeans several times during the year. These reports typically are four pages in length, discussing U.S. and world supply-demand conditions, market prospects, government programs and marketing alternatives. They can be obtained from the same address noted above for the USDA balance sheets.

Role of Advisory Services

A number of commercial advisory services are available to assist in keeping abreast of market conditions and price trends, and to help in making marketing decisions. Costs and types of services vary substantially from firm to firm. Services may include a weekly newsletter, recorded "hot line" messages with commentary on daily market developments and marketing recommendations, seminars, and advisors who are available for telephone consultation. In many cases, marketing recommendations from these services are based on chart formations such as those discussed in Chapter 13. The market recommendations often involve sale of the crop through futures contracts.

If you subscribe to an advisory service, be aware that you may need to adjust its recommendations to fit your individual business situation and financial risk-bearing ability. Typical recommendations from such services might be to "bring sales up to 60% of production as March futures hit $4.08 per bushel." If you're a highly leveraged farmer with heavy cash commitments for land payments, the 60% sales level may be too low. That would be particularly true if you are being offered profitable prices and further price strength will require widespread weather concerns in the spring. On the other hand, if your farm is fully paid for with no land debt and you think weather rallies are likely, sales of less than 60% might be reasonable. In that case, lower cash costs per bushel of production would give you greater risk-bearing ability than your neighbor who is committed to a heavy cash-flow for land payments.

Advisory services can be helpful in marketing grain. But remember that in the end, you're the one who has to pay the bills, live with the financial risk and meet the on-going needs of your business. These services can be an aid in decision-making, but the final decision should be made by you—based on your individual operation.

CHAPTER **8**

How Livestock Are Marketed

The livestock industry in the United States is important, large, complex and ever-changing. Livestock sales, including dairy products and poultry, account for about one-half of the total cash receipts from farm marketings.

In 1980, 33.8 million head of cattle were produced for slaughter, of which 23.9 million were grain-fed cattle. In addition to this, 96 million head of hogs were produced for slaughter, and 5.6 million head of sheep and lambs were fed, either on grass or grain, before moving to slaughter. Approximately 26 million cattle were marketed as feeders in 1980, 16 million feeder pigs were sold to hog finishers, and 3 million lambs were sold to sheep feeding feedlots.

Livestock are produced where the primary feed supplies are available. Hog production is heavily concentrated in the Midwest, where corn is marketed through hogs by many corn-hog farmers (Figure 8-1).

Cow-calf production is more widely dispersed geographically. It's a major enterprise in parts of the West and Southwest where lack of rainfall or rough terrain limits the production of crops other than grass and forage. But there are also large numbers of beef cows in parts of the Midwest and Southeast (Figure 8-2). Cattle feeding shows a more concentrated pattern, with a dozen states in the Midwest, Southwest and West accounting for nearly 90% of the marketings (Figure 8-3).

The geographic location of the livestock slaughtering industry is closely linked to livestock production patterns. This reflects a shift over the last 30 years of substantial slaughtering activity in metropolitan areas like Chicago to the areas where fed cattle and hog production is concentrated. In many cases, outmoded facilities were discarded

136   MARKETING FOR FARMERS

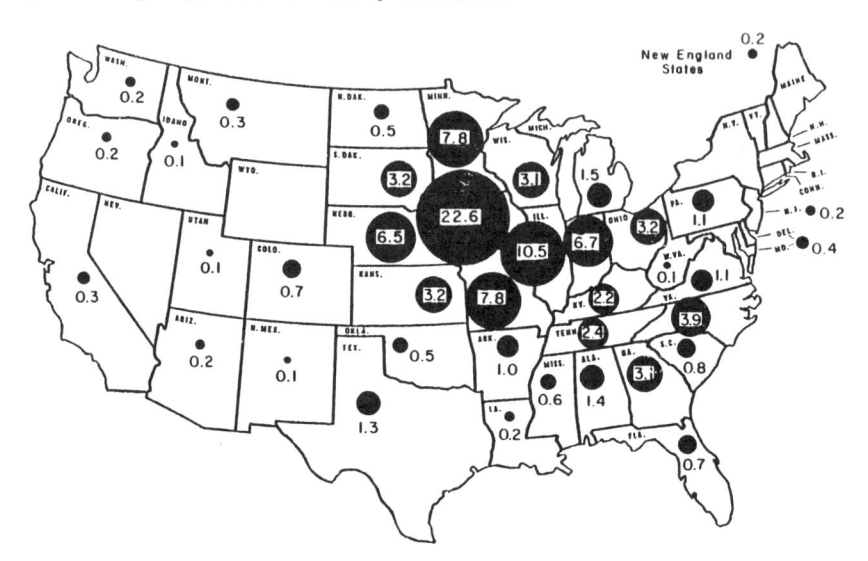

Figure 8-1. Pig Crop, Percent of Total by States, 1979.

Source: Engleman, Gerald, "Changes in Livestock Marketing in the United States and Prospects for the Future," AMS, USDA, Dec. 1980.

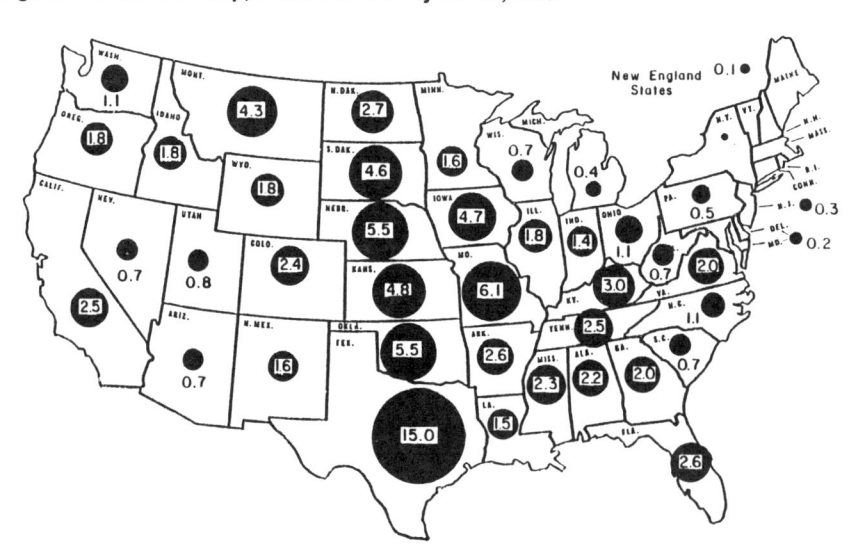

Figure 8-2. Beef Calf Crop, Percent of Total by States, 1980.

Source: Engleman, Gerald, "Changes in Livestock Marketing in the United States and Prospects for the Future," AMS, USDA, Dec. 1980.

How Livestock Are Marketed

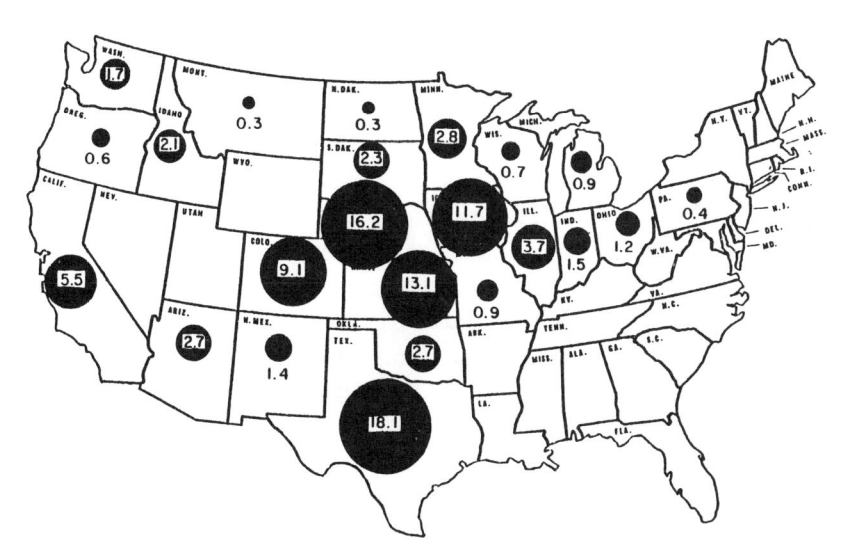

Figure 8-3. Fed Cattle Marketings, Percent of Total by States, 1979.

Source: Engelman, Gerald, "Changes in Livestock Marketing in the United States and Prospects for the Future," AMS, USDA, Dec. 1980.

and new, more efficient plants were built. Cost savings were realized from shipping carcasses or wholesale cuts of beef and pork rather than live animals.

In 1979, the four major cattle feeding states were also the four largest cattle slaughtering states. And the three top hog production states were the leaders in hog slaughter.

LIVESTOCK MARKETING CHANNELS AND PATTERNS

The large and diverse United States livestock production system is supported by a large and complex marketing system. In some ways this marketing system is not really much different than it was many years ago. But, many fundamental changes have evolved over the years and shifts are still occurring in response to changing needs.

Livestock producers have access to several types of outlets for their livestock. Most of the channels which existed in the early 1900's are still available and they have been joined by some new methods of marketing. Marketing functions performed within these various marketing systems include assembly, transportation, grading, financing, inspection, pricing, exchange of ownership, price discovery, market news reporting, risk bearing, and buying and selling.

The types of market outlets available to livestock producers today include:

Terminal public markets. These markets are also called public stockyards or central public markets. Livestock are consigned to commission firms that do the selling at these markets. A stockyard company owns and maintains the physical facilities, such as yards, alleys, scales, loading docks, and facilities for feeding and watering livestock. The proportion of livestock sold through terminal markets has declined sharply over the last 30 to 40 years, as shown in Table 8-1. In 1979, there were 28 terminal markets for livestock in the United States.

Auction markets. Auction markets, sometimes called sale barns, receive livestock from farmers and ranchers and sell to buyers on an auction basis, with bidding and selling open to the public. They may be owned privately by individuals, partnerships, corporations or cooperative associations. Auction markets are an especially important outlet for feeder livestock and for culled breeding stock. There were approximately 1,860 livestock auction markets in the United States in 1979.

Local markets or concentration yards. Facilities for receiving, holding and loading livestock are provided by operators of these markets. Livestock is purchased from farmers on a lot or graded basis and usually sorted and resold to packers, order buyers or other markets.

Country dealers. These are independent operators who buy and sell livestock. They may resell the livestock to any of the other outlets used by producers. Country dealers are also referred to as local dealers, truck buyers, traders, or in some areas as scalpers. Most of their dealing is with farmers and it usually is done at the farm. This is in contrast to local markets, which buy primarily at their own yards.

Packer buyers. Packer buyers are employed by meat packing companies. They travel through the country and buy livestock directly from producers, usually in their own feedlot. The livestock is then moved directly to the plant for processing.

Packing plants and packer buying stations. Livestock may be sold directly to the slaughtering plant or to buying points owned by the packer some distance from the plant. Livestock marketed to these outlets can usually be sold on either a live or carcass basis. A variety of forward pricing arrangements with some of the larger meat packers is also available to producers. Some other marketing agencies, including terminals and country dealers, also offer forward pricing contracts.

Order buyers. Order buyers act as agents of other livestock buyers in locating and procuring livestock. They commonly buy at terminal markets or auctions or from dealers and local markets; however, they also act as agents in buying livestock directly from farmers or ranchers.

Special auctions. Special auctions are held in some areas, where the livestock are sorted, graded and grouped into commingled lots before being offered for sale. They are used primarily for feeder cattle and calves and are held on a seasonal or infrequent basis.

Cooperative shipping associations. These organizations are owned and operated by farmers. They assemble livestock from producers, load the livestock and ship cooperatively to a market where the selling is usually handled by commission men. Thus, the main function of a cooperative shipping association is to assemble and forward livestock.

Cooperative selling associations. These are cooperatives which operate much like cooperative shipping associations; however, they usually perform more services in obtaining bids on livestock, selecting outlets for livestock, and providing information to producers. The precise functions performed vary from one area to another. A cooperative that takes title to the livestock is considered a local market, not a cooperative selling association.

Country commission firm or feedlot marketing. Under this system, producers are represented in the sale of their livestock at the feedlot by a professional sales representative. Price and other terms of trade are determined before the livestock leaves the feedlot. This is a relatively new marketing procedure and is being used in the commercial feedlot areas, as well as in Iowa and southern Minnesota.

Electronic auction marketing. This is a variation of the auction marketing system and is now being tested and used commercially on a limited basis in livestock marketing. An electronic device of some type, such as telephone, teletype, computer, or video technique, is used for price establishment and exchange of ownership.

The use of an interlocking system of telephones to link buyers and sellers is commonly referred to as a teleauction. Livestock sold by a teleauction system may be assembled at designated points or remain on the livestock producer's farm. In most cases, they are graded, sorted and sometimes commingled before being offered for sale by description via the conference call. Success of these sales is dependent on a grading system and the degree of confidence that traders have in it, plus the integrity of the buyers and sellers. Teleauctions are used in Missouri, Minnesota and Wisconsin in the sale of feeder pigs and in Wisconsin, Iowa, Minnesota, Oregon and Virginia in the sale of slaughter lambs.

Computerized marketing is being tested in the sale of various livestock. As with the teleauction, livestock must be graded and sorted, either at central points or at the livestock producer's farm. This is generally done by a disinterested party who is not involved in the trade. This information is then entered into the central computer through a terminal located at a central point. Once all livestock are assembled, graded and recorded, the computerized auction is held. Buyers are given information over TV-like screens on location, grade, number and weight for the lots being sold. Bids are made through input keyboards located in buyer offices. Once the highest bidder is determined by the computer, an exchange of ownership is completed.

Teletype auctions are identical in principle to computerized auctions. The difference is in the hardware used. Teletype machines have not been used in the United States to market livestock. However, this method has been used quite extensively in Canada to market slaughter hogs.

Video equipment is also being used in livestock marketing to provide a visual description of the animal. Pictures are taken of the animals on the ranch or in the feedlot by a party disinterested in the trade. These pictures are then projected on screens at the auction location. In addition to the video information, buyers are also given additional information about the weighing conditions, feed fed, location and delivery date. Bidding in these video auctions is carried on in a manner similar to other auctions, except that the livestock remains on the farm or ranch until after the price is established and location of the buyer is determined.

Bargaining associations. Bargaining associations are organized by agricultural producers to influence terms of trade in the sale or purchase of goods. While they have been quite popular in the trading of some agricultural commodities, they have had limited use in livestock trading, except for the marketing program of the National Farmers Organization (NFO).

Feeder Cattle and Feeder Pig Marketing Channels

Auction markets and order buyers are the primary marketing channels used to move feeder cattle from often small, widely dispersed cow-calf operations to feedlots. With both methods, small lots of feeders are assembled into the large, uniform loads required by the large feedlots. Direct feedlot purchasing from cow-calf operators is not common, since most feeder cattle producers are too small to make that an efficient purchasing method.

Feeder pig marketing channels are quite diverse. In some areas auctions are heavily used (either the standard auction or, in some cases, teleauctions). In other areas, most feeder pigs move directly from the farrowing operation to farm finishing facilities. Very large feeder pig producers normally sell direct to feedlot operators. Some feeder pigs are also handled by country dealers and order buyers, but auctions and direct marketing are the dominant marketing methods.

Changing Slaughter Livestock and Marketing Patterns

The relative importance of the various marketing systems used by U.S. livestock producers has changed rather markedly over time. The pattern which has emerged is a relative decline in receipts at terminal markets and a sharp increase in the percentage of total marketings which move direct to buyers. Information in Table 8-1 shows that this has been the trend for all slaughter livestock species, but to differing degrees.

The shift in livestock marketing patterns has been caused largely by (1) improvement in highways and truck transportation, (2) relocation of meat packing plants from terminal market locations to high density livestock production areas, and (3) improved market information and communication technology available to increasingly capable livestock producers.

Selling at terminal markets, as well as through auctions, requires an earlier commitment to sell livestock than in most direct marketing situations. There is also more uncertainty about the price, since it is determined by negotiation between commission agent and buyer, or by bidding, in the case of auctions. And a significant cost could be incurred if the livestock are withdrawn from sale after transport to the marketing point. By contrast, in most direct selling the price is likely to be known within a fairly narrow range before the livestock are moved from the farm.

Terminal markets now receive about 10% of total marketings of cattle, calves and sheep and about 15% of the hogs. The sharp decline in receipts at terminals began earlier for hogs than for other types of livestock, but has not progressed quite as far. This is because the bulk of the hog production takes place in areas where viable terminal markets still operate. Also, more cattle than hogs are sold by carcass pricing methods.

While receipts at terminal markets have declined for all types of slaughter livestock, these markets still remain important price reporting points in the marketing system. Prices are reported daily from terminal markets by USDA and private price reporting services.

Carcass grade and weight selling has increased for all types of livestock as is shown in Table 8-2. This form of marketing and pricing is used most in cattle marketing, with about 25% of the cattle sold this way. However, the extent of carcass grade and weight selling varies considerably from one state to the next. For example, in 1979 over 50% of the cattle purchased in some states by packers was purchased in this manner; in others, less than 1%. Three states—Nebraska, Iowa and Colorado—accounted for about 60% of all grade and weight purchases of cattle in 1979.

The percentage of total marketings purchased on a carcass grade and weight basis stood at about 12% for hogs in 1979. Again, the importance of this system was greater in some states than in others. The proportion was highest in Minnesota, where 28% of the hogs purchased by packers that year were priced on a carcass basis. Three states—Iowa, Minnesota and Nebraska—accounted for about 60% of the hogs purchased on a carcass basis in 1979.

Table 8-1. PERCENTAGE OF LIVESTOCK BOUGHT BY PACKERS BY TYPE OF MARKET OUTLET, 1925-1979.

Year	Terminal Markets	Direct & Country Dealers	Auction Markets	Terminal Markets	Direct & Country Dealers	Auction Markets
	—————Cattle—————			——————Hogs——————		
1925	90.7%	9.3%		76.0%	24.0%	
1935	83.6	16.4		56.0	44.0	
1945	76.8	23.2		37.3	62.7	
1950	74.9	25.1		39.9	60.1	
1960	45.8	38.6%	15.6%	30.3	61.0%	8.7%
1970	18.4	65.3	16.3	17.2	68.5	14.3
1971	15.9	68.6	15.5	16.9	69.3	13.8
1972	13.2	72.2	14.6	16.3	70.4	13.3
1973	11.9	73.0	15.1	17.3	70.3	12.4
1974	13.9	69.7	16.4	17.6	70.0	12.4
1975	14.4	65.9	19.7	16.3	71.6	12.1
1976	12.9	66.3	20.8	17.1	71.4	11.5
1977	12.0	69.4	18.6	15.6	71.7	12.7
1978	10.6	73.4	16.0	15.9	73.8	10.3
1979	9.5	76.4	14.1	14.7	74.6	10.7
	—————Calves—————			———Sheep & Lambs———		
1925	87.1%	12.9%		82.3%	17.7%	
1935	76.5	23.5		77.5	22.5	
1945	61.5	38.5		61.6	38.4	
1950	56.7	43.3		57.4	42.6	
1960	25.4	42.5%	32.1%	35.4	54.0%	10.6%
1970	11.4	34.0	54.6	15.1	72.5	12.4
1971	8.6	32.4	59.0	13.6	74.0	12.4
1972	7.7	31.6	60.7	13.7	74.3	12.0
1973	8.2	30.9	60.9	12.3	73.0	14.7
1974	6.5	30.4	63.1	11.4	75.1	13.5
1975	8.3	32.4	59.3	10.0	74.4	15.6
1976	7.7	30.0	62.3	9.8	75.2	15.0
1977	7.3	35.5	57.2	11.0	75.8	13.2
1978	9.0	37.3	53.7	10.1	78.6	11.3
1979	7.4	40.9	51.7	9.3	82.7	8.0

Source: *Packers and Stockyards Resumé*, USDA, AMS, Annual Statistical Special Issue, December 29, 1980.

Table 8-2. LIVESTOCK PURCHASED ON CARCASS GRADE AND WEIGHT BASIS AS A PERCENTAGE OF TOTAL PURCHASES, 1968-1979.

Year	Percentage of Total Purchases			
	Cattle	Calves	Hogs	Sheep
1963	7.9	2.5	2.6	5.2
1968	17.2	3.6	3.8	8.9
1969	19.6	3.9	4.3	6.6
1970	18.7	4.5	4.8	9.8
1971	20.5	5.8	4.9	7.4
1972	22.6	6.7	5.2	8.4
1973	23.4	5.6	5.8	7.9
1974	22.9	6.2	6.8	8.8
1975	24.3	9.1	8.9	10.5
1976	23.3	8.4	10.5	9.5
1977	23.2	9.1	8.9	8.8
1978	25.5	10.5	10.4	10.1
1979	27.2	17.7	11.5	24.6

Source: Ibid., table 8-1.

METHODS OF MARKETING

Most producers not only can choose among marketing channels and markets, but they also have a choice in the method by which livestock are marketed and priced.

The four main methods of marketing are:

1. Liveweight, mixed, or group marketing.
2. Live sort and select.
3. Carcass weight or hot carcass.
4. Carcass grade and yield.

Liveweight, Mixed or Group Marketing

A majority of the slaughter livestock sold in this country is sold by this method. Under the liveweight method of selling, the buyer offers a price per cwt on the entire lot or group of livestock being offered for sale.

Liveweight selling is simple, quick, and easy for the producer to understand. The buyer, however, has the problem of estimating the value of each animal in the lot, based on carcass price, dressing percentage and by-product value, and combining the information into one live bid. It takes considerable buyer skill to accurately estimate the blend price of a lot.

There is some tendency for buyers to use an averaging strategy and bid an average value for all lots purchased. By so doing they tend to underprice the high quality animals and overprice the poor quality animals. Thus, from the producer's standpoint, high quality animals should not generally be sold by this marketing method. However, it is a good way to sell livestock of below average quality.

Some producers choose this marketing method because they think they can fool the buyer into paying more than their livestock are worth. But a skilled buyer is not likely to be fooled more than once. Buyers purchase livestock regularly and continue to upgrade their estimating skills. They will not survive as buyers if they consistently over-price livestock. This makes it difficult to beat them at their own game.

Live Sort and Select (live weight)

With this method of selling, the farmer, commission agent, or the buyer sorts the livestock into uniform groups by quality grade, yield grade, and/or dressing percent. The buyer offers a live price per cwt for each group. After the price is established, the live weight is obtained and the value of the shipment determined.

This is a more accurate method of evaluating and pricing livestock than the mixed method previously discussed. High quality and low quality animals are more likely to be priced at their true value. The major disadvantage of this method of selling is that it takes more time and the costs may offset the gain.

Sort and select selling is commonly used at the terminal markets, where the commission agent sorts the cattle prior to offering them for sale to the buyer. In some cases the sorting is done by the buyer. While this might be superior to mixed selling, it leaves the responsibility for objective sorting in the hands of persons who could have a tendency to undergrade the livestock.

Sort and select selling is often similar to mixed selling in that only the obviously poor animals are sorted and priced separately.

Carcass Weight Selling (hot carcass)

Carcass weight selling is similar to live mixed selling except that a carcass price rather than a live price is established for a group of livestock offered for sale. The basic difference between live mixed selling and carcass weight selling is that the buyer does not need to estimate the dressing percent to establish the price for the livestock. However, the quality grade and the yield grade must be estimated and the cattle priced accordingly.

This method of selling is commonly used for slaughter cattle in the Midwest. It is seldom used in other parts of the country. It developed in large part because of the excessive mud that cattle in the Midwest often carry in the early spring, making it difficult for buyers to estimate the dressing percent of the animals. Many livestock producers prefer not to sell in the carcass, but under some conditions buyers are reluctant to price cattle on a live basis.

A major disadvantage of carcass weight selling for the producer is the difficulty in monitoring the weighing of the cattle. The producer has to trust that the packer will weigh the carcasses properly and maintain accurate identification of cattle from live to the carcass. One mishap or suspicion of error is enough to sour a producer on carcass selling.

Carcass Grade and Yield Selling

Discussion of this method of selling is divided into separate sections for cattle and hogs, since grade and yield selling systems are different for the two species.

Cattle. Very few cattle are sold by this method of selling. When they are, the buyer places a price on both the quality grade (Choice, Good, etc.) and yield grade (USDA, 1, 2, 3, 4 and 5). Each quality grade and yield grade combination will have a different carcass price. For example, the buyer may put a price of $111/cwt for a Choice yield grade 3 carcass, with a discount of $10/cwt if it is yield grade 4. After the animals are slaughtered, weighed and graded by a USDA grader, the value of each animal in the shipment is determined.

A major advantage of this method of selling is that the seller receives the actual carcass value of his livestock. This method of selling should be considered especially by producers who feel buyers are undervaluing their livestock. Cattle with dairy or exotic breeding are sometimes underpriced, because they do not appear to carry enough finish to reach Choice grade. However, they often produce a higher grading carcass than indicated by their live appearance.

Another advantage of carcass grade and yield selling is that the seller receives a detailed report on how the cattle graded. He can use this information in planning the feeding program, in selecting the type of feeders to purchase, and to upgrade marketing skills.

Hogs. Hogs are actually sold under a carcass *weight* and yield system, not a carcass *grade* and yield system. Many hog producers are not aware that the USDA hog grades are yield grades, not quality grades. When hogs are graded USDA No. 1, No. 2, No. 3, etc., they are evaluated on the basis of the yield of trimmed wholesale cuts from a hog carcass. The grades are very similar to USDA beef yield grades. While there are no official hog grades comparable to beef quality grades, some packers have standards which eliminate soft, watery pork or other undesirable hog carcass characteristics from their top grades.

Most packers prefer hog carcasses that weigh between 140 pounds and 170 pounds (about 200 to 240 pounds live). Carcasses which do not fall within the established weight ranges (either lighter or heavier) are discounted. The weight range desired, however, does vary from one packer to another; some prefer carcasses from hogs weighing 190 to 230 pounds, while others prefer heavier hogs weighing 210 to 240 pounds. The weight discount varies between packers and can vary seasonally, as well.

The other major pricing factor is the estimated yield (cutability) of primal hog cuts (loin, ham, belly, boston butt, and picnic) from a carcass. Each packing company has its own grading system, in contrast to cattle grading, which is based on USDA grades and is done by a USDA grader. Each packer also establishes its own price premium and discount schedule for different grades of hogs.

Hogs sold to packer under a carcass weight and yield program are evaluated (yield of carcass estimated) by a grader hired by the packer. Therefore, grading is entirely the responsibility of the packer who buys the hogs.

Carcass grade and yield (largely weight and yield) selling accounts for only about 10% of the slaughter hogs sold in the United States. But why do any hog producers sell under a marketing program where the buyer has the sole responsibility for accurately weighing and grading the hogs? The premiums paid for high performing hogs, with respect to dressing percent and yield grade, are obviously great enough to attract many top quality hog producers. Only hogmen who produce high quality hogs can gain the premium.

Carcass vs. Live Selling

Hogs. How can you determine if carcass weight and yield selling will net additional marketing dollars on your hogs? One method would be to occasionally split a group of hogs and sell some live and some in the carcass—and compare the returns. The comparison should not be based on the premiums reported on a grade and yield report sheet from the packer. The premiums reported often inflate the actual premiums, since the base price used is typically for a below-average hog.

It is difficult to compare carcass weight and yield returns between packers, since each packer uses a somewhat different method of pricing and evaluation. However, careful study of different packer programs can yield additional marketing dollars. Some packers prefer heavier hogs and will pay larger premiums for high quality heavy hogs. Other packers prefer lighter hogs and have premiums and discounts established to reward producers who market the lighter hog. So, it pays to select your markets, depending on the type of hog you have at a particular time.

If there is only one packer available who buys hogs on a carcass weight and yield basis, study his program carefully to select the weight and grade of hog that receives the highest premiums. Discounts are based on carcass weights and one additional pound can put the carcass in a discounted weight group. It's also possible that high dressing hogs can fall into a carcass weight group which is discounted, even if the live weight appears to fit the preferred weight.

As mentioned earlier, only producers with better than average quality hogs will increase their returns by using the carcass selling method. Producers who find this method profitable can also use their carcass weight and yield report to help them select breeding stock from their herds.

Cattle. The expected dressing percent is the main consideration in deciding whether carcass or live selling is the best method of pricing a particular group of cattle.

Assume you receive a bid of $70 per cwt live and a $107 per cwt carcass bid for a group of cattle that dress 62%. To compare the two bids, divide the live price by the dressing percent ($70 ÷ .62 = $112.90).

In this case, the live bid is better than the carcass bid. When the converted live price is lower, the carcass bid is the best.

As part of your marketing skill, you should learn to closely estimate dressing percent of cattle. The dressing percent of animals that are comparable in appearance will vary somewhat, but a close approximation usually provides sufficient basis to make the choice between the two pricing methods.

MARKET SUPERVISION

Traders in most livestock markets and under various livestock marketing systems operate under both federal and state regulations. The most common and far-reaching of these regulations is the federal Packers and Stockyard Act. The act, which is administered by the USDA, is designed to regulate business practices of livestock buyers and sellers who trade in interstate commerce.

Under the Act:

Stockyard owners, marketing agencies or dealers are required to furnish bond and cannot engage in discriminatory, unfair or deceptive practices while engaging in an act of weighing, feeding, shipping, buying, selling or handling livestock.

Meat packers cannot (1) engage in unfair or deceptive pricing practices, (2) give unfair preference to certain individuals, (3) apportion territories with other packer buyers, or (4) manipulate or control prices in a monopolistic manner.

Meat packers, when buying livestock on a carcass grade and yield basis, must (1) reveal the terms of the contract to the seller; (2) maintain identity of carcasses; (3) keep necessary records; (4) pay on a hot carcass weight basis; and (5) use uniform weight hooks, rollers and gambrels.

Meat packers who buy $500,000 or more worth of livestock each year must (1) carry a bond equal to the value of a 2-day kill, (2) pay a seller at the close of the business day following the sale, and (3) maintain accounts receivable and inventory in trust in the amount of purchases until checks to livestock producers have cleared the packer's bank.

If a producer has reason to believe that he has suffered damage from violation of the Packer and Stockyards Act, he may petition either the area P&S supervisor or the Secretary of Agriculture. This must be done within 90 days of the suspected violation.

Most states also have regulatory provisions requiring the licensing and bonding of livestock dealers, packers and agencies operating within an individual state. In some cases, these regulations cover similar potential violations as listed in the P&S Act, but carry the regulations to only within-state traders. In addition to regulations under the P&S Act, most states also have regulations covering the inspection and testing of scales used in livestock marketing transactions. Scales must be properly installed, maintained, operated, tested and inspected to assure correct weights.

THE FUTURE

There is little doubt that livestock marketing in the 1980's will continue to change. These changes will relate to the broad questions of where, when and how livestock are marketed and priced. They will be influenced by continued adjustments in livestock production units and in their locations; in technology, location and competitive structure of the meat packing industry; in changes in market institutions such as livestock and meat grading, market information dissemination, and market regulations; and in improved methods used by traders to communicate and negotiate livestock pricing and trading.

Increasing transportation costs will probably be dominant factors influencing where and how livestock will be marketed. Livestock slaughter facilities will continue to locate at points of dense livestock production rather than at terminal points located at or near population centers. Livestock from large production units will increasingly demand that marketing services be performed at or near the feedlot rather than at distant terminal points and that both the price and ultimate destination of livestock be known before they leave the feedlot.

Direct marketing will continue to be dominant, but in some areas various electronic devices will probably be used in livestock marketing. This marketing technique has the potential to increase pricing efficiency and competition while reducing the costs of marketing. Centralized competitive markets may become centralized market information and pricing points, with the physical product and traders being decentralized as they negotiate on a price and other terms of trade.

CHAPTER 9

Developing a Livestock Marketing Plan

Most farmers realize that their marketing decisions can mean the difference between making a profit or incurring a loss in their livestock operations. In recent years, both short and long term price changes have been dramatic. At times, with little obvious reason, agricultural commodity prices rise sharply or fall drastically, causing either large profits or losses for producers. Only a few years ago a 50¢ to $1 per cwt price change during an entire week was unusual, but in today's market, prices can often change $1 to $2 per cwt within a single day. These erratic and unpredictable price changes make it increasingly difficult to effectively market livestock.

It is important in these times of volatile prices to establish a market goal and develop specific market plans or strategies. As a livestock producer, you should address the marketing questions of where to sell, how to sell, what to sell, and when to sell. Not all producers will develop the same plans. The marketing plans or strategies must be an integral part of your total farming operation and be consistent with your production situation, type of livestock, financial situation, and personality.

ESTABLISHING GOALS AND OBJECTIVES

Many people are reluctant to set goals because they often set them too high and are disappointed if their goals are not attained. Others are not willing to take the time to think through their real goals and objectives.

Initially, livestock marketing goals should be simple and measurable. A marketing goal such as "increasing profits through better marketing" is a commendable goal, but is not definitive and will not help the producer determine how to improve marketing returns. A goal such as "increasing prices received" is not necessarily an adequate goal, because a higher price does not necessarily result in more profits if a producer's costs go up even more to get the higher prices.

All producers would like to improve their profits through better marketing. The first step is to examine your existing marketing program to determine how it can be changed to improve returns. In order to evaluate how well you are doing in marketing, it is necessary to keep some marketing records. The records need not be complex, but should include the prices received, what the livestock weighed and how they graded. With these records, plus published market information, you can begin to assess your market performance by comparing your prices to other reported market prices in your area during the same period. Did you receive substantial discounts or premiums? Did you consistently sell too early or late to get at least average market prices?

Marketing strategies that some livestock producers use are listed below. They are not recommended strategies, but illustrate how some farmers handle this aspect of their business.

1. Market livestock regularly, on a specific day, weekly, biweekly, or every month.
2. Market livestock always at a specified weight or grade (i.e., hogs at 220 pounds, cattle at 1,100 pounds, 85% Choice, etc.).
3. Market livestock when facilities are full and new livestock is coming to the feedlot.
4. Never sell when the market is rising.
5. Market when buyer says livestock are ready.
6. Market when money is needed.
7. Market when feed is used up.
8. Market when going to town anyway.

Livestock producers sometimes select some of the previously listed strategies because they simplify marketing decisions. Usually, little thought is involved in selecting such strategies. Some producers do not understand marketing very well or what causes market prices to change. The wide array of factors which can affect the market and can influence prices differently at different times can be confusing. Some producers feel that markets are too complex for them to analyze, and that following a set strategy, such as marketing at the same weight to the same market, will at least give them average returns.

A strategy of marketing hogs every two weeks, however, will not necessarily bring the producer average returns. And besides, it is questionable whether average returns are an acceptable marketing goal. Most farmers are not content with average corn, soybean, wheat and other crop yields. Why should they be satisfied with average livestock prices?

Some farmers are willing to accept average prices as a marketing goal because they feel inadequate in analyzing markets. But, if they make use of the known market facts and price relationships, they can improve their marketing returns without sophisticated price analysis. An alternative may be to pay for a professional marketing service.

A goal of obtaining the highest price for the period when livestock are marketed is almost impossible to attain. A more realistic goal is to receive better than average prices during the period. As you gain more skill in marketing, you should be able to improve the differential between your prices and average prices.

Livestock producers should also keep in mind that higher prices do not necessarily mean greater livestock profits. For example, assume a cattle feeder with steers weighing 1,050 pounds holds them to 1,100 pounds, hoping for a price gain in the market, and incurs a cost of $35 per head for the gain. If prices rose by $2 per cwt, the feeder would receive $22 per head more for the cattle, but would still lose $13 per head because of the cost of the added weight.

The market strategy selected to achieve a marketing goal must have some flexibility so that it can be adapted to changing economic conditions. The next step is to examine the markets available to you.

SELECTING A MARKET

The type and number of markets available to individual producers vary by regions of the country and by type of livestock. Some producers may have only one market within a reasonable distance from their farm and therefore have no alternatives to investigate. Producers in this situation should concentrate their efforts on the type of livestock to sell (i.e., which grade, weight, yield, etc.) and the timing of sales.

Other producers have more than one market and different methods of marketing from which to choose. How should they decide between alternative markets?

At least six specific factors need to be considered in determining which market to select. These are transportation costs, shrink, market charges or fees, marketing services available, methods of selling available, and competitiveness of the market.

Transportation Costs

Obviously, you should consider the distance you must haul livestock and the transportation costs when selecting a market. Usually, the greater the distance, the greater the cost. Therefore, the price at a more distant market needs to be higher to offset the additional hauling cost before it would be a reasonable choice.

The type of transportation facilities available to the producer can influence his market choice. If a farmer has only a small truck, no other truckers to hire, and sells only a few livestock at one time, he may have very few market options. The availability of the gooseneck trailer has expanded the market area for many producers. The cost of the trailer is small compared to other options and can be used on a small truck or pickup, thereby extending the distance at which producers can economically market livestock.

Transportation costs have risen sharply during the past decade and will continue to rise for the next several years. This will require more careful examination of these costs in evaluating various market alternatives. Prices available at different markets have to be adjusted to reflect any differences in transportation costs to the market.

Market Shrink

Market shrink is the weight loss animals incur during the marketing process. Producers often think all of the shrink loss occurs during shipment to market, but much of the weight loss occurs during sorting, loading, and the first few miles of shipment.

Weight loss or shrink can be affected by weather, disposition of animals and how the livestock are handled prior to and during shipment. Research indicates that the degree of shrink is affected by type of housing, degree of finish, weight of livestock (location and timing of weighing and any restrictions on feed and water), and the distance to market.

Under normal shipping conditions, the additional shrink from 50 miles to 150 miles is minimal. Most animals will normally have 2% to 3% shrink on the shortest of hauls. It normally requires considerable additional shipping distance to increase the shrink another 1%.

There are two basic types of shrink which occur in livestock; these are fill and tissue shrink. Fill shrink is the normal body excrement from the animal. There is no way of completely avoiding this weight loss, although it can be reduced by shortening the time from when animals leave the farm to when they are weighed.

Tissue shrink is primarily moisture loss from the tissue. It usually does not begin until the animal has been off feed and water (especially water) for some length of time. In normal marketing situations where the livestock are slaughtered within twelve hours after they leave the farm, tissue shrink is minimal. However, if the animals are stressed or if considerable time elapses during the marketing process, tissue shrink can become an important factor.

Animals held off feed and water on the farm or at the market for 12 to 14 hours can lose from 1% to 1½% to shrink. Lack of water causes most of the shrink; keeping feed away from the animals has little effect.

Shrink loss on marketing returns becomes more important as livestock prices rise. A 2% shrink loss when hogs are $30 per cwt reduces returns only 60¢ per cwt. But 2% shrink loss at $60 per cwt hogs is $1.20 per cwt. Therefore, as prices rise, the price difference between a nearby market and more distant market needs to increase to offset the greater shrink cost.

Shrink or fill weight can be a problem in livestock pricing if it is greater than estimated and the price is established before the final weight is taken. If excessive shrink occurs, the seller is penalized; if too much fill occurs, the buyer is hurt. Variation in shrink or fill is not a problem if the price is adjusted accordingly.

Pencil Shrink

Pencil shrink is a percentage weight adjustment from the actual live weight of an animal or a shipment of animals. When this is used, the buyer will place a price on livestock, but with a specified percentage weight adjustment when the animals are weighed. For example, a buyer may be willing to pay $70 per cwt for cattle weighed at the nearest scale, but will base the payment on the weight after it has been reduced by 2% (2% pencil shrink) from the actual scale weight. Pencil shrink is also applied often to cattle sold on farm scale weights—usually a 3% downward weight adjustment. The bid price would be lower without this pencil shrink adjustment.

The basic reason for using pencil shrink is to make the price paid for livestock delivered to a plant comparable to prices paid for animals that are weighed at the farm or near the farm.

Marketing Fees

Another part of the marketing costs is the fee charged by terminal (central public) markets, auctions, and other marketing agencies. The fees charged cover the cost of marketing services provided. For example, auctions usually charge a fee per head for use of the facilities and the auctioneer. The fees charged vary from one section of the country to another and by type of livestock.

Terminal market charges include commission fees, yardage, insurance, inspection, and feed and water. The fees vary by type and number of livestock consigned.

A marketing fee is also charged by various livestock marketing cooperatives which operate local buying stations or provide marketing assistance to livestock producers. The fee covers the cost of providing these marketing services and varies according to the nature of the services offered.

Marketing Services

A major decision producers need to make is whether to personally negotiate the sale of livestock with buyers or to make use of a marketing agent. Doing your own selling matches your skills against buyers who typically buy livestock every day, are in constant contact with the market and are skilled at evaluating livestock. The buyers are working for packing firms that want to purchase the animals for the lowest possible price. Many buyers receive special compensation based on their skill in buying livestock, that is, how much profit they can make for the company. To match the buyer's skill, you must be willing to spend time studying the market and upgrading your own marketing skills. If you are not willing to do this, you should consider utilizing the services offered by terminal markets, auctions or other marketing agencies.

Terminal markets and auctions concentrate many buyers and sellers together to compete for the livestock. For many producers, the fees

Developing a Livestock Marketing Plan

charged at these markets are well worth the cost. There are also market agencies which offer some of the same services as the central markets, but at the feedlot or farm. They can maintain contact with more buyers than the average producer and develop a more competitive market situation.

In addition to negotiating with buyers on the sale of livestock, some marketing firms also offer other services to producers, including:

1. Bonding of all sales.
2. Hedging and futures trading assistance.
3. Forward pricing contracts.
4. Assistance in purchasing feeder livestock.
5. Marketing advisory services.

The following questions should help producers decide whether to sell livestock themselves or use some type of marketing service. Unless all of the statements can be answered with a strong yes, the producer should seriously consider hiring a market service.

1. Are several buyers available within a reasonable distance of the farm?
2. Are you knowledgeable about the factors which influence price?
3. Are you willing to devote time to the study of market factors and to the bargaining process?
4. Do you have the knowledge and skills needed to estimate grade, weight, and dressing percent, or the willingness to upgrade your skills in these areas?
5. Do you have the temperament and skill needed for bargaining?
6. Are you willing to accept all of the responsibility for market decisions?
7. Do you recognize that buyers are not doing you a favor in buying livestock and want to buy at prices as low as possible?

Sorting and Selecting Livestock

One of the most important marketing activities for a livestock producer is to sort and select livestock before offering them for sale. The larger the producer, the easier it is, but it is a profitable effort for almost any size producer.

Livestock buyers usually react favorably to uniformity. A group of animals that is uniform has more eye appeal than a group that is uneven in size, quality or other characteristics.

If you have culls, cripples or other undesirable animals to sell, sell them separately rather than try to hide them in a group of high quality livestock. When a buyer does the "favor" of including poor quality animals in a bid, it probably reduces the producer's returns.

A TIMING STRATEGY

When to market; when to price! These are two of the more difficult decisions a producer must make. When caught in a weak market, producers often hold livestock, hoping for price improvement, and end up taking an even lower price. And when prices are high, some producers get greedy, hold their livestock for even better prices, and often watch prices decline. The longer the producer holds livestock the heavier they get and the greater the cost of gain. Excessive holding may also cause livestock to be discounted because they are overfinished.

Producers should develop a marketing strategy that will realistically examine the probabilities of price changes to determine when early marketing or delay is the more reasonable alternative. Eventually the month, week, day and time of day to market must be determined. The next section will briefly discuss each of these decisions.

Time of Day

Changing market conditions make it impossible to identify a certain time of day as always the best time to market. But there are some guidelines which should be helpful in choosing the time to sell. Packers normally try to fill (buy) their requirements early in the day and are usually the most aggressive before noon.

However, if receipts are low and they are not able to obtain their needs by noon, they can become very aggressive in the afternoon. Also, if buyers expect prices to decline they will be hesitant to have slaughter needs bought very far in advance. When they are caught short of supplies for this reason, they will become aggressive bidders later in the day.

Day of the Week

Terminal (central public) markets are usually most active during the early part of the week, but with sales of some types of livestock continuing throughout the week. Commission agents are aware of the number of livestock committed to the market and have some feeling of buyers' demands. Since they usually have some feel of the market, obtaining their advice and counsel before marketing can be beneficial.

Most auctions have sales only one day of the week. So, producers selling at auctions may not have the option of selecting a marketing day. Producers who market direct usually have more choices as to the day to sell livestock; but direct sales also tend to be larger in the first three days of the week. Marketing later in the week can be more risky, but at times can provide a higher market price.

Analysis of daily hog prices indicates that prices on Mondays and Fridays are slightly higher on average than the other days, with Wednesday the next highest. However, when prices are moving up seasonally and cyclically, the latter part of the week is the highest. When prices are declining seasonally or cyclically, the market appears highest in the early part of the week.

Using Probabilities of Price Changes

There are two approaches to developing a strategy on market timing. One way is to try to analyze all of the diverse market information, including market supplies, recent price changes in the cash and futures markets, short term demand influences and rumors. The other, and simpler, approach is to concentrate on historically known factors and patterns. The strategy selected may vary by type of market, weight of livestock, condition of livestock, type of livestock, and risk position.

Two kinds of livestock price patterns have existed over time with some degree of predictability and can be of help in developing a market timing strategy. These are seasonal and cyclical price patterns.

Price cycles are those price trends, either up or down, which extend for more than one year. Cattle price downtrends or uptrends last about five or six years. Hog price uptrends or downtrends have historically been only two or three years long.

Price cycles and production cycles for cattle and hogs are interrelated (see Figures 9-1 and 9-2). Production cycles occur because of the inability of producers to quickly adjust production in response to higher or lower prices. If cow-calf producers experience higher prices for calves sold, they usually respond by increasing the size of their cow herd. They expand by retaining more heifers for breeding or by reducing the cull rate of old cows. However, there is a lag from the time prices rise to the time producers can respond with more cattle. The number marketed increases over a period of years, until prices begin to decline. Lower prices cause producers to liquidate breeding stock, which eventually reduces numbers to a point where price and profit expectations cause a new cycle to begin.

The production and price cycle in hogs is much shorter because, biologically, hog numbers can be increased or decreased in a much shorter period.

Part of the marketing strategy of hog and cattle producers should be to market animals later during the uptrend phase of price cycles and earlier in the downtrend phases. Marketing animals later or at a heavier weight, when prices are rising cyclically, may improve the price received. Of course, the decision of how long to hold depends on the actual price level, weight and grade premiums or discounts, cost of gain and the seasonal price pattern.

Seasonal price patterns. You should consider both the long term price cycles and the seasonal price pattern in determining your marketing strategy. Livestock prices exhibit seasonal patterns within the longer cyclical patterns and may offset the cyclical price trend. Seasonal price patterns exist because of seasonal changes in supplies of livestock and seasonal differences in demands for meat within a year. Consumers, for example, eat more of certain kinds of cuts of meat in some months than they do in other months.

Seasonal changes in hog and cattle production have become more moderate in recent years. But the variations in production, along with seasonal demand changes, are still large enough to cause seasonal price variations.

The pattern for slaughter hogs is more predictable than it is for fed cattle. Tables 9-1 and 9-2 illustrate the seasonal price patterns for barrows and gilts at seven terminal markets and for choice steers in interior Iowa and southern Minnesota.

Developing a Livestock Marketing Plan 161

Figure 9-1. Year to Year Changes in Cattle Prices and Beef Production.

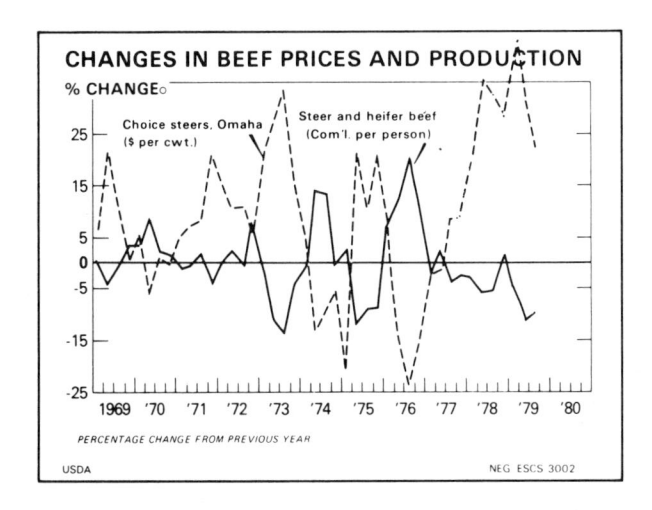

Figure 9-2. Year to Year Changes in Hog Prices and Pork Production.

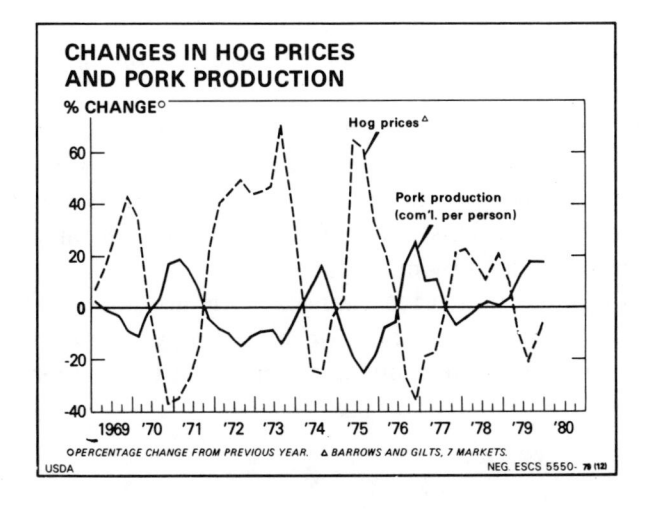

The two week price changes for hogs shown in Table 9-1 illustrate that hog prices typically rise in the first part of the year, decline in the early spring, rise again during the summer, decline in the fall and rise in the late fall and early winter. The price changes are divided into two week periods, with indications of the percent chance (probability) of price changes and the average price increase or decrease between the two week periods. The probability of price changes varies between different times of the year. In some periods, there is a very high probability that prices will rise and in others as low as a 6% or 12% chance.

You can use these probabilities to help decide whether to hold or market immediately. Using the seasonal price probabilities, along with knowledge of the hog or cattle price cycle, can improve your chances of making a correct market timing decision. For example, if hog numbers are decreasing cyclically (hog prices rising) and prices have an 88% chance of rising seasonally, you should be fairly confident that delayed marketing will bring higher prices. If, however, the seasonal pattern indicates that prices normally decline and prices are also trending down cyclically, you clearly should not delay marketing. If the seasonal hog price pattern indicates prices are rising but the cyclical trend is down, the seasonal pattern is more likely to prevail.

Seasonal price patterns for cattle are shown in Table 9-2. They are not as pronounced and consistent as the seasonal changes in hog prices. However, even if the two week price change for cattle indicates only a 50% chance for rise, it does let the producer know there is a 50-50 chance that the decision made will be correct. This, in combination with knowledge of usual cyclical price patterns, provides a more informed basis to make marketing decisions. With cattle, when the cyclical trend and the seasonal pattern give opposite price signals, the cyclical trend is more likely to be dominant.

These probabilities may not be true every year or for any specific year. But if you follow the same strategy consistently you should be able to increase market returns. Too often producers expect a strategy to work every time. This is not a realistic expectation with markets volatile and influenced by many factors.

Keep in mind that price changes alone are not a sufficient basis for decisions on whether to hold or market now. The price level, cost of gain, and price premiums and discounts need to be incorporated into the decision.

Market Discounts

Hogs are usually discounted if they fail to meet top grade standards. Some hogs do not have the genetic potential to reach the top hog grade (U.S. No. 1). Other hogs can reach the top grades, but if fed too long will become over-finished and drop to a lower grade.

Any hog not falling within the established weight range is normally discounted, although the amount of the discounts varies widely among buyers. Most hog buyers prefer hogs that are within the 200 to 240 pound weight range. Buyers who prefer heavier hogs have large discounts on light hogs, but have minimal discounts on heavier hogs. The reverse will exist for buyers who prefer lighter hogs. You should become familiar with the discount policy of potential buyers for your hogs as part of the information base for marketing decisions.

Cattle are discounted for certain quality and carcass cutability characteristics; they are seldom discounted because of weight alone. The amount of the price discounts varies according to market conditions.

The major price discounts on cattle relate to yield grade. As cattle reach their mature weight, they add more fat; the more fat they carry, the lower the yield grade. There are five USDA yield grades, 1 through 5. Cattle which are over-finished will fall into USDA yield grades 4 and 5, and at times the carcasses are discounted as much as $10 or more per cwt.

Cattle within each quality grade (Prime, Choice, etc.) can be discounted because of their yield grade. Often, cattle feeders try to feed their cattle until the group contains a specific proportion of Choice grade, say 90%. Holding the entire lot until that goal is reached increases the number of yield grade 4's and 5's. At times the discount for the additional 4's and 5's more than offsets the gains from obtaining a higher percent Choice. You should be mindful of these price relationships and adjust your marketing program accordingly.

Market Premiums

Cattle and hogs that attain a higher grade are usually paid market premiums. The size of premium varies over time and from buyer to buyer. You can often increase hog and cattle profits by marketing more livestock in the higher grades. But, achieving a premium for a higher grade should not be the only factor in your marketing decisions.

Table 9-1. HOG PRICE CHANGES BY TWO WEEK PERIODS (1961-1977).*

	Two Week Period	Number Years Prices Increased	Percent Probability of Price Increase	Avg. Price Increase $/cwt	Number Years Prices Decreased	Percent Probability of Price Decrease	Avg. Price Decrease $/cwt
Jan.	1st half	15	(88%)	$0.68	2	(12%)	-$0.51
	2nd half	13	(76%)	$0.74	4	(24%)	-$0.23
Feb.	1st half	8	(47%)	$0.93	9	(53%)	-$0.39
	2nd half	1	(6%)	$2.62	16	(94%)	-$0.88
Mar.	1st half	3	(18%)	$0.25	14	(82%)	-$1.10
	2nd half	5	(29%)	$0.29	12	(71%)	-$0.87
Apr.	1st half	6	(35%)	$0.68	11	(65%)	-$0.51
	2nd half	9	(53%)	$1.38	8	(47%)	-$0.51
May	1st half	14	(82%)	$1.65	3	(18%)	-$0.81
	2nd half	11	(65%)	$0.67	6	(35%)	-$0.50
June	1st half	16	(94%)	$1.46	1	(6%)	-$0.47
	2nd half	14	(82%)	$1.99	3	(18%)	-$0.22
July	1st half	11	(65%)	$1.03	6	(35%)	-$1.14
	2nd half	7	(41%)	$1.80	10	(59%)	-$1.00
Aug.	1st half	9	(53%)	$0.90	8	(47%)	-$0.72
	2nd half	3	(18%)	$0.55	14	(82%)	-$1.71
Sept.	1st half	4	(24%)	$0.97	13	(76%)	-$1.23
	2nd half	4	(24%)	$0.79	13	(76%)	-$1.24
Oct.	1st half	4	(24%)	$0.89	13	(76%)	-$1.16
	2nd half	2	(12%)	$0.25	15	(88%)	-$1.34
Nov.	1st half	7	(41%)	$0.46	10	(59%)	-$0.52
	2nd half	10	(59%)	$1.05	7	(41%)	-$0.44
Dec.	1st half	16	(94%)	$1.13	1	(6%)	-$1.27
	2nd half	7	(41%)	$0.46	10	(59%)	-$0.35

*Based on average price of barrows and gilts at 7 markets.

Developing a Livestock Marketing Plan

Table 9-2. CHOICE STEER PRICE CHANGES BY TWO WEEK PERIODS (1966-1977).*

	Two Week Period	Number Years Prices Increased	Percent Probability of Price Increase	Avg. Price Increase $/cwt	Number Years Prices Decreased	Percent Probability of Price Decrease	Avg. Price Decrease $/cwt
Jan.	1st half	8	(67%)	$0.93	4	(33%)	-$1.21
	2nd half	8	(67%)	$0.73	4	(33%)	-$1.07
Feb.	1st half	8	(67%)	$0.56	4	(33%)	-$1.29
	2nd half	4	(33%)	$1.38	8	(67%)	-$0.84
Mar.	1st half	6	(50%)	$0.84	6	(50%)	-$0.62
	2nd half	6	(50%)	$1.61	6	(50%)	-$0.70
Apr.	1st half	8	(67%)	$1.64	4	(33%)	-$0.48
	2nd half	7	(58%)	$1.31	5	(42%)	-$0.92
May	1st half	7	(58%)	$1.02	5	(42%)	-$1.12
	2nd half	8	(67%)	$0.59	4	(33%)	-$0.83
June	1st half	5	(42%)	$1.16	7	(58%)	-$0.52
	2nd half	9	(75%)	$0.92	3	(25%)	-$1.43
July	1st half	4	(33%)	$1.06	8	(67%)	-$0.83
	2nd half	7	(58%)	$1.73	5	(42%)	-$1.02
Aug.	1st half	6	(50%)	$0.55	6	(50%)	-$1.40
	2nd half	5	(42%)	$0.44	7	(58%)	-$1.54
Sept.	1st half	3	(25%)	$0.64	9	(75%)	-$1.28
	2nd half	2	(17%)	$0.97	10	(83%)	-$0.54
Oct.	1st half	2	(17%)	$1.24	10	(75%)	-$0.43
	2nd half	3	(25%)	$0.55	9	(75%)	-$0.70
Nov.	1st half	7	(58%)	$0.45	5	(42%)	-$1.07
	2nd half	8	(67%)	$0.65	4	(33%)	-$0.88
Dec.	1st half	7	(58%)	$0.97	5	(42%)	-$0.44
	2nd half	7	(58%)	$1.48	5	(42%)	-$0.59

*Based on prices of 1,100-1,300 lb. Choice steers, Interior Iowa-So. Minnesota.

Sometimes the cost of putting on additional weight to achieve the grade premium more than offsets the increased value of the animal.

For example, very few cattle feeders should be feeding cattle to Prime grade. There is a small premium for Prime; however, it often fails to offset the cost of gain. The same can be said about marketing Choice cattle, particularly above the mid-Choice. At times the *net return* would be greater if the proportion of Choice was less and there was a higher proportion of Goods.

Price premiums for hogs are different, since hog grades are based on cutability, not quality. Most hogs achieve their maximum grade by the time they reach 200 to 220 pounds. Some hogs maintain this grade as they go to 240 or 260 pounds. Others, because of their genetic background, will drop in grade as they put on extra weight. You should know the type of hog you produce and adjust your marketing plan to take this into account.

Cost of Gain

The heavier livestock become, the less efficient they are in converting feed to weight gain. The cost of gain goes up at an increasing rate as animals put on additional weight.

Table 9-3 illustrates the amount of feed required for each additional pound of gain on hogs and the added feed cost of gain at ration costs of 5¢ and 7¢ per pound.

Table 9-3. COST OF ADDED GAIN ON HOGS.

Weight of Hog	Feed per lb. Gain	Cost of Gain/cwt at Ration Costs of:	
		5¢/lb.	7¢/lb.
200 to 220 lbs.	4.2 lbs.	$21.00	$29.00
221 to 240 lbs.	4.4 lbs.	$22.00	$30.80
241 to 260 lbs.	4.8 lbs.	$24.00	$33.60
261 to 280 lbs.	5.2 lbs.	$26.00	$36.40

Table 9-4 illustrates the cost of added gain for typical beef steers.

Developing a Livestock Marketing Plan

Table 9-4. COST OF ADDED GAIN ON STEERS.

Weight of Steer	Feed per lb. Gain*	Cost of Gain/cwt at Ration Costs of: 5¢/lb.	7¢/lb.
850 to 900 lbs.	8.5 lbs.	$42.50	$ 59.50
901 to 950 lbs.	9.2 lbs.	$46.00	$ 64.40
951 to 1,000 lbs.	9.9 lbs.	$49.50	$ 69.30
1,001 to 1,050 lbs.	10.6 lbs.	$53.00	$ 74.20
1,051 to 1,100 lbs.	11.5 lbs.	$57.50	$ 80.50
1,101 to 1,150 lbs.	12.7 lbs.	$63.50	$ 88.90
1,151 to 1,200 lbs.	14.5 lbs.	$72.50	$101.50

*Feed requirements per pound of gain will vary by beef genetic type.

Marketing Formulas

Marketing formulas can help producers make decisions on when to market livestock.

Hogs. A simple formula can help producers decide when and at what weight to market hogs. Present prices, cost of gain, weight discounts and the probability of price change can be combined in the following way to indicate the probable return if hogs are held to a heavier weight.

Expected Profit Per Hog Equals:

Expected Added Weight (AW) X Present Hog Price (HP)
Minus, Expected Added Weight (AW) X Cost of Added Gain (AC)
Minus, Final Hog Weight (HW) X Weight Discount (WD)
Plus, Final Hog Weight (HW) X Expected Price Change (EP)

In equation form, this can be written as

Expected Profit Per Hog = AW X HP − (AW X AC) − (HW X WD) + (HW X EP).

To illustrate how the formula can be used, assume the present hog price is $42 per cwt and hogs on hand weigh 220 pounds. You are considering adding about 20 more pounds and estimate the cost of this gain will be 22¢ a pound. Some price decline is expected; and 240 pound hogs may be discounted 50¢ per cwt compared with 220 pound hogs. So, the inputs in this example are:

Hog Price (HP) = $42 per cwt or $.42 per lb.
Expected Added Weight (AW) = 20 lbs.
Cost of Added Gain (AC) = $22 per cwt or $.22 per lb.
Final Hog Weight (HW) = 240 lbs.
Weight Discount (WD) = 50¢ per cwt or $.005 per lb.
Expected Price Change (EP) = $.25 per cwt or −$.0025 per lb.

The values can be plugged into the equation shown, or the calculations can be made in the following form:

Expected Profit Per Hog Equals:

Expected Added Weight X Present Hog Price:	20 X .42 = $8.40
Minus, Expected Added Weight X Cost of Added Gain: 20 X .22 =	4.40
Minus, Final Hog Weight X Weight Discount:	240 X .005 = 1.20
Plus, Final Hog Weight X Expected Price Change:	240 X −.0025 = −.60

Expected Profit Per Hog $2.20

In the example, prices decline 25¢ per cwt and 240 lb. hogs are discounted 50¢ per cwt, but the return to the producer still increases $2.20 per hog by going to 240 lbs. Prices would have to decline $1.18 per cwt in this example before there would be a loss from adding the extra 20 lbs. The result will vary for different market situations.

Cattle. A similar but more complex calculation can be used for cattle. The cattle marketing formula is more complex because as cattle are held to heavier weight, they may reach a higher quality grade but a lower yield grade. Factors to consider in estimating the effect on returns from feeding a group of cattle to heavier weight are:

Present price of Choice cattle (Cp)
Present price of Good cattle (Gp)
Final number of Choice cattle (FC)
Number of Choice added by feeding (AC)
Final number of Good cattle (FG)
Number of cattle fed (N)
Final weight (FW)
Added weight (AW)
Cost of added gain (ADC)
Yield grade discount (YD)
Number of yield grade 4's and 5's added by feeding (ANY)
Expected price change (EP)

Appropriate values for each factor can be plugged into the following equation to estimate the impact of additional weight on feeding returns.

Added Return for the Total Lot = (AC) X (FW) (Cp − Gp) + (FC) (AW) X (Cp − ADC) + (FG) X (AW) X (Gp − ADC) + (ANY) X (FW) X (YD) + (N) X (FW) X (EP)

Although the formula appears complex, the calculations are not difficult. All prices, costs and discounts should be expressed in cents per pound. The final value will be the return expected from feeding the cattle to the heavier weight.

DEVELOPING A PRICING PLAN

In addition to deciding *when to deliver livestock*, livestock producers must also consider the question of *when to price* livestock. This is because forward pricing alternatives are available. The decision is generally based on (1) price goals of the individual, (2) analysis of alternative ways of reaching those goals, and (3) market risk.

Goal setting is very important. Without price goals, a livestock producer will probably not be able to make satisfactory pricing decisions. Goals must be set individually and be realistic for the person involved. A realistic goal for one person may be unrealistic for another. The goals may depend on the seller's need for cash or could reflect a desire to cover costs plus a small profit.

If your goal is to always hit the peak of the market in either cash or forward pricing, you will probably be frequently disappointed. However, a goal of forward pricing when you can cover the cost of production plus a reasonable profit can often be achieved sometime during the feeding period, even if it is not possible at the time the cattle are placed in the feedlot or pigs farrowed.

Market Risk

Any time a farmer buys feeder cattle, farrows pigs, or buys feeder pigs, he is taking a market risk. The producer makes the decision to produce livestock under the assumption that prices will be profitable at the time the finished product is marketed. The price is at least expected to pay a favorable return for the use of land, labor and capital. However, because prices are fairly volatile, there is a good chance prices will be different than expected.

The ability to bear market risk, like the ability to bear production risk, is highly dependent on the producer's capital base. Producers who have a large equity base are able to bear considerable market risk without jeopardizing their farming business. Under-capitalized farmers with a high debt to equity ratio find it increasingly difficult to carry the price risk that exists in livestock operations. This has caused some farmers to discontinue livestock production. Others are turning to methods of marketing which reduce market risk.

Forward Pricing

Hedging and forward contracting are two methods of reducing market risk. By forward contracting or by hedging in the livestock futures market, you can expand the period of time in which to make the pricing decision. You can decide when the price is satisfactory for pricing livestock, or when you no longer are willing to take further price risk. You do not have to wait until the livestock reach market condition before you establish their price.

There are important differences between hedging and contracting. When considering forward pricing, you should select the method that most closely fits your operation and expertise.

Forward contracts are offered by meat packers, livestock marketing agencies and other agricultural firms. A major advantage of forward contracts is that you can work directly with a local buyer or agent, rather than deal with the impersonal futures market. The major disadvantage is that the contracts offered by different firms or agencies have somewhat different specifications. This results in a wide variety of forward contracts.

When forward contracting you sign a specific contract with a firm or agency for actual delivery of the livestock at a specified time. The price is usually a certain amount under the price of the futures contract closest to the expected marketing date.

To hedge, a producer must sell and buy futures contracts on one of the two futures exchanges that offer livestock contracts. These are the Chicago Mercantile Exchange and the Mid-America Commodity Exchange. The size of the cattle and hog contracts on the Mid-America Exchange is one-half as large as those on the Chicago Mercantile Exchange.

Developing a Livestock Marketing Plan

A major advantage of hedging, compared with forward contracting, is that all contracts on the futures market are standardized with respect to volume, quality, delivery terms and other details. However, the size of the contract may not make hedging feasible for some small producers.

Producers who use the futures market for hedging should fully understand how futures markets work. General characteristics of futures markets are discussed in Chapter 6, and the use of livestock futures markets for hedging is discussed in detail in Chapter 10. Table 9-5 compares some features of forward contracting and futures contracts.

Table 9-5. COMPARISON OF HEDGING AND FORWARD CONTRACTING.

	Forward Contracting	Hedging
1. Whom to contact	Local buying or marketing firm	Commodity broker
2. Price of livestock	Specific price estabished	Price varies as basis changes
3. Funds required	No margin deposit	Initial margin deposit required, and additional margin if necessary
4. Contract terms	Each firm has different specific terms	Standardized
5. Delivery	Required	Optional
6. Flexibility of contract	Not cancellable	Hedge can be lifted any time
7. Type of livestock	As specified in contract	More flexibility in kind of livestock that can be hedged
8. Number of livestock	Varies by contract agency	Only two contract sizes
9. Knowledge required	Understand contract specifications	Need to understand contract and futures trading

You need to determine which of these two forward pricing tools is best adapted to your operation. If you have little knowledge of futures markets, use forward contracts, initially. As you gain experience, you may be able to increase your returns by using a combination of hedging and forward contracting.

By taking a close look at your options and using the appropriate tools, you can make your marketing strategy more effective. Keep records of your marketing program so that you can study and improve it. With the wide variability in prices, even a well designed marketing plan will not always work out as expected. But if the program is based on sound reasoning and followed consistently, it should yield improved returns.

CHAPTER **10**

Using Livestock Futures

A new dimension was added to livestock marketing with the introduction of livestock futures markets in the mid-60's. It provided a way for producers and feeders to remove some of the uncertainty about the price they would receive for livestock when it was sold. Prior to the introduction of livestock futures, producers could price livestock only when it was physically ready for market. And they had to carry the entire price risk during the production or feeding operation. But futures markets have made it possible to expand the pricing period so that producers can take advantage of favorable prices if they become available and at the same time shift much of the price risk to others.

The basic purpose of futures markets and how they work was discussed in Chapter 6. These general concepts and procedures apply to livestock futures markets as well and do not need to be repeated. But we will apply them to live slaughter cattle, hogs and feeder cattle as we discuss how you might use these markets in pricing livestock.

GENERAL CHARACTERISTICS OF LIVESTOCK FUTURES

The markets for live cattle and hogs have several characteristics that are different from those of most commodities traditionally traded in futures markets. These differences influence the kind of market performance that can be expected and may limit the degree of price protection available through hedging. They relate to or affect such things as the comparability of cash and futures market positions, the price-quality relationship existing in the cash markets and the concept of basis.

Cash Basis

Cattle and hog production are continuous, year-round processes. By comparison, in grain markets the supply available for an entire marketing year is known once the harvest is completed. This production-utilization pattern affects the nature of the "cash basis," or price difference, between cash and futures markets.

Basis that results from location and quality differences between the futures market and the cash market for particular lots of cattle or hogs is quite important and relevant. However, basis related to time period, which is especially important to grain markets, is not relevant in livestock futures markets. First, there is no storage period and, therefore, no cost of storage that must be reflected in futures prices. In addition, there does not seem to be much reason to expect cash and futures markets in livestock to show a consistent relationship from one period of time to another. The exception is at the maturity of a contract. Then, the two markets must be in close accord or substantial delivery of product will occur. At other times cash prices may logically be either above or below a particular futures contract, depending on current conditions. Inverted markets in livestock futures are fairly common. They are relatively rare in stored commodities.

The pattern of cash-futures price relationships in livestock markets may also be quite different from one year to the next; and prices of individual contracts may be fairly independent of each other. This is true because of the continuous nature of the production process. Thus, supplies and utilization in one period do not necessarily affect the market in later periods.

Cash and Futures Positions

Futures markets for livestock differ from many traditional futures markets in another way. The cash and futures positions are not comparable—until the livestock achieves the weight and quality characteristics specified in the futures contract. Until then, the cash market position is represented by feeder cattle or hogs in some stage of transition to the product defined by the contract. Hedging therefore provides a measure of price protection during a production process instead of for a storage or merchandising operation. However, there is some uncertainty about how closely the final product will conform to contract specifications. This limits the precision with which a hedging position can be estimated.

Price-Quality Relationships

Prices in the cash markets for live cattle and hogs are typically within a fairly wide range for a particular weight and grade category. By contrast, the futures market is represented by a single point within this range.

A cattle feeder, for example, who hedges by selling steer contracts does not know with certainty how his cattle will compare with the quality-weight combination represented by the futures price. Unless quality and price relationships can be accurately predicted, this condition can limit the price protection obtainable from hedging.

Price relationships between different weight-quality combinations within a live cattle or hog grade are not constant over time. Thus, Choice 1,050-pound steers may sell at the top of the price range at one time, but near the lower end of the range a few weeks later. This situation also tends to limit the precision with which a hedging position can be estimated.

GENERAL HEDGING CONSIDERATIONS

The discussion in this section is limited to placing a hedge at the beginning of a feeding or production period and lifting the hedge when the livestock are ready for market. These are not the only times you can place or lift hedges. The hedge can be placed whenever the futures market offers a satisfactory return or when prices appear to have peaked, based on chart patterns, moving averages, or other market analysis information. However, you should be aware that until you place the hedge you are absorbing all the market price risk.

The same can be said for lifting hedges. Because of a favorable basis you may decide to lift a hedge early rather than wait until livestock are physically ready for market. However, this shifts all of the price risk back to you, which may defeat the purpose of the original hedge. Skill can be gained in placing and lifting hedges as you use this marketing tool.

You should carefully study forecasts of future prices before hedging. Obtain price forecasts from several sources, including reputable market analysts with private firms, land-grant universities and the USDA. You must also estimate the total cost of putting livestock on the market, whether they are slaughter cattle, feeder cattle or hogs. This is necessary to realistically evaluate the profit potential from hedging at any particular time. And, it will help avoid the pitfall of inadvertently hedging in a loss. A feeder, however, might decide to lock in a negative return if it will help minimize a loss.

After obtaining price forecasts and estimating the cost of production, you can compare the estimates of a hedged return and the unhedged return. If the estimated hedged return is lower than the expected return from an unhedged position, you must decide if you are willing and able to absorb the extra risk from an unhedged position. The amount of risk a feeder can carry varies widely and is heavily dependent on his overall financial situation. A feeder with limited capital would be more likely to hedge even though the hedge return might be smaller than the expected unhedged return. An established feeder who fully owns or has large equity in a farming operation may choose to stay in a higher risk cash position rather than a lower risk hedged position. On the other hand, if the estimated return from hedging is higher than the expected unhedged return, the lower risk alternative would be best under either capital situation.

The decision is not necessarily an either/or decision of hedging or not hedging. It can also be a decision on whether to hedge all of the livestock to be marketed or only a portion of it. A cattle feeder who has purchased 100 head of steers may choose to sell only one 40,000 pound contract, representing about 37 head of cattle. This would provide price protection through hedging on about a third of the cattle actually planned for market. In a partial hedge of this kind, if cash prices rise, extra profits will be realized on the unhedged portion. If cash prices decline, however, there will be price protection and better returns on a least a third of the feeding operation.

Most analyses of the returns from routine hedging over extended periods of time indicate that returns are lower than non-hedged returns. However, net returns from always staying in an open cash position are likely to show more year to year variation. Hedging, as a marketing management tool, should not be used routinely. It should be used on a selective basis when it appears to offer a favorable pricing option. When used in this way, there is greater potential to increase net returns.

ANALYSIS OF EXPECTED HEDGE RETURNS

The futures market price for any commodity repesents a price for a particular product at a specified market. For example, the live beef

Using Livestock Futures

contract reflects the price at any of six par delivery points for 1,050 to 1,200 pound Choice steers. The live hog contract reflects a Peoria, Illinois price for U.S. No. 1 to 3 barrows and gilts weighing from 200 to 230 pounds; and the feeder cattle contract represents 575 to 700 pound feeder steers at Sioux City, Iowa and Omaha, Nebraska.

Since futures prices represent prices at specific points and for a specific quantity and quality, you should adjust the futures price to reflect your local market and the type of livestock fed. This procedure is called localizing the futures price. The localized futures price, not the quoted futures price, should be compared with production costs for an estimate of the potential hedging return.

Localizing Factors

The main localizing factors are transportation, shrink, delivery marketing costs, brokerage fees, interest on margin deposit, quality discount and delivery point discount. These factors are subtracted from the relevant futures price to estimate a localized futures price.

Transportation. Only the added cost of transporting livestock to the delivery point should be used in this adjustment figure. For example, assume it costs a feeder 25¢ per cwt to transport livestock to a local market and 50¢ per cwt to deliver to a contract delivery point. The producer would subtract the 25¢ it costs to haul livestock to the local market from the 50¢ transportation costs to the delivery point, leaving 25¢ to use as a localizing factor for transportation costs.

Shrink. The shrink adjustment is handled in the same way as transportation costs, with only the additional shrink loss from shipping to the delivery point used in localizing the price. For example, if Choice steers shrink 3% in going to the local market and 4% to the more distant delivery point market, the weight loss from the 1% additional shrink times the live price should be used as the localizing factor.

Delivery marketing costs. Livestock delivered on a futures contract must be delivered to a designated public market and assigned to a livestock commission firm on that market. The seller pays the livestock commission fee, yardage, feed, water, insurance and a grading fee. These charges must be deducted from the futures price because they must be paid if delivery is made. Marketing costs vary depending on the type of livestock. The delivery marketing cost for hogs is about 75¢ per cwt; for slaughter steers, about 50¢ per cwt, and for feeder steers about $1 per cwt, depending on the weight of animals delivered.

Quality discount. If the livestock hedged are of lower quality or a different weight than the par contract, an adjustment from the par price must be made.[1] For example, if a producer delivered 37 head of 1,100 pound animals, but the delivery unit contained eight head of Good steers, there would be a quality discount on the price. The discount for up to 10 head of Good steers is $3 per cwt times the average weight of the delivery unit, or $264 discount (8 x 11.00 x $3.00 = $264). To convert the dollar discount to a price per cwt, divide the total delivered on the contract by this amount, i.e., $264 ÷ 40,000 lbs. = $.0066/lb or $.66 cwt. The same procedure is used to adjust for discounts on any weight and dressing percent deviation from the par contract.

Although heifers are not deliverable on a live cattle futures contract, they can be hedged by a similar localizing procedure. A feeder hedging Choice heifers should deduct the normal difference between Choice steers and Choice heifers in estimating the hedged price.

Delivery point discount. If a hedger's delivery point is likely to be other than a par delivery point, the par price should be adjusted by the value of the discount established by the Exchange. For example, the hog contract par delivery point is Peoria, Illinois and hogs delivered to Sioux City, Iowa; Omaha, Nebraska; St. Paul, Minnesota and St. Louis, Missouri are discounted 25¢ per cwt. The other livestock contracts have different discounts to their alternate delivery points, and these should be used to localize the futures price.

Brokerage fee. One of the costs of participating in a futures market is the fee charged by brokerage firms for handling futures transactions. This fee is also included as a localizing factor as it will affect net hedging returns.

Brokerage fees for live cattle and feeder cattle are about 12¢, and for hogs about 15¢, per cwt. Federal Trade Commission regulations make the brokerage fee negotiable between the trader and broker, therefore the specific fee will vary.

---

[1]Par contract is the full value of the futures contract without any discounts.

Using Livestock Futures

Interest on margin deposit. A margin deposit is required for every contract bought or sold on a futures market. The margin required can vary as the price of livestock varies. Also, if the market moves against a trader's position, additional margin money is required. Since the money is deposited in an escrow account, an interest charge should be deducted for this deposit.

It is difficult to estimate exactly how large the interest deduction should be because costs will vary depending on the extent of price changes, the length of time the contract is held and the current interest rate.

Evaluating a Potential Hedge

Once a feeder has estimated production costs, localized costs, selected a futures contract, and developed a price forecast, a course of action can be decided. The following example will illustrate the procedure to follow in analyzing a live cattle hedge.

Example 1. Analyzing Live Cattle Hedge Return.

1. October live beef futures price (contract selected by estimating the month the cattle will be ready for market)	$70.00/cwt
2. Cost of feeding (should be taken from feeder's records if available and contain cost of feed, feeders and all non-fed costs)	$62.50/cwt
3. Localizing costs	Dollars/cwt
a. transportation (depends on producer's location)	$ 0.50
b. shrink (calculated for producer's location)	0.70
c. delivery marketing cost	0.50
d. quality adjustment (obtained from estimating type of livestock producer will sell and adjusting from par)	0.33
e. delivery discount (no discount if delivery made at Omaha, Sioux City or Peoria)	0.00
f. brokerage fee	0.12
g. interest on margin deposit (estimated by length of time, degree of price change and interest rate)	0.25
Total localizing cost	$ 2.40

4. Adjust futures price to obtain localized
   futures price
   October futures price $70.00
   Localizing costs .... -2.40
   Localized futures price $67.60
5. Net return from hedge
   Localized futures price $67.60
   Cost of feeding costs .... -62.50
   Estimated net hedge return .... $ 5.10/cwt
6. Forecasted price obtained from private and
   university economists
   Expected October cash .... $68.00   to $72.00
7. Expected return without hedging .... $5.50 to $9.50

A feeder should go through the seven steps in Example 1 before making a decision. In the example, the feeder could lock in a return of about $5.10 per cwt by hedging. The estimated profit without hedging ranges from $5.50 to $9.50 per cwt. While the net return through a hedge should be fairly close to $5.10 per cwt, the net return from an unhedged position can vary widely. Since there is considerable difference between the expected profit from a hedged and unhedged position, a producer might choose to hedge an assured profit for at least a portion of the cattle.

The same procedure used for live cattle in Example 1 can be used for short hedges on hogs and feeder cattle. The localizing values, however, will be different.

Localized Futures Prices vs. Basis

In Example 1, the localized futures price was used in estimating the potential return from hedging. For most commodities, a potential hedge return is estimated by using basis.

Basis is the differential between a futures price and a cash price. This is a concept which has been used by hedgers in the grain market for years. Basis patterns for grains are relatively stable from year to year, reflecting storage costs and normal market utilization of a storable commodity.

If basis is used to analyze a potential hedge return, the basis is substituted in place of the localized costs. The basis used is the expected differential between the cash price and the futures contract price at the time the hedge is lifted, as in Example 2.

Example 2. Hedging Live Cattle.

1. October live beef futures price	$70.00
2. Cost of feeding	$62.50
3. Basis (normal)	$ 2.50
4. Obtain localized futures price	
Futures price	$70.00
Basis	-2.50
Less brokerage & interest on margin	.35
Localized futures price	$67.15
5. Approximate hedge return	
Localized futures price	$67.15
Cost of feeding	-62.50
Estimated hedge return	$ 4.65
6. Forecasted price obtained from private and university economists	
Expected October cash	$68.00 to $72.00
7. Expected non-hedge return	$5.50 to $9.50/cwt

Futures markets for livestock have a more recent origin than those for grains, so there is a more limited history of price relationships on which to estimate basis patterns. Also, grains are produced seasonally and are storable, whereas livestock are not storable and are produced year-round. As a result, the basis on livestock may vary from one contract month to the next and may be less predictable. Under these conditions, using localizing factors may be a safer procedure for estimating livestock hedging returns than using basis.

It is possible that when a hedge is lifted, the actual localizing costs may be either smaller or larger than the basis. A hedger who is in position to deliver will do no worse, and quite often better, than the estimated hedge return arrived at by the localizing procedure.

HEDGING EXAMPLES

Four basic types of hedges are illustrated in this section. These are short (selling) hedges in live beef, live hogs and feeder cattle and a long (buying) hedge in feeder cattle. These examples assume that the hedger will complete the hedge by taking an offsetting futures position rather than delivering on the contract and that actual basis is the same as the localizing costs.

Live Beef Cattle (Short Hedge)

Assume a producer has 200 head of feeders and expects to market them in October. The steers are expected to weigh about 1,100 pounds at market time. The producer's localizing basis, or expected futures-cash price differential, will be $2 per cwt at the time the cattle are marketed, and the price on the October futures is $73 per cwt. The producer feels that the $71 price, taking into account localizing costs and cost of feeding, will provide a favorable hedge return. He decides to hedge only three contracts, or 120,000 pounds (40,000 pounds per contract), and remain open with about 100,000 pounds.

In Example 3, the price declines after the hedge is made.

Example 3. Live Cattle Hedging—200 Head (Falling Prices).

	Futures Transactions	Cash Transactions
Sold October futures (place hedge)	$73.00/cwt	(no action)
Bought October futures		Sold cattle
(remove hedge)	70.00/cwt	$68.00/cwt
Futures gain	$ 3.00/cwt	

Gross Hedge Price		Cost of Futures Trading	
Cash price	$68.00/cwt	Interest on margin	$.15/cwt
Futures gain	+3.00/cwt	Brokerage fee	.12/cwt
Gross hedge price	$71.00/cwt	Trading cost	$.27/cwt

Net Hedge Price per Cwt

Gross hedge price	$71.00
Trading cost	-0.27
Net hedge price	$70.73 or $.7073 per lb.

a. Gross return from partial hedge:
  40,000 lbs. x 3 (contract) x $0.7073   = $ 84,876 hedged
  (1,100 lbs. x 200 hd. − 120,000 lbs.) x $0.68 = $ 68,000 unhedged
                          Total $152,876
                          Per cwt price $69.49/cwt

b. Gross return if no cattle were hedged:
  1,100 lbs. x 200 hd. x $0.68   = $149,600
                          Per cwt price $68.00/cwt

The producer gained $3,276 by hedging about 60% of his 200 head cattle feeding operation. In this case, he would have gained more if he had hedged a larger part of his operation.

Example 4 uses the same basic data as in Example 3, but assumes prices rise after the hedge is made.

Using Livestock Futures

Example 4. Live Cattle Hedging—200 Head (Rising Prices).

	Futures Transactions	Cash Transactions
Sold October futures (place hedge)	$73.00/cwt	(no action)
Bought October futures (remove hedge)	76.00/cwt	Sold cash $74.00/cwt
Futures loss	-$ 3.00/cwt	

Gross Hedge Price		Cost of Futures Trading	
Cash price	$74.00/cwt	Interest on margin	$0.30/cwt
Futures loss	-3.00/cwt	Brokerage fee	0.12/cwt
Gross hedge price	$71.00/cwt	Trading cost	$0.42/cwt

Net Hedge Price

Gross hedge price	$71.00/cwt
Trading cost	-0.42/cwt
Net hedge price	$70.58 or $.7058 per lb.

a. Gross return from partial hedge:

40,000 lbs. x 3 (contract) x $0.7058		= $ 84,696
(1,100 lbs. x 200 hd.—120,000 lbs.) x $0.74		= $ 74,000
	Total	$158,696
	Per cwt price	$72.13/cwt

b. Gross return if no cattle were hedged:

1,100 lbs. x 200 hd. x $0.74		= $162,800
	Per cwt price	$74.00/cwt

The hedged return was only $158,696, whereas remaining in an unhedged position would have returned the producer $162,800, or $4,104 more than the hedged return. The unhedged return is greater because cash prices rose after the hedge was made.

The hedge return would have been lower than $158,696 if all of the cattle had been hedged. But since only three contracts were hedged, the producer gained from the cash price advance on the unhedged portion of the operation.

Live Hogs

Assume a producer has 600 hogs, including 300 that will be ready to market in August and 300 in September. Since there is no September contract, the producer would have to hedge part of the hogs with an October contract, even though the contract matures after the hogs are ready to market. This means that delivery would not be an option on the hogs hedged with October futures.

Assume the August futures price is quoted at $47 per cwt and the October contract is at $46. The producer's basis, obtained from past basis history and localizing costs, would be $1 per cwt for the August contract removed in August and $2 per cwt for an October contract removed in September. The localized futures prices of $46 per cwt for August and $44 per cwt for September look favorable to the producer and he decides to hedge.

Once the decision to hedge has been made, the producer must then decide how much of the expected marketings should be hedged. Each hog contract on the Mercantile Exchange is 30,000 pounds, or from 130 to 150 hogs per contract.

Assume in this case that the decision was to hedge about half of the hogs and to divide them between the contract months. Assume also that after the hedge is made and before it is fully lifted, hog prices decline during August but recover some in September. In August, when the producer lifted part of the hedge, August futures were $45 per cwt; but the October contract moved up to $47 per cwt in September, when an offsetting contract was purchased.

Example 5. Live Hog Hedge (August and October Contracts).

August Marketings

	Futures Transaction	Cash Transaction
Sold August Futures (place hedge)	$47.00/cwt	(no action)
Bought August Futures (remove hedge)	$45.00/cwt	Sold cash $44.00/cwt
Futures profit	+$ 2.00/cwt	

Gross Hedge Price		Cost of Futures Trading	
Cash price	$44.00/cwt	Interest on margin	$0.05/cwt
Futures profit	+2.00/cwt	Brokerage fee	$0.12/cwt
Gross hedge price	$46.00/cwt	Trading cost	$0.17/cwt

Net Hedge Price	
Gross hedge price	$46.00/cwt
Trading cost	-0.17/cwt
Net hedge price	$45.83/cwt or $.4583/lb.

a. August marketing return for 300 hogs marketed at 220 lbs:

Hedged portion ($.4583 x 30,000 lbs.) (one contract)	= $13,749.00
Unhedged portion ($.4400) x (66,000-30,000 lbs.)	= 15,840.00
Total August marketing return	$29,589.00
Per cwt price	$44.83/cwt

Using Livestock Futures

| | September Marketings ||
	Futures Transaction	**Cash Transaction**
Sold October Futures (place hedge)	$46.00/cwt	(no action)
Bought October Futures (remove hedge)	$47.00/cwt	Sold cash $45.00/cwt
Futures loss	-$ 1.00/cwt	

Gross Hedge Price		**Cost of Futures Trading**	
Cash price	$45.00/cwt	Interest on margin	$0.15/cwt
Futures loss	- 1.00/cwt	Brokerage fee	$0.12/cwt
Gross hedge price	$44.00/cwt	Trading cost	$0.27/cwt

Net Hedge Price

Gross hedge price	$44.00/cwt
Trading cost	- 0.27/cwt
Net hedge price	$43.73/cwt or $.4373 per lb.

b. September marketing return for 300 hogs marketed at 220 lbs:

Hedged portion ($.4373 x 30,000 lbs.) (one contract)	= $13,119.00
Unhedged portion ($.4500) x (66,000 - 30,000 lbs.)	= $16,200.00
Total September marketing return	$29,319.00
Per cwt price	$44.42/cwt

c. Total return (partially hedged) for August and September marketings
29,589 + $29,319 = $58,908 or $44.63/cwt

d. Total return if marketings in August and September had not been hedged.
(66,000 lbs. x $.4400) + (66,000 x .4500) = $58,740 or $44.50/cwt

e. Total return if entire hog marketings would have been hedged.
$59,109.60 or $44.78/cwt

The return from the partial hedge operation was about the same as the unhedged return because the price decline in August was offset by a price rise in September. If there had been price declines both months, the fully hedged and partially hedged options would have appeared more favorable.

Feeder Cattle (Short Hedge)

A cow-calf producer with 160 cows considers using the futures market to hedge the sale of feeder cattle. If the November feeder steer futures price is $80 per cwt and the localizing costs are $4 per cwt, this would mean a localized futures price of about $76 per cwt could be hedged.

The producer has 144 calves and plans to hold 30 heifers for replacement and to market 114 head (73 steers and 41 heifers) which are expected to weigh 600 pounds.[2] If the cattle would be heavier than 700 pounds, the basis would have to be increased to reflect a discount on heavier weights.

The producer can use the $76 per cwt price to evaluate the hedging potential. Since the plan is to market 114 calves that weigh 600 pounds per head, the total weight to be marketed is 68,400 pounds (114 head x 600 pounds).

One futures contract is 44,000 pounds with a 5% variation allowable. Thus, the producer should sell only one contract, since selling more than one would create a speculative position on part of the contract. This means that about 24,400 pounds of the expected feeder cattle production would not be hedged.

Assume the producer decided to hedge, and prices declined after the hedge was made. Example 6 illustrates the results from partially hedging the operation.

Example 6. Hedging Feeder Cattle (Short Hedge, Falling Price).

	Futures Transaction	Cash Transaction
Sold November futures (place hedge)	$80.00/cwt	(no action)
Bought November futures (remove hedge)	$79.00/cwt	Sold Cash $75.00/cwt
Futures profit	+$ 1.00/cwt	

Gross Hedge Price		Cost of Futures Trading	
Cash price	$75.00/cwt	Interest on margin	$0.10/cwt
Futures gain	+ 1.00/cwt	Brokerage fee	$0.12/cwt
Gross hedge price	$76.00/cwt	Trading cost	$0.22/cwt

Net Hedge Price	
Gross hedge price	$76.00/cwt
Trading cost	- 0.22/cwt
Net hedge price	$75.78/cwt

a. Total return from marketing 114 feeder cattle:

Hedged portion ($.7578) x 44,000 lbs.	= $33,343.20
Unhedged portion ($.7500) x 24,400 lbs.	= $18,300.00
Total return	$51,643.20
Per cwt price	$75.50/cwt

---

[2]To simplify calculations, it was assumed that steer and heifer weights and prices were the same. Under actual conditions, heifer weights would be somewhat lighter and the price on heifers approximately $4 per cwt below steers.

The expected hedging price was $76 per cwt, but the average price received was slightly less at $75.50. The return was less than expected because of hedging costs and because only about two-thirds of the feeder cattle were hedged.

If the producer had delivered on the contract instead of offsetting the hedge with a purchase, and the delivery costs were the same as localizing costs, the net price on the hedge would have been the same.

Sold November futures contract	$80.00/cwt
Delivery cost (transportation, shrink, etc.)	- 4.00/cwt
Futures price	$76.00/cwt
Cost of futures trading	
Brokerage $0.12/cwt	
Interest on margin $0.10/cwt	- 0.22/cwt
Total cost $0.22/cwt	$75.78/cwt

If the producer had not hedged a portion of his feeders, the gross return for the 114 calves would have been:

(68,400 lbs. x $.75) = $51,300

Feeder Cattle (Long Hedge)

Cattle feeders can use the feeder steer contract to hedge the purchase of feeder cattle. This is a long hedge, in contrast to the short (selling) hedge illustrated before.

Assume a cattle feeder wants to feed steers and will need about 300 head in November to fill the feedlot. The feeder is flexible regarding the weight of cattle to be fed.

The feeder's localizing costs are $3/cwt to the nearest par delivery point at Sioux City or Omaha. Adding the localizing costs to the futures price will set an approximate price for the feeder steers. If the November futures price is $80, this means the feeder can set a purchase price at the farm of about $83 per cwt ($80.00 + $3.00 = $83.00). The following example will illustrate how the hedge might turn out if prices fall after the hedge is made. A weight of 650 lbs. is assumed, with the feeder buying three futures contracts.

Example 7. Feeder Cattle (Long Hedge and Falling Prices).

	Futures Transaction	Cash Transaction
Bought November futures (place hedge)	$80.00/cwt	(no action)
Sell November futures (remove hedge)	$76.00/cwt	Buy cash $79.00/cwt
Futures loss	-$ 4.00/cwt	

Gross Hedge Price		Cost of Futures Trading	
Cash price	$79.00/cwt	Interest on margin	$0.10/cwt
Futures loss	$ 4.00/cwt	Brokerage fee	$0.12/cwt
Gross hedge price	$83.00/cwt	Trading cost	$0.22/cwt

Net Hedge Price	
Gross hedge price	$83.00/cwt
Trading cost	$ 0.22/cwt
Net hedge price	$83.22/cwt

Total cost of partially hedging and buying 300 steers:

Hedged portion (44,000 lbs.) x 3 (contracts) x $.8322	= $109,850.40
Unhedged portion (63,000 lbs.) x $.79	= $ 49,770.00
Total cost	$159,620.40
Per cwt price	$81.86/cwt

In this case, if the cattle feeder had not hedged, the feeder steers could have been purchased for $79 per cwt; because he hedged, the cost was $81.86 per cwt. However, if prices had risen after the hedge was made, the hedge price would have been less than the unhedged price.

Removing a Hedge

The discussion up to this point has focused mainly on the procedure to follow when placing a short hedge (selling a contract). After placing a hedge, producers can generally ignore price movements in the futures market until they are ready to lift their hedge. They must be in a position, however, to respond to margin calls when necessary. Generally, the hedge should be lifted only if the livestock are ready to sell on the cash market. When the hedged livestock are ready to be marketed, the hedger must determine the best way to remove the hedge.

A feeder may have a choice of two methods for lifting short hedges—either by delivering livestock as specified in the contract or by buying an offsetting futures contract for the same month. Delivery, however, is feasible only if livestock are hedged in a contract delivery month. A producer with livestock which meet the contract specifications and are hedged in a contract delivery month can select the most favorable of the two alternatives. Example 8 illustrates the data needed to decide which procedure to use to lift a hedge.

Example 8. Deciding How to Remove a Hedge.

Item		
(1) Futures price at which the feeder would have to purchase to lift his hedge		$72.00
(2) Localizing factors (costs that would be incurred if cattle are delivered)		
(a) Transportation (added)	$0.50/cwt	
(b) Shrink (added)	$0.70/cwt	
(c) Delivery marketing cost	$0.50/cwt	
(d) Quality discount estimate	$1.50/cwt	
(e) Delivery discount	—	
Total localizing costs	$3.20/cwt	
(3) Adjusted futures price		
Futures price		$72.00/cwt
Localized cost		$ 3.20/cwt
Adjusted futures price		$69.80/cwt
(4) Cash price bid obtained from a packer or estimated return from commission firm or auction		$70.00/cwt
(5) Comparison of cash and adjusted futures price		
Cash price		$70.00/cwt
Adjusted futures price		-69.80/cwt
Price difference		$ 0.20/cwt

In example 8, since the price difference under item (5) is positive, the producer would sell on the cash market and buy back a futures contract. The hedge would actually net $0.20 more than was anticipated when it was placed.

If the adjusted futures price (item 3) and the cash price (item 4) are equal, the result would be the same for either method of removing the hedge. Most producers, however, would rather buy back a futures contract because the localizing costs in item (2) are estimated, and there would be some uncertainty about the actual delivery cost.

If the difference between the cash price and adjusted futures price in item (5) is negative, the producer should consider delivery on the contract. As a practical matter, if the value (item 5) is negative by less than $0.50 to $0.75 per cwt, the producer will probably choose to buy back the contract rather than take the delivery risk.

It is not necessary for a feeder to consider the original hedge price in determining which alternative to use in lifting a hedge. The feeder only needs to examine his delivery cost, cash price and the futures price of the contract to be purchased.

A feeder who has hedged livestock that does not meet the contract specifications or whose livestock will be marketed in a non-delivery period has only one option—to buy a futures contract to offset the hedge. A feeder in this position must accept whatever basis exists. If it's unfavorable, the hedge can become very unprofitable.

LIMITATIONS OF LIVESTOCK HEDGES

Effective hedging in any commodity is dependent on either having a predictable basis for the commodity or being able to effectively deliver on the contract. If the futures contract is designed so that delivery is feasible, it will generally have a fairly predictable basis at the par delivery point and during the delivery period. The following section discusses possible limitations of livestock futures markets for effective hedging by producers.

Live Slaughter Cattle

Delivery months. Even a casual appraisal of the record on live cattle futures since their beginning will show that the basis relationship has not been consistent between years or between months during a year. Since the basis cannot be predicted accurately, the feeder must estimate the approximate basis at the time the hedge is made and, if the basis is unfavorable at contract maturity, consider delivery on the contract.

Delivery on the live cattle contract is not difficult for producers with steers which were fed to reach the Choice grade. The contract specifications allow a wide range of weights and dressing percents and up to eight head of Good steers at reasonable discounts. Many cattle feeders and traders have made deliveries without major difficulty.

There are times during the year, however, when cattle feeders are not able to make delivery. The Mercantile Exchange offers trading in only six contracts during a year, so delivery is not an option for feeders who have steers to market in the months without contracts. For example, there is no July live beef futures contract. So if a feeder with cattle that will be ready to market in July wants to hedge, he must sell either a June or August contract. Since neither contract matures at the time the steers will be ready for market, the feeder will not have the option of delivering if the basis is unfavorable when it's time to lift the hedge. The feeder will have to buy back an offsetting contract regardless of the cost. The general situation is the same for feeder cattle and live hog futures, since contracts for these commodities are not available every month.

Good grade steers. Cattle feeders who feed lower quality steers that will not make Choice grade will not be able to deliver on a contract. If they decide to hedge, their return will be dependent on having a favorable basis when the hedge is lifted. If the basis is unfavorable, they must buy a futures contract to complete their futures transaction. This kind of hedging is more risky, since the hedge return is dependent on the price differential between Good and Choice steers and the basis when the hedge is lifted.

Hedging heifers. Heifers cannot be delivered on a live cattle futures contract. So, the case for hedging heifers is the same as for Good steers. The final hedge return will be based on the price relationship between steers and heifers and the basis at the time the hedge is lifted. Therefore, feeders attempting to hedge heifers by using the live cattle futures market are taking more risk than those who hedge Choice steers.

Hogs

Major disadvantages of the live hog futures contracts available at the Chicago Mercantile Exchange are: (1) the contract size is too large for many producers, (2) contracts are not available for each month of the year and (3) the grade specifications are too low.

Most hog producers, except very large operators, will find it difficult to deliver on the hog contract. It calls for delivery of 30,000 pounds of live hogs, which would mean from 130 to 150 head, depending on the weight. While most hog producers market many more than 130 to 150 hogs per year, many of them would not be able to put together the number needed on any one day to meet the contract specifications.

The Mid-America Exchange in Chicago offers trading in both live hog and live cattle contracts that are half the size of the Mercantile Exchange contracts. The 15,000 pound live hog contract would represent 65 to 75 head of hogs. All other contract specifications are identical to the Mercantile Exchange contract. This provides an alternative for producers whose volume will meet this contract but is too small for the larger contract.

To provide effective hedging potential, contracts should be available for each month of the year. Hogs are produced year-round and cannot be stored from one month to the next. Attempting to hedge in a contract which matures before or after the hogs are sold on the cash market is risky.

These delivery limitations make it difficult for hedgers to put pressure on the futures market and cause a consistent relationship to cash prices at contract maturity. Precise hedging is not possible without a predictable basis relationship and broad potential for delivery. A hog producer expecting to hedge a small positive return, for example, could end up with a loss because of an unfavorable basis relationship.

Feeder Cattle

Hedging sales. The futures market on feeder cattle can be used by cow-calf producers or backgrounders to set prices for feeder steers. A reasonable degree of pricing precision appears possible for those months in which contracts are available. Delivery appears feasible and can be carried out if the basis is unfavorable when contracts mature. Hedging sales expected in months when futures contracts are not available is more risky.

The effectiveness of hedging with feeder cattle futures is limited some by comparatively small trading volume. As a result, basis patterns are erratic and may encourage deliveries on contract by cow-calf producers or backgrounders, rather than taking an offsetting position in the futures market.

Effective hedging of non-par cattle (ex. heifers or steer calves) is dependent on a predictable basis between the futures price at contract maturity and the cash value of such cattle. Since the basis is not consistent or predictable, hedging these kinds of feeder cattle can be risky. Actual hedge returns may vary widely from the expected return.

Hedging purchases. The feeder cattle futures market appears less effective for hedging the purchases of feeders than for selling feeders. This is because some of the delivery conditions in the contract may cause a buyer some unusual expenses, should he decide to take delivery.

For example, the buyer of a feeder cattle contract has neither control over where delivery is made nor the weight of animals delivered.

There are eleven delivery points, ranging from Sioux City, Iowa and Omaha, Nebraska as par delivery points to Amarillo, Texas at 50¢ per cwt discount and Montgomery, Alabama at a $6 per cwt discount. The holder of a contract receiving delivery cannot designate the delivery point he prefers, but has to accept the cattle wherever the seller decides to deliver.

The weight of cattle which are delivered on the contract is also determined by the seller. The average weight of a contract delivery unit can vary from 550 to 800 pounds, with 550 to 700 pounds as par. If the cattle delivered are heavier than the par weight, the delivery unit is discounted. The delivery unit must be fairly homogenous, and no steer in the delivery unit can weigh 50 pounds less or more than the delivery unit average. The hedger accepting delivery, however, has no control over whether heavy or lighter steers will be delivered.

These limitations of the feeder cattle contract are not a criticism of the Mercantile Exchange contracts. With the wide range of weights, grades and classes of feeder cattle in the market, it may be impossible to develop one feeder cattle contract that can be used effectively to hedge all types of feeder animals.

Effect of Geographic Location

Some possible difficulties in hedging, even when delivery is an option or at least locationally feasible, have been discussed previously. Location of the hedger in relation to delivery points can also affect hedging potential. If a cattle feeder, cow-calf or hog producer is located a considerable distance from a par or reasonable alternate delivery point, hedging becomes a less precise marketing tool.

Two factors determine the hedging outcome for producers whose location is such that delivery is not feasible. These are the price relationship between cash and futures at the par delivery point and the cash price relationship between the producer's market and the par cash market. If the price difference between the local cash market and the par market is quite variable, it will be difficult to hedge precisely. Variations in the price differential can potentially wipe out any expected hedge profit or might double the profit.

For example, the cash market price for Choice slaughter steers in the Texas-New Mexico area is above the Omaha cash market at times and is below at other times. It is difficult for hedgers in this area to closely estimate hedge returns.

A somewhat similar situation exists for the eastern Corn Belt, or in other feeding states located east of the delivery points. Cash markets are usually slightly higher than at the par delivery point, but if price relationships change after a hedge is placed, there is no way to maintain the expected hedge return. Hedging slaughter cattle on the Mercantile Exchange or Mid-America Exchange contracts can be more precise for cattle feeders located in Illinois, northern Missouri, Iowa, southern Minnesota, southern South Dakota, Nebraska, northeast Kansas, Colorado, northern Texas and Oklahoma than it can for other areas of the country. The same is true for hogs; hedging is a less useful marketing tool for producers located a considerable distance from a delivery point.

LIVESTOCK BASIS

As pointed out in earlier discussions, basis information is vitally important for effective hedging. If the basis variation is as potentially large as the cash price variation, hedging is as risky as staying in an open cash position.

Tables 10-1 and 10-2 contain some historical basis information for cattle and hogs. Although the basis data is for Iowa and southern Minnesota, it can be adapted to other areas of the country by simply comparing local cash prices with prices on the Interior Iowa-Southern Minnesota direct livestock market. If your local cash prices are above the Iowa price, subtract the difference from the basis shown in the table; and if local cash prices are normally lower, add the difference to the basis in the tables.

How to Use the Table

The data in Tables 10-1, 10-2 and 10-3 are based on a ten-year history of daily basis. The year is divided into 24 marketing periods, providing basis information for each of these periods. The tables show the time period for which the basis applied, The futures contract which would be used for that period, the average basis, the extremes in basis over the ten years and the probability that the basis will be $3 per cwt or less, $2 per cwt and less, $1 per cwt and less, etc.

A close look at the live cattle basis in Table 10-1 will illustrate how to use the data. The mean basis for each marketing period could be used, but the probabilities of basis provide a better approximation of what the actual basis might be. The first marketing period in Table 10-1 is January 1 to January 15 and the contract traded for that marketing period is February. The mean or average basis was $0.85 per cwt and the range in basis was from $8 per cwt to -$3 per cwt. This means that the cash price ranged from $8 per cwt under the futures to $3 per cwt above during that period.

The next value horizontally on the table is 83, which indicates there is an 83% probability that the basis will be less than $3 per cwt. Or stated another way, there is only a 17% (100 - 83 = 17) chance that the basis will be larger than $3 per cwt. This all means there is a good chance that the cash price will be less than $3 per cwt under the futures price in this time period. The next value horizontally is 73, which means there is a 73% chance that the basis will be $2 per cwt or less and only a 27% chance the basis will be wider than $2 per cwt. The probability of a basis of $1 per cwt or less is 63%; for 0 or less, 39%; for -$1 or less, 24%; and for less than -$2 per cwt the probability is only 4%.

It is apparent from the data that the probabilities and the basis vary from one marketing period to another.

The basis values for live hogs in Table 10-2 were developed in the same way as for live cattle. In general, hogs show more basis variation than cattle from one marketing period to another.

Since the tables present different basis probabilities, producers can select the basis desired—depending on how much basis risk they want to avoid. The two-thirds rule may be a good guide to use—that is, using a basis that has a 67% chance of being at a certain value or less. Or, stated the opposite way, there is only a 33% chance that the basis will be wider than the one used.

Table 10-3 illustrates the estimated basis for live cattle and hogs in interior Iowa and southern Minnesota if the 67% rule is used. The data can be used to estimate the potential return from a hedge and to decide whether you should hedge.

The basis on cattle and hogs is generally less stable during non-delivery periods. This does not mean the basis is either wider or narrower, but that it is less predictable. And an inconsistent basis increases the hedging risk. The basis risk historically has been greater for live hogs than for live cattle.

When to Lift Hedges

As the time of marketing livestock and possibly lifting a hedge approaches, a producer can compare the current basis with the historical probabilities of various basis levels (Tables 10-1 and 10-2). If the probability for the current basis is high, it indicates the basis will probably narrow and that the producer should delay lifting the hedge. The reason for delaying is that, with high probability, there is a good chance the basis will narrow and improve the hedge return.

On the other hand, if the current basis is small and the probability of this basis is low, it may be best to lift the hedge early to take advantage of the favorable basis. An example will illustrate how the information can be used.

Assume a producer used the April contract to hedge live cattle he expected to market during the March 1 to March 15 period. The basis used to estimate hedge return would be $1.50 per cwt (Table 10-3).

Suppose that on March 1, the producer observed that the current basis was $3.10 per cwt. Data for that period in Table 1 indicates a 95% chance that the basis will be $3 per cwt or less. The producer should therefore delay lifting the hedge, expecting the basis to narrow.

Suppose, however, that the current basis is zero. Table 10-1 shows that there is only a 10% probability that the basis will be this narrow. In this case, the hedge should be lifted since there is only a small chance of a more favorable basis. Any delay in lifting the hedge would likely result in lower hedge returns.

Proper timing of hedge lifting should receive careful analysis by livestock producers who hedge. Livestock producers who chart futures prices should recognize that chart patterns alone are not a sufficient guide for deciding when to lift hedges. It is the cash-futures price relationship, not just the movement of futures prices, that is important to decisions on lifting hedges.

While the data in Tables 10-1, 10-2 and 10-3 do not eliminate the risk, they can be used as a guide and should improve the effectiveness of hedging operations.

Table 10-1. LIVE CATTLE BASIS (1968-1978).
Interior Iowa & Southern Minnesota Choice Steers.*

Period	Contract	Mean Basis $/cwt	Basis Range $/cwt	$3/cwt or Less	$2/cwt or Less	$1/cwt or Less	Zero or Less	$-1/cwt or Less*	$-2/cwt or Less*
						(Probability)			
1/ 1- 1/15	Feb.	0.85	8 to -3	83	73	63	39	24	4
1/16- 1/31	Feb.	0.66	5 to -3	91	81	62	35	8	2
2/ 1- 2/20	Feb.	0.68	4 to -2	100	95	69	16	1	0
2/21- 2/29	Apr.	0.87	4 to -2	96	85	57	17	4	0
3/ 1- 3/15	Apr.	1.22	5 to -1	95	80	43	10	0	0
3/16- 3/31	Apr.	1.15	4 to -2	97	77	47	10	4	0
4/ 1- 4/20	Apr.	0.98	4 to -2	97	89	54	8	2	0
4/21- 4/30	June	1.31	7 to -2	72	67	65	39	5	0
5/ 1- 5/15	June	0.77	4 to -3	90	78	63	36	7	1
5/16- 5/31	June	0.86	6 to -2	90	83	62	34	6	0
6/ 1- 6/20	June	0.36	4 to -9	99	95	76	28	9	3
6/21- 6/30	Aug.	-0.18	5 to -5	88	82	73	48	26	22
7/ 1- 7/15	Aug.	-0.30	5 to -6	93	86	74	54	31	19
7/16- 7/31	Aug.	0.36	6 to -6	87	71	67	54	27	14
8/ 1- 8/20	Aug.	0.56	5 to -4	94	89	66	30	11	4
8/21- 8/31	Oct.	-0.31	5 to -5	89	88	81	71	36	14
9/ 1- 9/15	Oct.	-0.41	5 to -5	93	83	77	73	35	17
9/16- 9/30	Oct.	-0.04	2 to -4	—	100	85	46	14	7
10/ 1-10/20	Oct.	0.55	3 to -3	101	95	75	20	4	1
10/21-10/31	Dec.	0.73	5 to -5	90	78	52	34	16	11
11/ 1-11/15	Dec.	0.97	5 to -3	95	84	44	25	4	1
11/16-11/30	Dec.	1.58	5 to -1	90	69	26	3	0	0
12/ 1-12/20	Dec.	1.23	4 to -1	98	81	37	9	0	0
12/21-12/31	Feb.	1.16	8 to -3	85	68	53	39	13	5

Source: J. Marvin Skadberg, Iowa State University.
*Negative values indicated that the cash price is above the futures.

Table 10-2. LIVE HOG BASIS (1968-1978).
Interior Iowa & Southern Minnesota.

Period	Contract	Mean Basis $/cwt	Basis Range $/cwt	$3/cwt or Less	$2/cwt or Less	$1/cwt or Less	Zero or Less	$-1/cwt or Less*	$-2/cwt or Less*
						(Probability)			
1/ 1- 1/15	Feb.	1.63	9 to -3	77	63	47	19	7	2
1/16- 1/31*	Feb.	0.84	7 to -3	87	80	61	31	9	1
2/ 1- 2/20	Feb.	1.03	4 to -2	96	86	52	10	1	0
2/21- 2/29	Apr.	-0.89	3 to -5	99	97	89	62	40	28
3/ 1- 3/15	Apr.	-0.25	3 to -4	100	99	80	47	25	18
3/16- 3/31	Apr.	0.85	5 to -2	96	87	53	21	5	0
4/ 1- 4/20	Apr.	1.73	4 to -2	91	60	22	4	1	0
4/21- 4/30	June	4.46	8 to 0	10	5	1	0	0	0
5/ 1- 5/15	June	3.83	9 to -1	20	5	1	1	0	0
5/16- 5/31	June	2.74	7 to 0	65	28	3	0	0	0
6/ 1- 6/20	June	2.43	5 to 0	74	30	2	0	0	0
6/21- 6/30	July	1.41	4 to -2	95	73	35	11	3	0
7/ 1- 7/20	July	1.56	5 to -1	88	69	33	8	0	0
7/21- 7/31	Aug.	0.28	6 to -4	89	86	73	51	20	7
8/ 1- 8/20	Aug.	0.84	6 to -4	97	92	54	17	3	2
8/21- 8/31	Oct.	-1.94	1 to -8	—	—	99	91	69	35
9/ 1- 9/15	Oct.	-0.82	5 to -5	98	98	94	70	41	22
9/16- 9/30	Oct.	0.30	4 to -4	99	93	69	35	15	2
10/ 1-10/20	Oct.	1.36	6 to -2	94	79	32	7	3	0
10/21-10/31	Dec.	1.34	6 to -3	90	69	43	13	4	2
11/ 1-11/15	Dec.	2.54	8 to -1	75	44	18	2	0	0
11/16-11/30	Dec.	3.01	10 to 0	64	29	5	0	0	0
12/ 1-12/20	Dec.	2.51	7 to -2	69	31	9	3	1	0
12/21-12/31	Feb.	0.81	6 to -3	87	75	60	36	10	5

Source: J. Marvin Skadberg, Iowa State University.

Using Livestock Futures

Table 10-3. ESTIMATED BASIS FOR LIVE CATTLE AND HOGS, Iowa—Southern Minnesota (67% probability).*

Period	Live Cattle ($/cwt)	Live Hogs ($/cwt)
1/ 1 to 1/15	1.00	2.00
1/16 to 1/31	1.00	1.00
2/ 1 to 2/20	1.00	1.25
2/21 to 2/29	1.25	0
3/ 1 to 3/15	1.50	0.50
3/16 to 3/31	1.50	1.25
4/ 1 to 4/20	1.25	2.25
4/21 to 4/30	1.00	5.00
5/ 1 to 5/15	1.00	4.50
5/16 to 5/31	1.00	3.00
6/ 1 to 6/20	0.75	2.75
6/21 to 6/30	0.50	1.75
7/ 1 to 7/20	0.50	2.00
7/21 to 7/31	1.00	0.75
8/ 1 to 8/20	1.00	1.25
8/21 to 8/31	0	-1.00
9/ 1 to 9/15	0	-0.50
9/16 to 9/30	0.50	1.00
10/ 1 to 10/20	0.75	1.75
10/21 to 10/31	1.25	2.00
11/ 1 to 11/15	1.50	2.50
11/16 to 11/30	2.00	3.00
12/ 1 to 12/21	1.75	3.00
12/21 to 12/31	2.00	1.25

*Estimated basis level with a 67% probability that actual basis will be no more than shown.

CHAPTER **11**

Livestock Markets: Sources of Information and Market Factors

Supply and demand are the basic factors for discovery of meat and livestock prices. But what additional factors play a role? And what brings about changes in supply and demand?

Supply

The number of yearling feeder cattle or feeder pigs or lambs placed on the market affects price. Age, weight, and condition of livestock are other supply factors. Each of these may affect the price. Seasonal patterns and the phase of a cycle are also important.

Supplies of different classes of livestock, of imported meat, and of other competing products are part of price establishment. While many are familiar with the wide swings in hog supplies, some tend to forget that in recent years, cow slaughter almost doubled from 1973 to 1975 and was chopped almost in half from 1975 to 1979. Such changes take place as a result of individual decisions by thousands of producers. These decisions are influenced by current and expected market prices and simultaneously influence the actual supply, and thus price.

Market supplies of various classes of livestock and meat are determined by earlier decisions relating to breeding herds, land use, feed availability, cost of off-farm inputs or new technology. Weather also is a major determinant of supply. It affects pastures and ranges, feedgrain production, basic livestock numbers, death losses, and rates of gain. The 1978-79 winter was unusually harsh in many livestock feeding areas and extended the time on feed to reach market weights.

The 1980-81 winter was unusually mild and dry in some areas, and many cattle went to slaughter 10 to 30 days earlier than expected. The increased market supplies, some overfinished, caused wide discounts. Such weather influences cause shifts in short term supplies and can drastically affect price.

Processing changes livestock to more useful items such as meat for consumers, hides for leather and other products. Price is the main lever to assure that this "given" quantity of product does not back up in the "pipeline." If price is too low, it will empty the meat counters; if too high, it will cause meat to remain unsold on the counters.

Interest costs can also be a significant factor in livestock price discovery. High interest rates and more dollar needs because of the increased investment per animal can significantly influence both supply and demand sides of the market. The increased cost of money reduces the demand for feeder animals, lessens placements on feed and slows the buildup of breeding herds. Interest costs also affect the inventory policy of processors, retailers and others in the meat channels. This can slow the flow of meat through "pipeline" channels and drastically affect prices.

Changes in storage stocks of meat are part of the potential supply picture. However, such stocks are small in relation to use except with pork bellies, sometimes hams, and boneless beef for processing purposes. Initial and storage costs are fundamental factors that affect these flow patterns.

Figure 11-1 shows per capita consumption of beef, pork, poultry and total meat. These consumption levels are largely a reflection of actual supply to the consumer, rather than of demand. They include both domestic production and imports. Supply availability is affected if breeding numbers are being increased or decreased. Death losses and exports also affect U.S. consumption. All meat that is placed on the market will move to consumers in less than 30 days, except for small amounts held in commercial storage. Once meat is purchased by the consumer, it is considered used; however, there is an unknown quantity of meat held in family freezers for later consumption.

There has been a rising long term trend in consumption of beef and poultry and a static trend for pork consumption. Beef hit an all-time peak consumption of 129 pounds per person in 1976, then declined to 106 pounds in 1979 and 103 pounds in 1980 (carcass weight equivalent). Pork consumption increased from 60 pounds in 1978 to 74 pounds in 1980. Increased poultry meat consumption is, to a considerable extent, a result of significant technical management breakthroughs that lowered the relative cost of poultry production.

Demand

Demand is the amount of product that consumers are willing to take off the market at a certain schedule of prices during a period of time. Demand for livestock products is influenced primarily by five factors: (1) human population; (2) income of consumers; (3) substitution of other products; (4) taste and preferences; and (5) habits, culture, and other environmental characteristics. Demand for livestock by-products, and for meat to a limited degree, is influenced by the demand in other countries. Some of these factors are difficult to measure, but they are still significant. Rapid changes in supply, plus double-digit inflation, may mask what is happening to "real" prices and demand for each meat.

Demand is most relevant at the consumer level. Demands at various other stages from producer to consumer are derived from this level. Increases in population have been a most reliable source of rising demand in the past. Population is now increasing less than 1% a year, and our median age is rising.

Changing consumer incomes have provided an important base for increased demand for meat. There is a positive correlation between meat demand and per capita disposable income. Meat tends to be purchased for cash; therefore, unemployment, debt load and other expenditures may at times limit available dollars for meat purchases.

Shifts in preferences for meat and for particular cuts of meat take place, but we frequently only guess at what they are. Shifts made to hogs that produce leaner, meatier pork have helped the demand for pork. Increasing business at "tablecloth" restaurants in the 1960's and 1970's, with beef a major menu item, increased the effective demand for loin and rib items. The increase in number and sales volume of fast food restaurants in the 1970's increased the demand for ground beef, at the same time that demand for beef roasts declined. At the beginning of the 1980's, diversification of menu items in fast food outlets increased the amount of pork and poultry sold through this channel. Customs, religious beliefs, ethnic background, and food and family backgrounds can have an influence on demand. Preferences in the 1980's will be influenced by a weight and health-conscious society.

Figure 11-1.
CONSUMPTION OF MEAT, POULTRY AND FISH (Retail Weight Equivalent).

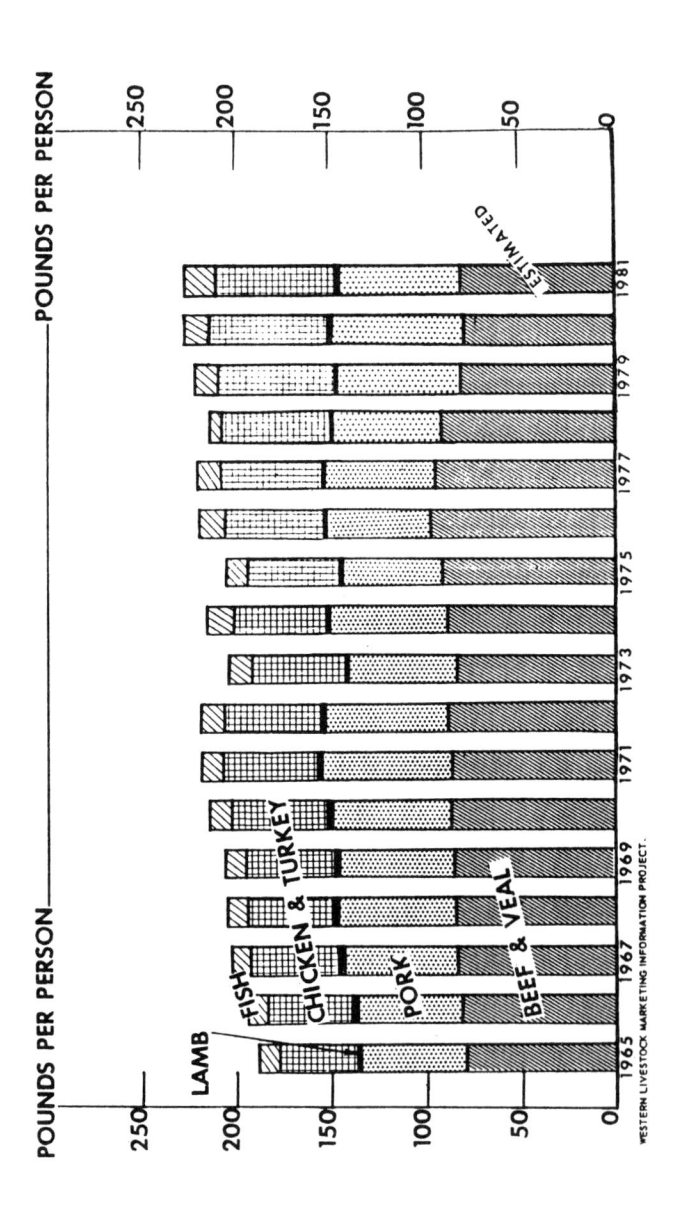

Technology sometimes helps products to more closely match consumer preferences. New beef items include a variety of beef patties and simulated steak from beef muscle and trimmings. This has increased the array of beef items for customers at restaurants and meat counters. Pork has long provided a wide array of choices. Poultry is now appearing in more diverse forms—quite a change from the time when broilers and turkey were sold only as whole birds.

Increases in energy costs have adversely affected the demand for beef. When sharp increases in energy prices occurred in 1977 and again in 1980, some of the consumer dollars to pay for that energy appear to have come from lower expenditures for beef and other products bought for cash. Transportation and other meat handling, processing and distribution costs are boosted when energy prices rise.

The supply and price of other meats, of non-meat proteins, and of other foods play a role in the price of specific meats. Lower price for a competing product would tend to reduce the price of whatever meat item we are producing and marketing.

Government policy, programs and pronouncements have an impact at various stages from production to consumption. Cost of production and consumer prices have been raised by limiting some technology applications such as feed additives, insecticides and predator controls. Regulations and taxes raise costs throughout the production, processing, distribution and consumption channels. Food stamp and other programs have added to the demand for meat. Policies of other governments also must be taken into consideration. Australia's export policies and Japan's meat import policies are examples.

DATA AND ITS SOURCES

This section is divided into two parts. The first part is on data relating to United States livestock production, assembling, processing, distribution, consumption and prices. The second section relates to data on other countries.

United States Livestock Data

Basic breeding stock and total inventory numbers are estimated and published by the U. S. Department of Agriculture for the following dates:

Cattle and Calves—January 1 and July 1
Hogs and Pigs—December 1 and June 1 (U. S.)
                    March 1 and September 1 (14 States)
Sheep and Lambs—January 1

These reports also include estimates of calf crops, pig crops and lamb crops.

Quarterly information is published for cattle on feed in each of 23 states. Monthly data is published for each of seven cattle feeding states: California, Arizona, Texas, Colorado, Nebraska, Kansas and Iowa.

Livestock supplies are reported daily and weekly for major market assembly points and country trading areas. Volume and price information is provided for feeder and finished livestock.

Livestock slaughter and meat production are estimated on a weekly and monthly basis. Daily livestock slaughter is also estimated on a "same day" basis. Storage stocks are estimated monthly.

Daily, weekly and monthly average prices also are estimated for livestock, wholesale meat and by-products. An important additional series is the USDA's weekly retail beef and pork prices.

Additional data series relevant to the meat area include feed supplies and prices, dairy and poultry product supplies and prices, feeding costs in different areas, range condition reports, slaughter weights and meat consumption.

Relevant data also is obtained from government sources other than the USDA. Population figures and consumer prices for different groupings are estimated by the U. S. Department of Labor. Various income series, Gross National Product estimates, transfer payments, and various price deflators are developed by the U. S. Department of Commerce.

Private sources are valuable in the area of daily and weekly wholesale meat and by-product prices. Price and volume of commodity futures transactions are reported for the Chicago Board of Trade, Chicago Mercantile Exchange, and other futures markets. Some industry organizations, such as the National Cattlemen's Association, sponsor service divisions offering supply and price information and analysis.

Various university and private publications report regular and special analyses relating to the livestock and meat complex. Many informal exchanges of information take place between various individuals in the industry.

Selected Publications and Data Series

In a compilation such as this, it is not possible to list every pertinent publication. Bulletins issued by private organizations and firms are not included. State and federal publications often may be obtained free of charge.

The weekly *Livestock Meat and Wool Market News* contains a wide array of livestock data. It can be ordered from Livestock Division, AMS, USDA, Washington, D.C. 20250. The following statistical series from this report are especially useful in analyzing the livestock and meat economy.

Estimated Federally Inspected Slaughter can be used to plot slaughter trends on a weekly basis in nine areas of the U. S. Total meat production and average live and dressed weight data also are available for the U.S. as a whole. Data is frequently picked up in many trade publications.

Cattle, Hogs and Sheep Slaughtered by Class is useful in determining changes in type of livestock moving to slaughter. For example, if slaughter was up in any week, the reason could be a significant increase in only one class of slaughter, such as cows.

Weekly Receipts of Salable Livestock at 39 Public Markets. Today more livestock are moving to market by direct or country sales. Therefore, numbers marketed at public markets do not necessarily indicate a trend.

Confirmed Direct Sales contains information for 13 areas of the country; includes sales for current and later delivery.

Live Feeder and Slaughter Prices includes several series available for different locations, weights and grades.

Wholesale Dressed Meat Prices are gathered and available from government and private sources and include prices for carcasses and for cuts. An increasing amount is being sold as cuts.

Hide, Pelts and Variety Meat Prices. By-product values are an important factor in livestock values.

Import and Export Volume lists monthly imports and exports of live animals and meat.

The *National Feeder Cattle and Calf Summary*, *Feeder Lamb Summary*, and *National Feeder Pig Summary* include information on the volume of sales and prices of feeder livestock for the major markets and market areas in the United States and are available from AMS, USDA, 701 Livestock Exchange Building, Kansas City, MO 64102.

Livestock and Meat Futures. Futures prices are reported by many local newspapers and radio stations. A daily report showing the opening, high, low and close, volume, and open interest on livestock futures contracts is available on a subscription basis from the Chicago Mercantile Exchange.

Livestock estimates of several kinds are developed by the USDA's Crop Reporting Board. They are available from your state Crop and Livestock Reporting Service or from Crop Reporting Board, Economics and Statistics Service, USDA, Washington, D.C. 20250.

Cattle and Calves on Feed—Monthly reports on number on feed, placements and marketing covering Arizona, California, Colorado, Nebraska, Texas, Iowa and Kansas. Quarterly reports for 23 states include number on feed for each state by class and weight group; also reports marketings and placements for the previous quarter and expected marketings for the current quarter.

Livestock Slaughter Reports—Estimates of monthly commercial livestock slaughter and meat production. Data on slaughter by states included, and slaughter by class.

Lambs on Feed—Report for seven states released in November and March, and for 24 states in January.

Hogs and Pigs Reports—Report of 50 states released in December and June. Report for 14 states released in March and September.

Cattle Inventory—Issued twice a year; lists the number of cattle on January 1 and July 1. Includes a breakdown by class and weight, and estimate of calf crop.

Sheep and Lamb Inventory January 1—Issued once a year for January 1. Includes a breakdown by class and estimate of lamb crop.

Range and Pasture Conditions—Monthly report covers range feed conditions and is included in the monthly *Crop Production Report.*

Livestock and Meat Situation, Agricultural Outlook and Farmline. Order from Economics and Statistics Service, USDA, Washington, D.C. 20250. *The Livestock and Meat Situation* contains statistics of production and consumption; prices of cattle, hogs, and sheep; tables on supplies and distribution of meat by months; and other selected statistics for meat animals and meat products. Also, has timely special articles of interest to livestock producers and feeders. Complete analysis of the livestock situation is a major feature. *Agricultural Outlook* and *Farmline* cover a broader range of topics and data; there is a charge for these two publications.

Extension Service Publications. Newsletters and other publications providing periodic analysis of livestock markets and market outlook are available from the Cooperative Extension Service in many states. Some have a subscription charge while others are available without cost. Some examples are:

Western Livestock Roundup. A monthly publication on the livestock, meat and feed situation; available from Cooperative Extension Services in many Western states.

Iowa Farm Outlook. A twice-monthly newsletter on market conditions and outlook for grain and livestock; available from the Cooperative Extension Service, Iowa State University.

Weekly Outlook (Illinois). A weekly newsletter on market conditions and outlook for Midwest farm products; available from the Cooperative Extension Service, University of Illinois.

Missouri Agricultural Outlook. A twice-monthly newsletter on market conditions and outlook for grains and livestock; available from the Cooperative Extension Service, University of Missouri.

Corn Husker Economics. A weekly newsletter on market outlook and economic and management issues; available from Cooperative Extension Service, University of Nebraska.

Market Viewpoints. A publication with emphasis on the livestock market situation and outlook. Available from the Cooperative Extension Service, Oklahoma State University.

Commercial Market Advisory Services. Livestock market information and market outlook are available from a number of commercial advisory services, such as the Doane Agricultural Report and others. The costs and services provided vary from one service to another, but they are generally oriented to helping clients keep up to date on market conditions and to help them in their marketing decisions.

Foreign Production and Import/Export Prospects

Production and export or import prospects are published for various meat and by-product items by the USDA. The United States imports beef, pork and lamb, while exports to other countries are primarily by-products and breeding stock. Hides are the single most important export product. Prices, consumption and feed conditions in other countries are frequently of interest.

From a production cost standpoint, current and prospective exports in the feedgrain and soybean complex are also important. As discussed in Chapter 2, corn exports have shown large increases in the 1970's. These now amount to about one-third of total corn production. Corn exports are now approaching the size of the total crop in the early 1950's.

Daily and weekly prices of imported meats are reported by private sources. Additional information relating to the foreign livestock and meat situation on both the demand and supply sides also is available from the U.S. Meat Export Federation, which has offices in this and several other countries.

INTERPRETING LIVESTOCK STATISTICS

You can use various data series to examine reasons for past changes in demand, supply or price; to analyze the current situation; and to estimate alternative future developments. In examining prospects for several years ahead, you need data on current numbers and component changes in basic breeding herds. Long term estimated costs and probable future demand for the product are also important factors.

Within the cattle herd, cow numbers and calf crops are the most important variables for long term analysis. Estimates of cow slaughter and a derived estimate of heifers entering the cow herd each year are helpful. (A parallel with the sheep flock is to look at ewe numbers, ewe lambs being kept for flock replacement, and lamb crops.) A balance sheet including annual inventory numbers, calf or lamb crops, slaughter and estimated death losses is useful for looking at these numbers and alternative prospects. Figure 11-9 shows historical cattle number cycles.

With hogs, changes are more rapid than with cattle or sheep. The breeding cycle is much shorter and seven to eight pigs are commonly produced each six months from one sow. In studying hog market prospects, you should give special attention to sow farrowings, total pig crops, a four to six year production cycle, and seasonal marketing patterns. A number balance sheet is less useful than with cattle and sheep.

Developments in various regions of the country are important in examining long range prospects for livestock production, and different factors may influence production in one region compared to another. Changes in cattle and sheep breeding herds in the West are slow because of the normally severe winter weather, limited roughage production potential and fewer alternatives for resource use. In the Southeast, cattle production has been affected more by the sharp increase in fertilizer costs than in other regions. Hog production is tied closely to corn production. Yet, much corn also floats down the Mississippi River to export, and away from hog producers. Increasing predators have been a limiting factor on sheep production throughout the country.

For shorter term analysis, USDA estimates of cattle on feed and feedlot placement and of pig crops and hog inventories can be used to forecast future slaughter or marketing levels. A fairly simple way of using these data is to compute historical ratios of slaughter to cattle or hog inventories of particular weights. These relationships between hog inventories or cattle on feed and later marketings have been fairly consistent from year to year.

Table 11-1 shows average ratios of quarterly hog slaughter to market hog inventories for the 1976-80 period. When new inventory estimates are released, the average ratio can be applied to develop a quick and approximate forecast of future slaughter. Similar relationships can be computed for pig crop data.

Relationships between cattle on feed and subsequent fed cattle marketings are shown in Table 11-2. The ratios have been consistent enough to be useful in making approximate forecasts of future marketings.

To illustrate the basis for the ratios in Table 11-1, the December 1, 1978 inventory of 60 to 179 pound hogs was estimated by the USDA to total 22,529,000 head. Commercial hog slaughter during the January-

March quarter of 1979 was 20,040,000 head. The ratio of slaughter to inventory was 20,040,000 ÷ 22,529,000 = .89. The average of this particular ratio for the 1976-80 period was .91, as shown in table 11-1.

The ratios in table 11-2 are computed in a similar way from estimates of cattle on feed and fed cattle marketings in 23 feeding states. For example, on January 1, 1979, a summation of the steers on feed weighing over 900 pounds and heifers over 700 pounds, plus one-half of the steers weighing 700 to 899 pounds, totaled 7,034,000 head. Fed cattle marketings in the January-March quarter of 1979 totaled 6,747,000 head. The ratio of fed cattle marketings to cattle on feed was 6,747,000 ÷ 7,034,000 = .959. The average of this particular ratio for the 1976-80 period was .996, as shown in table 11-2.

If ratios of this kind are used, they should be updated periodically to reflect any trends or changes in the relationships. And it should be recognized that unusual weather conditions or significant changes in breeding stock (in the case of hogs) will alter the relationships somewhat.

There is some margin of error in all current crop and livestock estimates and in historical data series. Crop and livestock estimates are based on sampling procedures rather than a complete count. This needs to be recognized rather than assuming the data to be an exact reflection of the actual situation. For example, when the USDA estimates of January 1, 1980 cattle inventories were released, there were many people who said that the data showed an increase from a year earlier. The number reported was 110,961,000 (total cattle) compared with 110,864,000 for a year earlier, an increase of less than one-tenth of 1%. With such a small change, the actual numbers may have been either up or down by a small amount because of sampling error. Survey estimates are also subject to non-sampling error.

Table 11-1. RATIO OF HOG SLAUGHTER TO MARKET HOG INVENTORIES (U.S. 1976-80 Average).

\multicolumn{3}{c}{Inventory of 60-179 lb. Hogs.}	\multicolumn{3}{c}{Inventory of Hogs Under 60 lbs.}
Inventory Date	Slaughter Period	Slaughter/ Inventory Ratio	Inventory Date	Slaughter Period	Slaughter/ Inventory Ratio
Dec. 1*	Jan.-Mar.	.91	Dec. 1*	Apr.-June	1.03
Mar. 1†	Apr.-June	1.12	Mar. 1†	July-Sept.	1.28
June 1*	July-Sept.	.97	June 1*	Oct.-Dec.	.98
Sept. 1†	Oct.-Dec.	1.12	Sept. 1†	Jan.-Mar.	1.16

*based on inventories in 50 states
† based on inventories in 14 states

Livestock Markets: Information

Table 11-2. RATIO OF FED CATTLE MARKETINGS TO CATTLE ON FEED (23 States, 1976-80 Average).

Heavier Steers & Heifers*			Lighter Steers & Heifers†		
On-Feed Date	Marketing Period	Marketing/ On-Feed Ratio	On-Feed Date	Marketing Period	Marketing/ On-Feed Ratio
January 1	Jan.-Mar.	.996	January 1	Apr.-June	1.394
April 1	Apr.-June	1.042	April 1	July-Sept.	1.440
July 1	July-Sept.	.985	July 1	Oct.-Dec.	1.776
October 1	Oct.-Dec.	.988	October 1	Jan.-Mar.	1.946

* One-half of steers 700-899 lbs., all steers over 900 lbs. and all heifers over 700 lbs.
† One-half of steers 700-899 lbs., steers 500-699 lbs. and heifers 500-699 lbs.

SEASONAL SUPPLY AND PRICE CONSIDERATIONS

Seasonal supply and price patterns can give you an indication of the most likely price trend from one month to the next. The usual seasonal variation in the price of several kinds of livestock is shown in the following charts.

Seasonal supply and price fluctuations in some livestock categories are lessening. The major reason for this is the wider geographic distribution of production, allowing the impact of seasonal weather factors in one area to offset other areas. A second reason is that an increasing proportion of production of some kinds of livestock is by larger sized operations (see Figure 11-6, Fed Cattle Marketings by Size of Feedlot). Larger operations (such as commercial feedlots) will usually operate at a more even volume throughout the year than family farm operations.

Marketings of feeder cattle in specific areas are still highly seasonal. In the northern parts of the United States and in Canada, most calves are born in the spring and either marketed as calves in the fall or as yearlings the following fall. Winter severity and the need for roughage during the winter months cause seasonal marketing of feeder animals and of excess cows before severe winter weather sets in.

In parts of California and Arizona, fall and winter grass growth provides good grazing. Dry weather in the spring then stops grass growth and leads to a spring marketing pattern for feeders. The mild weather in the South Central and Southeast results in a more variable marketing pattern. Dry weather and lack of grass growth will cause earlier summer marketings than in a year in which frequent moisture allows continued grass growth. The seasonality of marketings in different areas will partly smooth out the marketings of feeder cattle for the U.S. as a whole. Figure 11-7 (Placements of Cattle on Feed, by quarters) shows the pattern by the time cattle go on finishing rations.

Seasonality has been further smoothed out by the time cattle come out of feedlots and go to slaughter. Fed cattle marketings show less seasonal variation than placements on feed (see Figure 11-8). Cow marketings show some seasonal variation, with highest levels of slaughter in September-December.

Fed cattle prices have not shown a very consistent seasonal pattern. Prior to 1976, price weakness in the late winter and spring was often followed by price strength during the summer. In each year from 1976 through 1979, however, there was winter or early spring price strength, then weakness or, at best, a flat price pattern in the summer.

Demand for beef follows a seasonal pattern, but it varies with different beef cuts. The demand for rib and loin cuts of beef is weak in the winter and early spring, then strengthens in the summer. Chuck and round cuts are weak in the summer. As we have eaten more at fast food outlets, the demand for ground beef has increased. More barbecuing at home probably has helped demand for steaks and ground beef versus roasts. Demand for briskets has tended to be stronger in the late fall and winter.

The farrowing of pigs and pork production have historically followed a pronounced seasonal pattern, but seasonal changes have become more moderate. Fifteen years ago, March-May sow farrowings accounted for a third of the yearly total farrowings. In 1979 and 1980, farrowings in these months made up only 28% of the total. Monthly hog slaughter has also evened out considerably.

Seasonal price patterns result largely from the seasonality of pork supplies. Demand for pork is less seasonal now than in earlier times of less refrigeration and before air conditioning, when cooking heat was more of a problem. However, demand still appears to be stronger in the winter than in summer, and seasonal demand variations are important for some products. For example, demand for cured hams is typically strong around the Easter and Christmas holidays and may be somewhat better in the summer than in winter.

Seasonal weather patterns have provided marked seasonal patterns for the lamb crop and lamb marketings. This has been a problem in processing, marketing, and consumption of lamb. The industry is making

Livestock Markets: Information

progress in reducing this seasonality, which would also reduce the wide seasonal price patterns.

Religious and political holidays also tend to affect demand for meats. Easter lambs or ham, turkey at Thanksgiving and beef for Father's Day are examples.

Figure 11-2. Seasonal Price Index for Choice Slaughter Steers, (Omaha, 1970-79 Average).

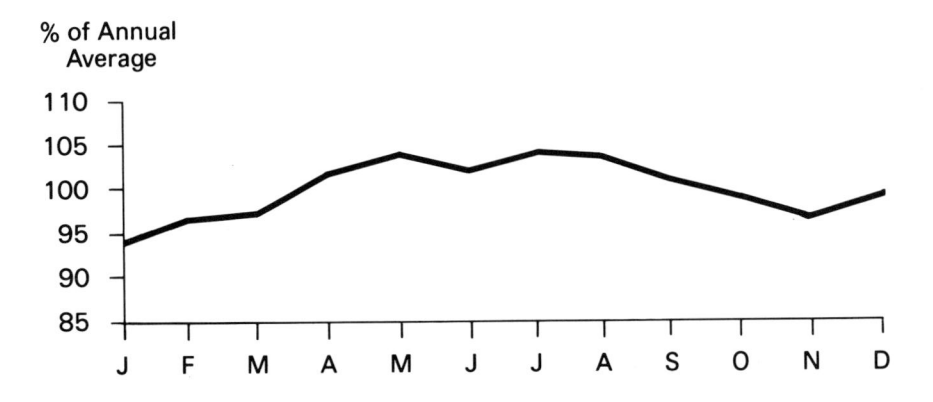

Figure 11-3. Seasonal Price Index for 400-500 lb. Steer Calves, (Kansas City, 1967-78 Average).

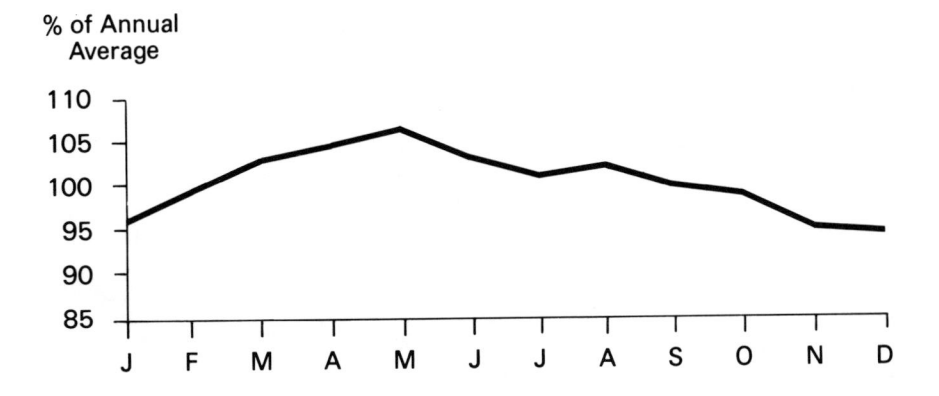

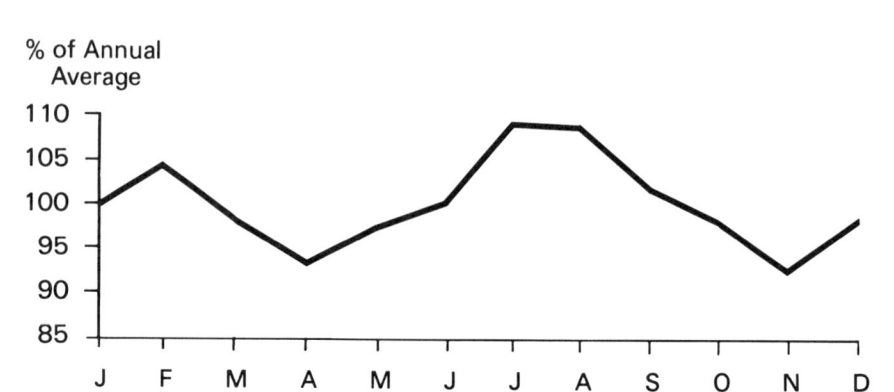

**Figure 11-4. Seasonal Index of Hog Prices.
(Average of Barrows and Gilts at 7 markets, 1970-79 Average.)***

*Sioux City, Omaha, Kansas City, St. Louis, south St. Paul, Indianapolis and south St. Joseph.

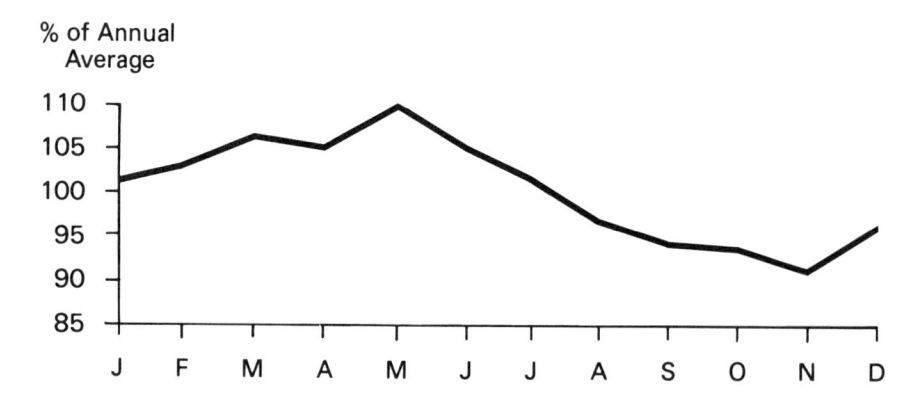

**Figure 11-5. Seasonal Price Index for Choice Slaughter Lambs,
(South St. Paul, 1967-78 Average.)**

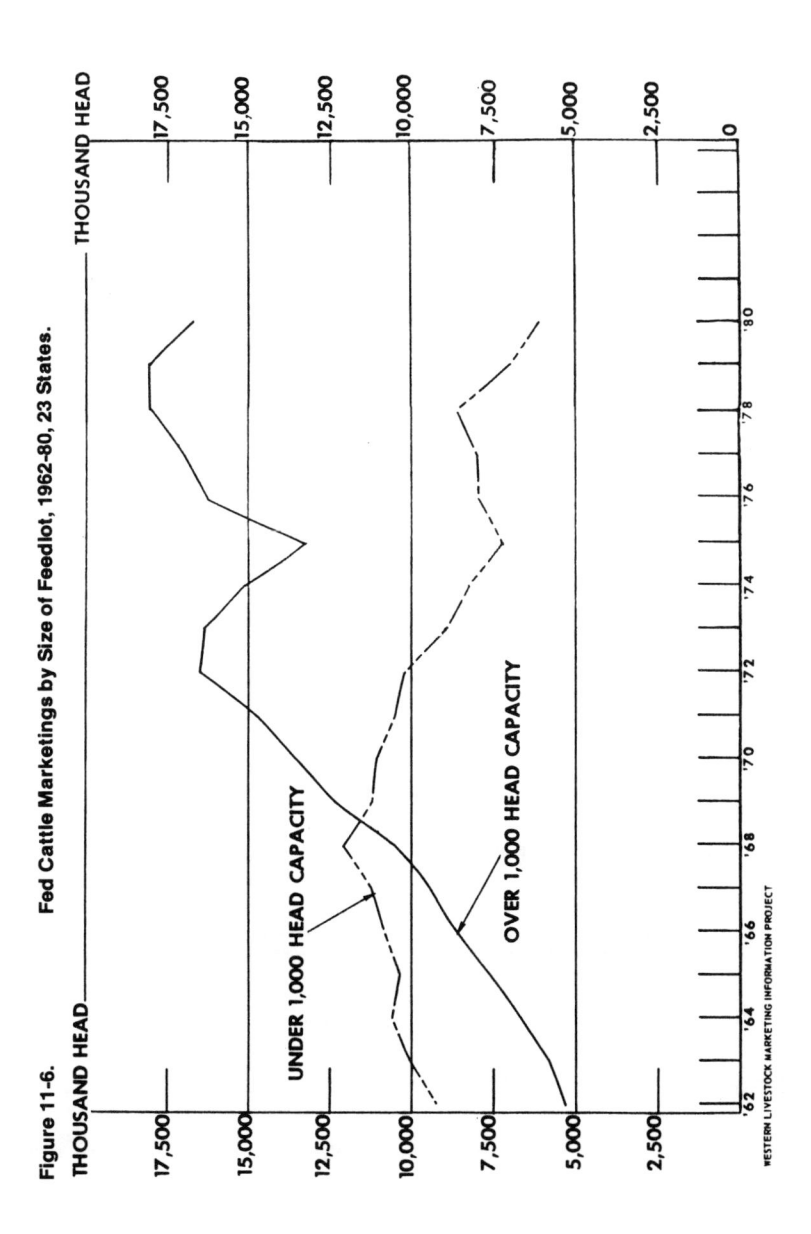

Livestock Markets: Information 217

Figure 11-6. Fed Cattle Marketings by Size of Feedlot, 1962-80, 23 States.

WESTERN LIVESTOCK MARKETING INFORMATION PROJECT

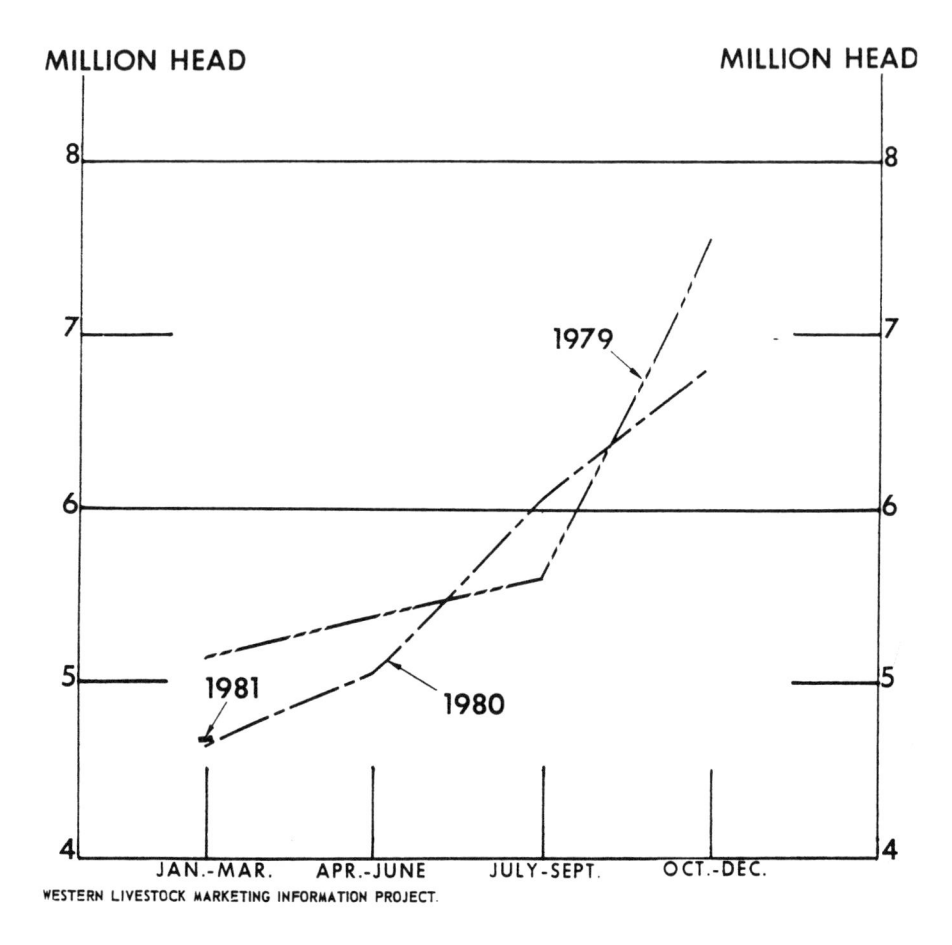

Figure 11-7. Quarterly Net Placements of Feeder Cattle, 23 States.

WESTERN LIVESTOCK MARKETING INFORMATION PROJECT.

CYCLICAL SUPPLY AND PRICE TENDENCIES

Cattle inventory numbers in the past have run in cycles of 9 to 14 years, as shown in Figure 11-9. These cycles are an important part of production and price changes. Recent cycles have been less regular than earlier ones.

The 1958-67 cycle is the only one that did not have a liquidation phase. After the peak in 1965, numbers showed no significant change for the next two years. They then started the buildup phase of what we define as a new numbers cycle.

Livestock Markets: Information

Figure 11-8.   **Quarterly Marketings of Fed Cattle in 23 States.**

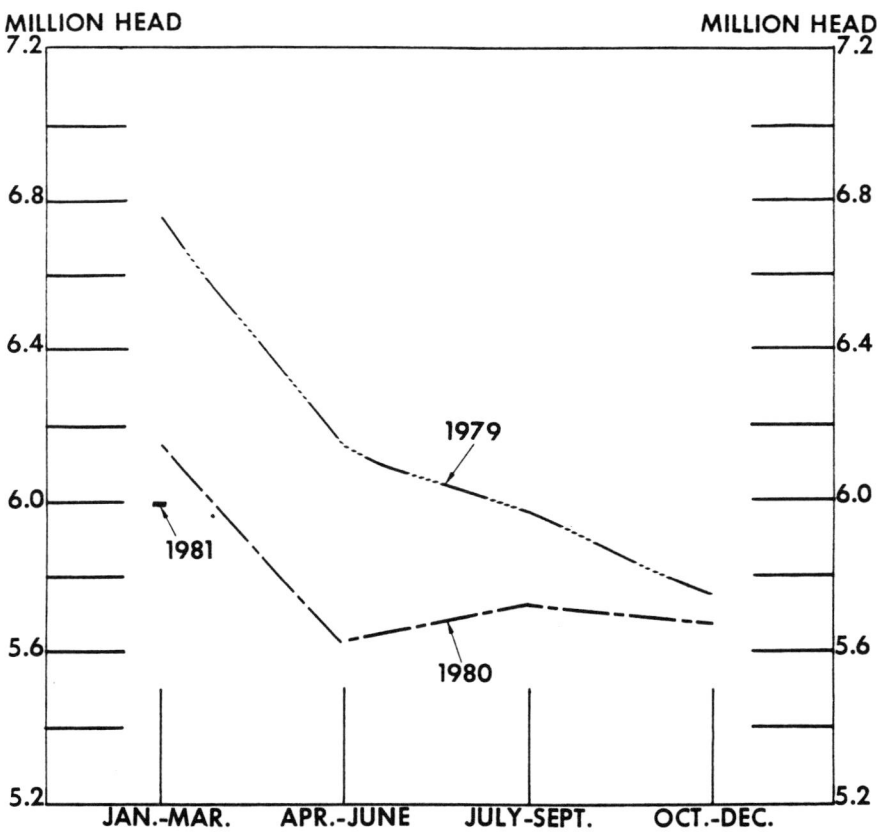

[Chart showing quarterly marketings of fed cattle for 1979, 1980, and 1981, in millions of head, ranging from 5.2 to 7.2 million head across the four quarters.]

WESTERN LIVESTOCK MARKETING INFORMATION PROJECT.

The cycle from 1967-79 included the sharpest liquidation phase of any cycle. The buildup phase of a new cycle started in 1979, and expansion is expected to continue into the mid-1980's or longer.

The increase in cattle slaughter and beef production usually lags behind the start of a new cattle inventory cycle by two or three years. Price is usually more directly related to changes in livestock moving to slaughter than to changes in inventory numbers.

In the buildup phase of a cycle, additional cows and heifers are being kept for the breeding herd; this initially reduces slaughter of these classes. Eventually, either drought or unfavorable prices cause individual herd owners to decide to reduce their breeding herds. This is done

Figure 11-9.   **Cattle on U.S. Farms by Cycles.**

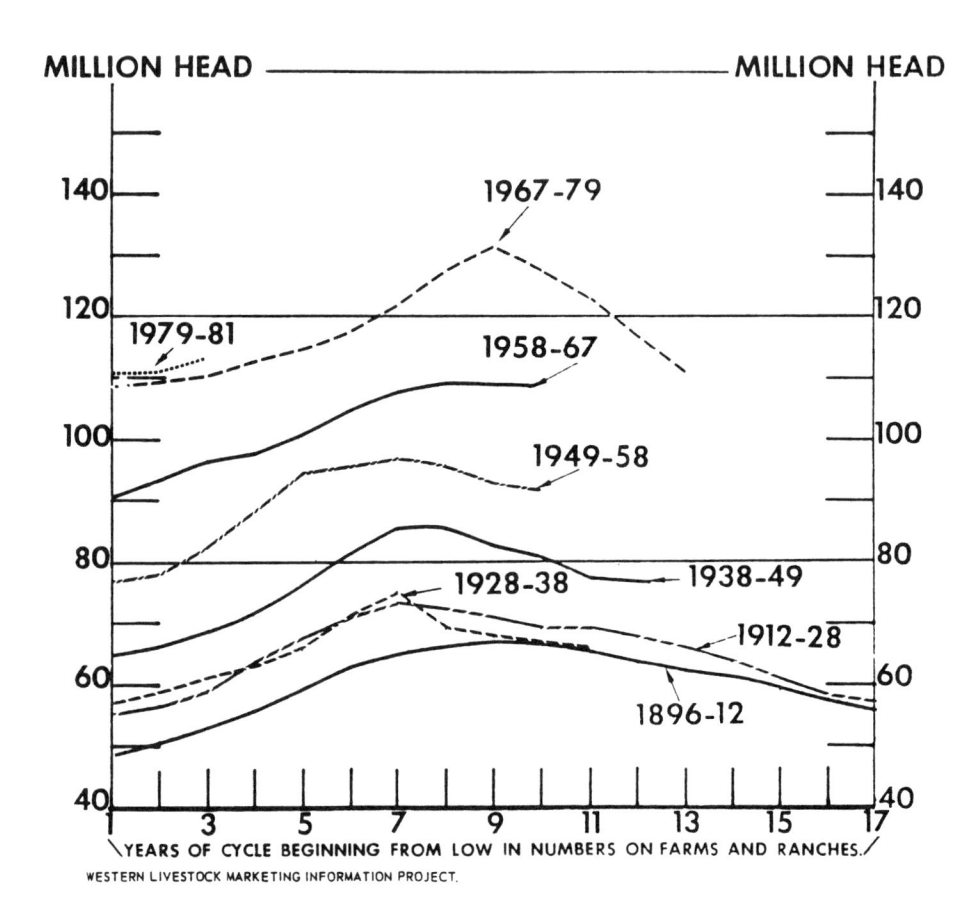

by sending more cows and heifers to slaughter. The initial liquidation immediately increases slaughter numbers and meat production.

Hog number cycles are not consistent in length, but tend to range from four to six years. Pork production increases follow pig crop increases by six to seven months, since that is the marketing age of barrows and gilts for slaughter. Changes in breeding stock have some impact on slaughter, but not as much so as with cattle.

Sheep flocks and bands also change, but do not go through limited period cycles as cattle and hogs. Sheep and lamb numbers and slaughter increased in 1979 and 1980 after declining each year since 1960.

DEVELOPMENT OF PRICE EXPECTATIONS

Factors commonly considered in making judgments of future meat prices at the retail level are: (1) the prospective supply of a particular product and of closely competing products, (2) consumer incomes and how they are likely to be spent, (3) changes in consumer prices for other food and nonfood items, and (4) population. Livestock prices or wholesale meat prices may be estimated in a similar manner or may be derived from the retail price estimates by making allowance for retailer and processor price spreads. Because of the uncertainty of many of these factors, there is a high degree of variability between expected and actual prices.

The location, time and type of product on which an expected price is to be based must be identified. Cow herd owners are interested in a price reference point for a particular weight and quality of feeder calves or yearlings, as well as the selling conditions. Hog producers want to know feeder or slaughter hog prices of a particular weight and quality at a particular location. A feedlot operator is concerned with a price reference point for an array of feeder animals, for feed costs, and for finished animals. The management of a slaughter plant looks in one direction at the expected cost of slaughter animals and in the other direction at the expected price of carcasses or primal and subprimal cuts.

So time, place, form, and possession cost must be considered in determining the expected price. In livestock production, it takes time (25 to 35 months or more) to produce finished beef. The desired weight and grade can change rapidly during the production process. For instance, a surplus of livestock of a grade or weight at certain market locations will change price expectations.

At the retail level, prices are adjusted to clear the retail counters with a reasonable rate of turnover. Expectations of price are secondary at the retailer and slaughter level. The retailer's concern is that he buys meat at the same price as, or for less than, his competition. He is concerned primarily with the short run rather than the long run. The slaughterer must bid for the retailer's business. Place of slaughter and comparative labor and transportation costs are important in his price bids.

Price expectations can be changed by shifts in government policies. Promotion of feedgrain exports or of agreements with the Soviet Union or other nations for long term exports of grain may cause higher domestic feed prices, the principal input cost of livestock finishing. Programs related to health, the environment, or trade activities all contribute to changes in costs or expected prices, and welfare programs such as food stamps can influence demand and prices for end products. Foreign government policies can also affect costs or product prices.

Price expectations will not be static very long in a dynamic economy. Risk is a part of price expectations. So are doubts, fears and lack of understanding of economic forces. Actual prices are a result of interaction of the forces of demand, supply and government policy, few of which remain the same for long. In a free market, resulting prices will seek that point at which product flows reasonably well through the channels, within rules and influences set by the government.

Key elements in actually developing a price forecast for cattle or hogs are estimates of the quantitative relationships between prices and particular price factors. For example, how much will hog prices usually change if the pork supply changes by 1%? Or what effect does a 1% change in per capita disposable income have on prices of cattle or hogs?

These relationships can be estimated statistically, based on historical data. While they may change over time, some recent estimates of the price effects (also called price flexibilities) for various cattle and hog price variables are shown in Tables 11-3 and 11-4. These show a range of the estimated impact on cattle or hog prices of a 1% change in the particular variable. For example, a 1% change in the supply of pork is estimated to result in a change in live hog prices of from 1.70% to 2.30% — in the opposite direction. And a 1% change in the supply of beef is estimated to affect hog prices by .30% to .60% — also in the opposite direction.

Table 11-3. HOG PRICE FORECASTING GUIDES.

Percent Change in Hog Price Associated with a 1% Change in:*

Pork supply per person	-1.70 to -2.30
Beef supply per person	- .30 to - .60
Chicken supply per person	- .30 to - .60
Disposable income per person (current $)	+ .30 to + .40
U.S. Population†	+1.00

*A negative sign indicates the price effect is in the opposite direction to the change in supply; a positive sign indicates the price effect is in the same direction as the change in income or population.

†Population growth in recent years has been about .8% per year.

Table 11-4. CATTLE PRICE FORECASTING GUIDES.

*Percent Change in Fed Cattle Price Associated with a 1% Change in:**

Beef supply per person	-1.60 to -2.00
Pork supply per person	- .30 to - .50
Chicken supply per person	- .10 to - .30
Disposable income per person (current $)	+ .60 to + .70
U.S. Population†	+1.00

*A negative sign indicates the price effect is in the opposite direction to the change in supply; a positive sign indicates the price effect is in the same direction as the change in income or population.

†Population growth in recent years has been about .8% per year.

Assume the USDA's Hogs and Pigs Report indicates pork production two quarters ahead will be 8% smaller than the previous year. The impact of this change alone would be estimated to increase hog prices by 13.6% to 18.4% from the year—earlier period (8.0 x 1.70 = 13.6 and 8.0 x 2.30 = 18.4).

In each case, the individual price flexibilities assume all other variables are unchanged. So the net impact of different price variables must be added to arrive at a final estimate of price change. These relationships can be used to develop forecasts of general price level, as illustrated in Figures 11-10 and 11-11. Markets are often affected by other factors, however; so the average relationships shown in Tables 11-3 and 11-4 may not fit conditions every month or quarter. As a result, price forecasts developed from these relationships must always be viewed as a general guide and not as a highly precise indication of future price levels.

In summary, consumer demand, supply of product, and retailer and processor price spreads are important to price establishment. The main factors frequently used in estimating future prices are: income per person; population; supply or price of competing products; priority demands on consumer incomes; supply of product placed on the market; and demand as it is derived through grocery stores, restaurants and processors to producers. All the meat placed on the market by producers will move through to consumption. Price levels and price changes are the gears that move this production through to consumers.

The cattle cycle, general direction of sheep and lamb numbers, and expectations of sow farrowings provide a framework for changes on the supply side. Shorter run changes in production are indicated by quarterly pig crop reports, by annual or semi-annual reports of cattle and sheep numbers and calf and lamb crops, by cattle and lamb on-feed reports, and by weekly and daily slaughter reports.

Historical relationships between livestock and meat prices and various supply and demand factors are helpful in understanding industry relationships and responses. Supply forecasting has been reasonably accurate, but price forecasts leave room for much improvement. Various factors such as supply of slaughter animals, demand for meat, and marketing aspects related to both producer and consumer sway prices. At times the impact of these factors is difficult to foresee.

Figure 11-10. HOG PRICE FORECASTING WORKSHEET.

1. Per capita pork supply	
% chg. from yr. ago x price effect:	- 8.0 x -2.00 = +16.00
2. Per capita beef supply	
% chg. from yr. ago x price effect:	+ 3.0 x - .50 = - 1.50
3. Per capita chicken supply	
% chg. from yr. ago x price effect:	+ 2.0 x - .50 = - 1.00
4. Per capita disposable income	
% chg. from yr. ago x price effect:	+10.0 x + .40 = + 4.00
5. Population	
% chg. from yr. ago x price effect:	+ .80 x +1.0 = + .80
6. Net percent effect on hog price	
(sum of 1 through 5)	+18.30
7. Hog price forecast	
price in year earlier period	= $41.00
price change = price in year-earlier period x	
estimated net percent price effect, or	$41.00 x .183 = + 7.50
price forecast = $41.00 + $7.50	= $48.50

Figure 11-11. CATTLE PRICE FORECASTING WORKSHEET.

1. Per capita beef supply	
% chg. from yr. ago x price effect:	+ 3.0 x -1.80 = - 5.40
2. Per capita pork supply	
% chg. from yr. ago x price effect:	- 6.0 x - .40 = + 2.40
3. Per capita chicken supply	
% chg. from yr. ago x price effect:	+ 3.0 x - .20 = - .60
4. Per capita disposable income	
% chg. from yr. ago x price effect:	+10.0 x + .60 = + 6.00
5. Population	
% chg. from yr. ago x price effect:	+ .80 x +1.0 = + .80
6. Net percent effect on cattle price	
(sum of 1 through 5)	+ 3.20
7. Cattle price forecast	
price in year-earlier period	= $67.00
price change = price in year earlier-period x	
estimated net percent price effect, or	$67.00 x .032 = + 2.14
price forecast =	$67.00 + $2.14 = $69.14

CHAPTER **12**

Technical Price Analysis

The utilization of various types of charts, trading volume, open interest, and mathematical formulas in forecasting the price behavior of commodities is commonly known as technical price analysis. This is in contrast to fundamental analysis, which concerns itself solely with supply/demand considerations such as physical stocks of grain, projected crop and livestock production, and federally inspected slaughter of livestock for specified periods of time.

The bullish or bearish bias of a pure technical analyst is the result of careful scrutiny of charts and mathematical formulas without regard to fundamental considerations. He is concerned with the psychology of the market rather than its supply and demand factors. The chartist believes that all of the opinions of all traders in a marketplace are reflected in the high, low, and close of each particular trading period (daily, weekly, monthly, etc.). Through analysis of an aggregation of these trading periods (i.e., a chart) you can study the change in traders' opinions which appears as the various chart formations and, in anticipation that what has historically occurred will occur again, you can predict future price behavior.

It is well known that major government reports (supplying fundamental information) can have quite dramatic effects on agricultural price behavior. For this reason they are well-respected and caution is exercised regarding trading positions on the eve of such reports. Technical developments can also cause a market to react dramatically, and it is therefore of equal importance for the trader to be informed as to what technical influences may exist on the market in question.

The marketplace is not one of a comparatively small number of chartists and other technicians, but has in its population a vast number of people who rely on technical information to assist them in their trading activities. The proverb "charts work because chart traders make them work" has never been so true. New technical tools are constantly emerging, some quite simple, while others are of a very sophisticated nature. The point is that an increasingly larger portion of the influence on prices in the marketplace is coming from the technical side. Therefore, the concepts of technical analysis can be of considerable benefit to those who will take some time to learn what they are and how to use them.

VOLUME AND OPEN INTEREST

Before beginning a study of bar chart analysis, it is important to be familiar with the concepts of trading volume and open interest. Although they are of a secondary nature to other tools of the market technician, they can be of tremendous help in making the final decision as to what prices are going to do. In fact, some of the most common bar chart formations are dependent upon the action of volume and open interest in order to hold a high degree of reliability.

Trading volume is defined as the number of futures contracts traded in a particular commodity on a particular trading day. Of course, a trade consists of a buyer and seller agreeing upon some price at some time within the bounds of the trading session. Each time a transaction is completed, volume increases by the size of the trade. That is, when a buyer and seller of one live hog contract agree on a price, volume in live hog futures increases by one. If the transaction involved fifty contracts, volume would increase by fifty. With the exception of grains, volume is expressed in number of contracts traded. Grains are reported in bushels.

Consider the usefulness of trading volume in technical price analysis. You can think of volume as the "pressure gauge" of a market. For example, in the early stages of a major bull market, a combination of two things is occurring simultaneously. First, new buyers are bidding aggressively to establish long positions in order to take advantage of the expected further advance in prices. On the other side of the coin, people with short positions suddenly find themselves on the wrong side of the market and scramble to offset their positions in order to minimize their losses. It is the activity of these two different groups that causes volume to suddenly increase, which creates the power required to send the market on its way. Demand is greater than supply, therefore prices rise. As long as this bullish attitude remains, the uptrend can be expected to continue. As prices reach a major resistance area or, fundamentally, some bearish rumor or news item "hits the floor," the majority of longs attempt to liquidate their positions, immediately resulting in a large volume figure and lower prices. At this point, the market has lost virtually all of its upside momentum and begins to sink from the absence of any underlying support. Only if bullish sentiment can somehow regain control will the uptrend be able to continue. Otherwise, the market has experienced a major price reversal.

Similarly, in a bear market, sellers dominate the marketplace as new shorts enter and old longs liquidate their positions in expectation of lower price levels, i.e., supply is greater than demand. Again, as long as this (bearish) sentiment dominates, the market will trend lower.

Volume can be a valuable tool in the analysis of short term price behavior as well. A day of light volume is a signal for the trader to be cautious of what may appear to be a significant price move on that day. Although the day's action may look like a reversal, breakout, or some other crucial form, it is not. Without good volume, formations are insignificant because the "push" is not there. Trading sessions around holidays are notorious for their light volume-false signal days. After such a day occurs, you can be quite certain that the market will return to the price level originally prevailing. You are only asking for trouble if you establish a position in the direction of such a false move in price.

Open interest is the number of futures contracts outstanding in a commodity. Like volume, it is expressed in number of contracts or, in the case of grains, bushels. If open interest rises as prices rise, it is an indication that an increasing number of traders maintain a bullish sentiment and are establishing long positions in the market. The same holds true in a bear market. As prices fall and open interest rises, the general feeling is becoming increasingly bearish.

The level of open interest can change in the following ways:

1. When a new long and new short agree on a price, a new contract is made and open interest increases. For example, the new long may be a bullish speculator and the new short may be some country elevator which just purchased the cash commodity and wants to lock in a price.

2. Open interest decreases if the buyer is an old short who is liquidating his previous sale and the seller is an old long likewise offsetting his position.
3. Open interest will also decrease if a short makes delivery and a long takes delivery.
4. There is no change in open interest if the buyer is a new long and the seller is an old long selling back his position. Similarly, if a new short sells to a liquidating old short there is no change in open interest.

Volume and open interest are most reliable when used in combination with each other. The following examples will best explain the analysis procedure and will act as a summary of these concepts:

1. Volume and open interest both *increase* as prices *increase*—shorts are covering (buying back) their positions and new longs are entering the market simultaneously, thus heavy volume. This is a *bullish* signal.
2. Volume and open interest both *increase* as prices *fall*—longs are liquidating (selling) and new shorts are establishing positions simultaneously. Once again this results in relatively heavy volume and is considered a *bearish* signal.
3. Volume *increases* and open interest *decreases* as prices *increase*—short covering. The rise in prices is only temporary and a drop to some nearby support level is imminent. A bottom may be in the making.
4. Volume *increases* and open interest *decreases* as prices *fall*—long liquidation. This is a temporary fall in prices. They will eventually move back up to some recently made resistance level. This is a sign of a possible top.

A word of caution regarding open interest is in order. For some commodities such as grains there is a degree of seasonality in the number of contracts outstanding. At the time a crop is being harvested there is a lot of hedging activity as grain elevators protect their cash purchases and farmers lock in a price on a portion of their crop. This increases open interest and, to the unwary analyst, may look like the beginning of a major move. It is, in fact, a seasonal phenomenon and is not indicative of any market trend.

BAR CHART ANALYSIS

The bar chart is the most common tool used by the technical analyst due to its ease of construction and accuracy in reflecting the price action for the time period under consideration.

The chart is constructed on a graph having price on the vertical axis and time on the horizontal axis. The high and low prices are plotted and a vertical line is drawn between them to indicate the price range. The closing price is then drawn as a small horizontal line at the appropriate level. This is shown in Figure 12-1.

Figure 12-1.

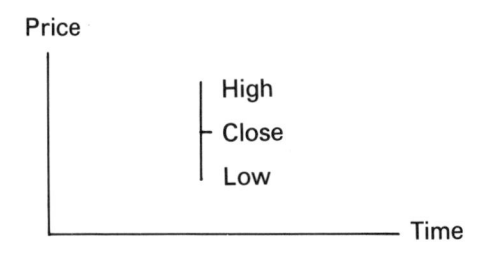

```
Price
  |       | High
  |       ├ Close
  |       | Low
  |_____ Time
```

The high, low, and close of each element in a bar chart may represent prices occurring anywhere from a few minutes to as much as a year in duration. The most common is the daily chart which denotes price activity of individual trading sessions.

Although the daily bar chart is of immense value to the analyst, you should not overlook the potential value of charts of other time intervals, especially weekly and monthly charts. They are quite useful in predicting areas of support and resistance and play a major role in determining longer term price objectives and trends. Charts of price behavior involving time periods of less than one day are important to the speculator who may maintain a trading position for a relatively short period of time, but are not of any major value to the hedger.

Bar chart analysis consists of an examination of a series of days, weeks, months, etc., represented by the individual elements in the chart. As time progresses, new factors are interjected into the market, changing traders' ideas and opinions. This causes prices to rise and fall, resulting in the formation of chart patterns which form the basis for the forecasting of future price behavior. As mentioned in the opening comment, the chartist believes that what has happened in the past will happen again. The remainder of this section will be concerned with the description of several of the basic bar chart patterns.

Support and Resistance

An area of *support* is a price level at which buying interest will increase due to previous significant market activity at that level. *Resistance* is the opposite concept where selling interest increases at points of previous market activity. Support and resistance occur at old lows and highs (respectively), gaps, areas of price consolidation, and other points where significant chart patterns occurred at some previous time.

Figure 12-2 shows support and resistance levels for the July 1981 Kansas City wheat futures contract. Note the difficulty the market had in penetrating the $4.30 per bushel support level which was the life-of-contract low at the time. It made one attempt in early March, but failed, and another in mid-May, where some trading did occur below $4.30 but the market twice refused to close below that level.

The downside gap made on March 2 proved too much for the bulls in this market on several occasions. Three tops were formed at the $4.60 level as bullish enthusiasm could not overcome the significant resistance that the gap provided.

After a particular contract expires its influence on the market prevails, since old areas of support and resistance still influence traders' decisions. This is where weekly and continuation bar charts are invaluable, since they indicate these areas and offer the trader the opportunity to develop a trading strategy to take advantage of something that would otherwise be overlooked. A continuation chart, as its name implies, is one of a perpetual nature in that the nearby (spot) futures contract is plotted until its expiration, at which time the next contract is plotted. For example, if a trader is using the December option in his corn continuation chart, at the time of its expiration the March contract would be used.

Trendlines

Probably the most important use of the bar chart is its ability to show the direction of prices over time, or trend. This direction is indicated by the *trendlines*, a straight line connecting the extreme lows in an uptrend and the extreme highs in a downtrend. As long as the trendline remains intact the trend can be expected to continue. It is important

Technical Price Analysis

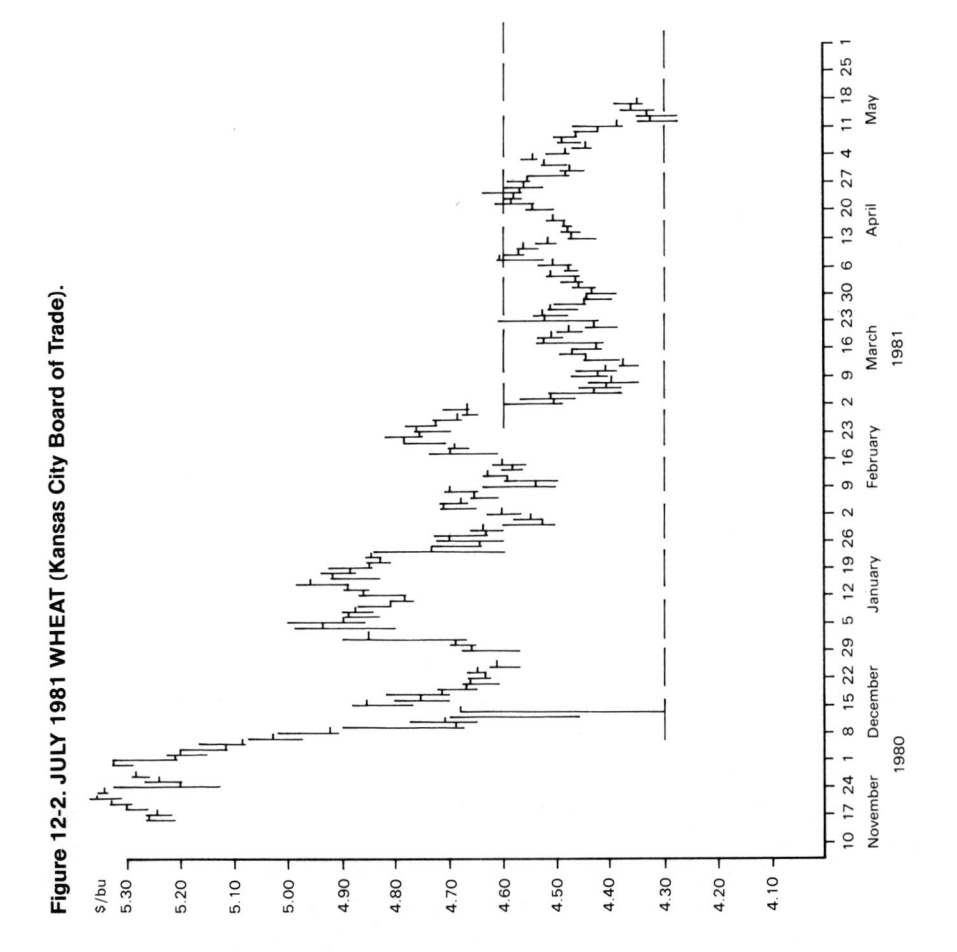

Figure 12-2. JULY 1981 WHEAT (Kansas City Board of Trade).

to stress that the decisive factor regarding the soundness of a trendline is the closing price of the commodity in question. On any particular day, prices may, in fact, penetrate a trendline. This does not constitute a violation. Only if the market *closes* above or below a trendline is there doubt whether the trend will continue. Some technicians consider two closes as a violation of trend and a signal that a price reversal is imminent.

Construction of trendlines, although simple, is not an exact science. Where one chartist believes that a trendline lies, another will disagree. Actual placement is left to the individual. The important thing is to recognize the trend early enough to take advantage of it. Once the market has made some kind of top or bottom, usually indicated by a reversal of some kind, prices will begin to move in the opposite direction of the most recent general trend. Soon after, the old trendline will be broken, which gives sound basis to assume a further move in the new direction. As the market proceeds, intraday trading creates extremes of highs and lows. It is on these extremes that the trendline is drawn.

The March-April uptrend in July 1981 CBT Corn (Figure 12-3) exemplifies the construction of a trendline. The minor reversal which occurred on March 11 (Point A) was the first sign that the market might turn from its bearish bias. The next day the market closed above its downtrend line giving an even more positive indication. Prices rose until resistance was met at the gap made on March 2. As the market turned lower the astute chartist would be watchful for a significant break in the market upon which a trendline might be drawn. This came on March 30 (Point B). The tentative trendline would now exist as a straight line connecting Points A and B. The aggressive chartist would immediately draw the line and adjust his trading strategies accordingly. The more conservative chartist would wait for some time before drawing the trendline. He would watch the price activity after the suspected low was made and arrive at a conclusion only after prices were safely on their way up again.

Regarding trading strategy with trendline analysis, liquidate your short or long position immediately after prices penetrate and close above or below the respective trendline. Placing trailing stop-loss orders at a reasonable distance away from the trendline is one method of achieving this. Aggressive traders could initiate new positions on any corrective movement back toward the old trendline after it had been violated. Conservative traders would wait until the correction had been completed and prices had resumed their new direction.

Technical Price Analysis 233

Figure 12-3. JULY 1981 CORN (Chicago Board of Trade).

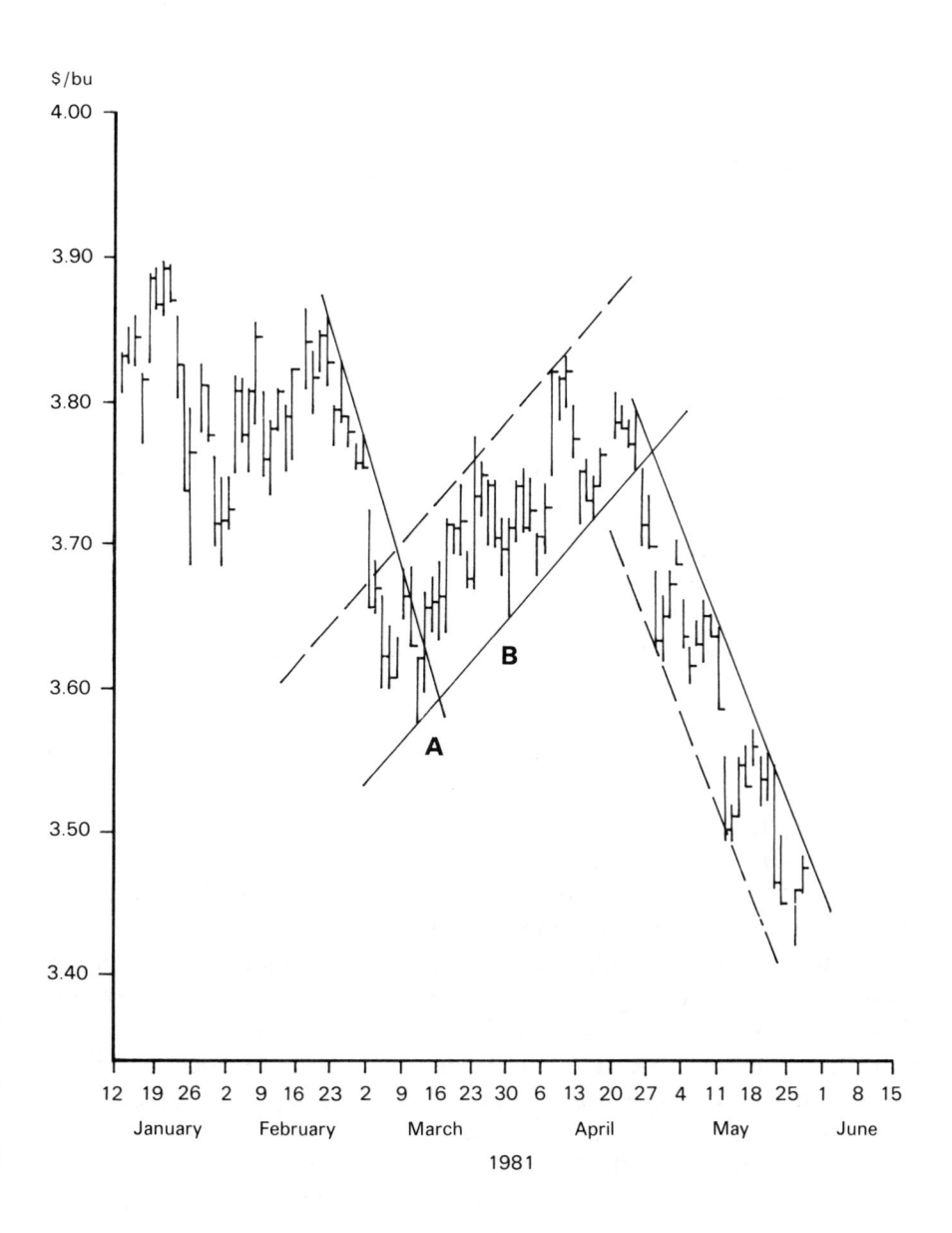

The dashed lines represent *channel lines*. These lines lie parallel to the trendline and define the upper or lower bounds of the trading range, or channel. Note how the market is turned away as it approaches the channel lines in our example.

Key Reversal

An indicator that is easy to identify yet is quite critical in price analysis is the *key reversal*. It is unique among chart formations in that it comprises only one element of the bar chart, that is, a key reversal on a daily bar chart is completed in only one day. This is the result of an abrupt change in traders' opinions due to some external factor injected into the market. Things such as some extremely influential rumor, liquidation ahead of a major report, or profit-taking in the face of heavy chart support or resistance may be the cause.

The distinguishing characteristic of a key reversal is that its price range extends both above and below the previous day's range. This is the result of the abrupt change in sentiment. For example, in a major bull market, early on the day of the reversal, prices will again trade higher as demand still reigns. Suddenly, the causative factor is introduced and liquidation begins. At first it is slow, but gradually picks up momentum as more and more traders decide to get out. If enough demand cannot enter the market at some price level to support the wave of selling the market will continue to drop to the extent that a limit-down day may result. The classic examples often referred to are those of soybeans in the markets of 1973 and 1977, in which prices went from limit-up early in the session to limit-down at the close, to signal an end to those respective bull markets.

Key reversals are not uncommon in most commodities. Although the extreme limit-up-limit-down day may not be experienced quite so often in any one commodity, more moderate, yet significant, examples appear quite frequently. Figure 12-4 illustrates a typical key reversal in the August 1981 Live Cattle contract (Point A). Note the characteristic "outside day" price range as compared to the previous day. This, in conjunction with the close below the previous day's close, is a strong signal that lower prices are to follow.

As mentioned in the discussion of trading volume, it can be the decisive criterion as to the validity of some chart patterns. The key reversal is one such example. If a key reversal occurs on heavy volume, it is a sign that a large proportion of traders was responsible for the

Technical Price Analysis

Figure 12-4. AUGUST 1981 LIVE CATTLE (Chicago Mercantile Exchange).

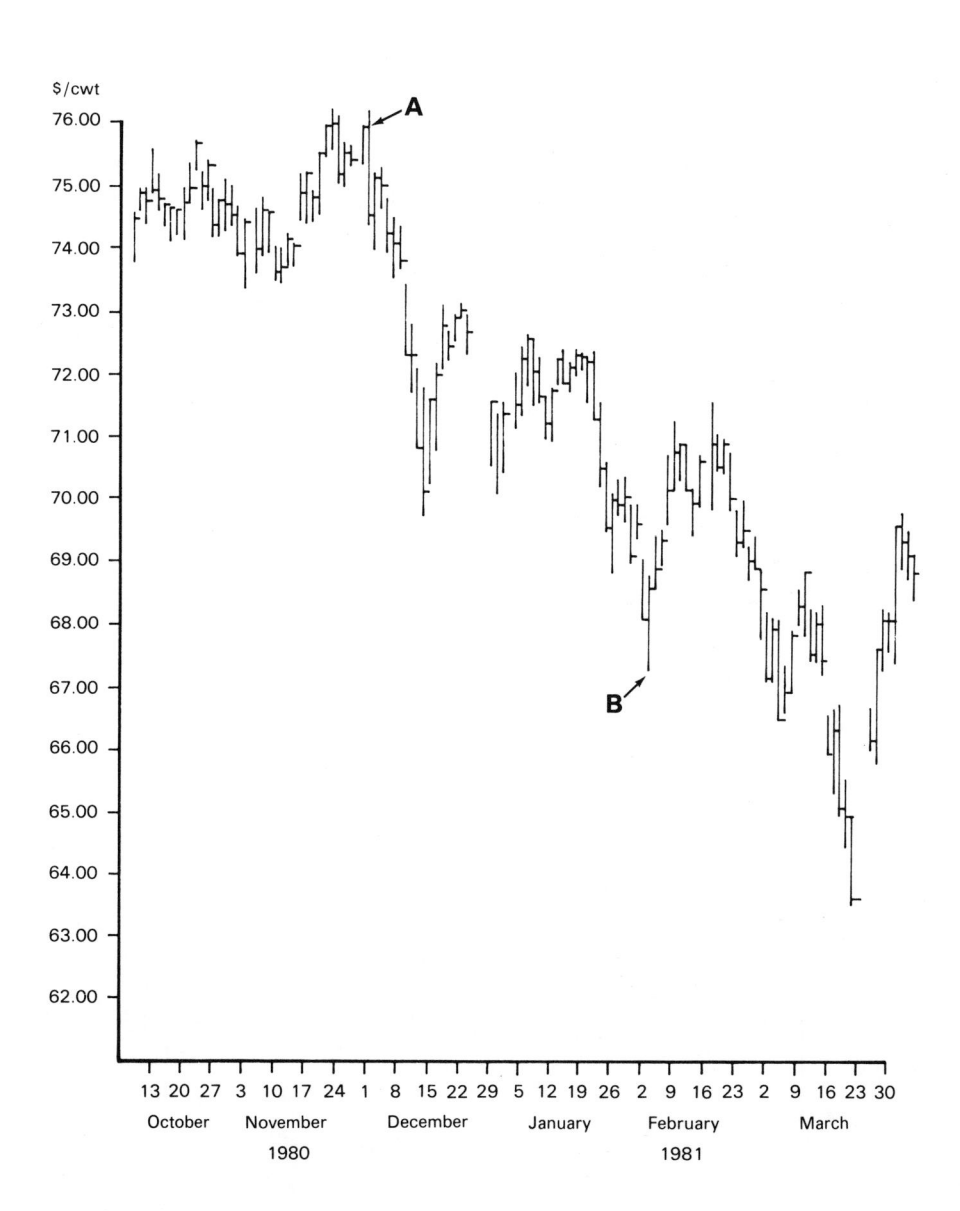

change in direction and, thus, a large number of people have lost the enthusiasm to make prices move in the original direction. Therefore, the reversal in question is relatively sound. As for our example, volume on the day of the reversal was recorded at 31,072 contracts versus an average of 20,195 contracts for the previous five trading days, an adequate rise in volume to consider the reversal valid.

Also shown on this particular chart is an example of a closely related concept known as the *hook reversal*. It appears at Point B. The hook reversal is very similar to the key reversal in that, on the day that it occurs, the prevailing price trend continues but, again, some factor is injected into the market to cause an abrupt change in direction. The only difference between these two types of reversals is that the hook reversal does not extend both higher and lower than the previous day's price range, as does the key reversal. It will extend only in the direction of the prevailing trend. A close above the previous day's close is required for a bullish hook reversal (as in our example) and a close below the previous day's close is required for a bearish hook reversal.

In summary, we have the following:

Bullish key reversal—high above previous day's high, low below previous day's low, close above previous day's close.

Bearish key reversal—high above previous day's high, low below previous day's low, close below previous day's close.

Bullish hook reversal—low below previous day's low, close above previous day's close.

Bearish hook reversal—high above previous day's high, close below previous day's close.

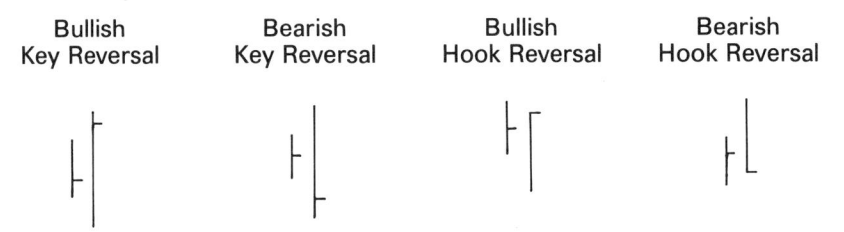

Bullish Key Reversal	Bearish Key Reversal	Bullish Hook Reversal	Bearish Hook Reversal

Gaps

Gaps are a very common occurrence in all commodity markets and have a great degree of reliability regarding their use in forecasting price trends and objectives. The gap sequence that occurs in a major market move consists of three types of gaps. The first is the *breakaway gap* which appears as the initial thrust out of the existing market activity, usually some period of consolidation, as Figure 12-5 demonstrates. A close above major resistance or below major support in conjunction with the gap is a strong indication that a move of significant proportion is in the making.

As the market proceeds in its new direction there are periods of quite extensive daily moves. It is at this time that the *measuring gap* appears. The measuring gap is the result of a powerful thrust in the market which leaves a large gap between the high of the previous day and the low of the day on which the gap occurred in a bull market, and between the low of the previous day and the present-day high in a bear market. The measuring gap is useful in predicting the extent of the whole move, as its name implies. It is considered to be halfway in the move so that, once the measuring gap occurs, simply determine the distance from the gap to the beginning of the move and add it to the price at the gap to arrive at the ultimate price objective. In our example the measuring gap was made at the $7.11½ to $7.16 range, or an average price of $7.13¾. The move began at $6.38½. The difference comes to 75¼¢. Adding this to our $7.13¾ gives us a price objective of $7.89. In this case the price advanced even further so that one must consider the computed price objective as an estimate and not an exact measurement.

The third, and final, gap of the sequence is the *exhaustion gap*. As the major move draws to a close, the vast majority of traders is bullish (or bearish in a declining market). Extreme buying (or selling) pressure causes the market to gap on the open as overzealous traders struggle to jump on the bandwagon. However, chartists now realize that the measuring gap objective is close at hand and begin liquidating their positions. Weakness becomes apparent and a top is formed.

You should be aware of some additional rules regarding gaps. As was mentioned above, the measuring gap is considered halfway in a move. After the market has run its course and reversed direction, the old measuring gap area will serve as an area of support or resistance which coincides with the concept that a market will retrace its move by 50%.

Also, once a gap is made the market will continually strive to fill it. It may take only a few days or many years, but the chartists know that the gap still exists and will include it in their strategy. Again, the value of weekly and continuation bar charts must be stressed.

238   MARKETING FOR FARMERS

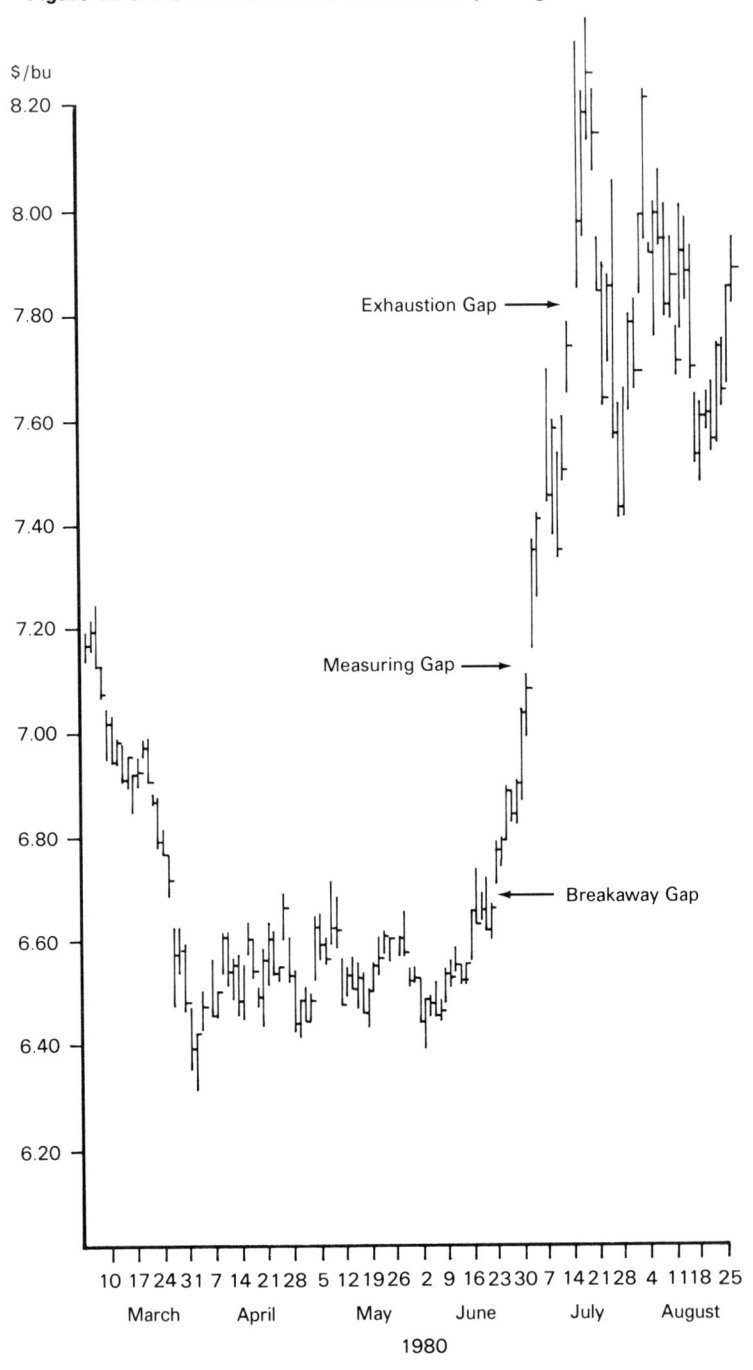

Figure 12-5. NOVEMBER 1980 SOYBEANS (Chicago Board of Trade).

Pennants and Flags

Geometrical chart formations are of immense value in the analysis of prices using bar charts. This category includes *pennants, flags,* and *triangles,* all of which are common to the various commodities of interest to the agriculture industry.

Pennants and flags appear as consolidation formations in trending markets, that is, in markets having an obvious direction. Prices reach a level at which the bias in favor of the prevailing trend is overcome by profit-taking and the feeling by some that the move has run its course, which causes them to take positions opposite to the prevailing trend. This results in a sideways market. Only when some catalytic factor is introduced into the market will this consolidation be penetrated and prices begin to move in one direction or the other. A period of low volume usually accompanies the formation of a pennant or flag as trading enthusiasm diminishes significantly due to lack of direction in price.

The value of pennants and flags is in their ability to measure the length of the ensuing move if prices should resume the prior trend once a breakout occurs. Upon retracing price behavior immediately before the pennant or flag is formed, you can see a nearly vertical series of elements on the bar chart known as the "flagstaff." This is shown in Figure 12-6 as the distance from Point A to Point B. After the consolidation occurs and prices resume their original direction by penetrating the appropriate trendline (in our case the uptrend line BC) the length of the "flagstaff" can be added to the point of breakout to determine an estimated price objective. In our example the "flagstaff" ranged from a $3.64½ high on May 11 to a low of $3.49¼ on May 12, or an overall length of 15¼¢. When the market broke out on May 21, confirming a resumption of the downtrend, the 15¼¢ could be subtracted from the penetration level of $3.52¾ to arrive at an estimated objective of $3.27½.

Triangular formations are very similar to the pennant and flag patterns in that they represent periods of price consolidation and are useful in predicting future price objectives. The triangle appears as one of three types: symmetrical, ascending, or descending. The latter two types are mirror images of each other and are dependent upon whether a bull or bear market is in the making.

240   MARKETING FOR FARMERS

Figure 12-6. JULY 1981 CORN (Chicago Board of Trade).

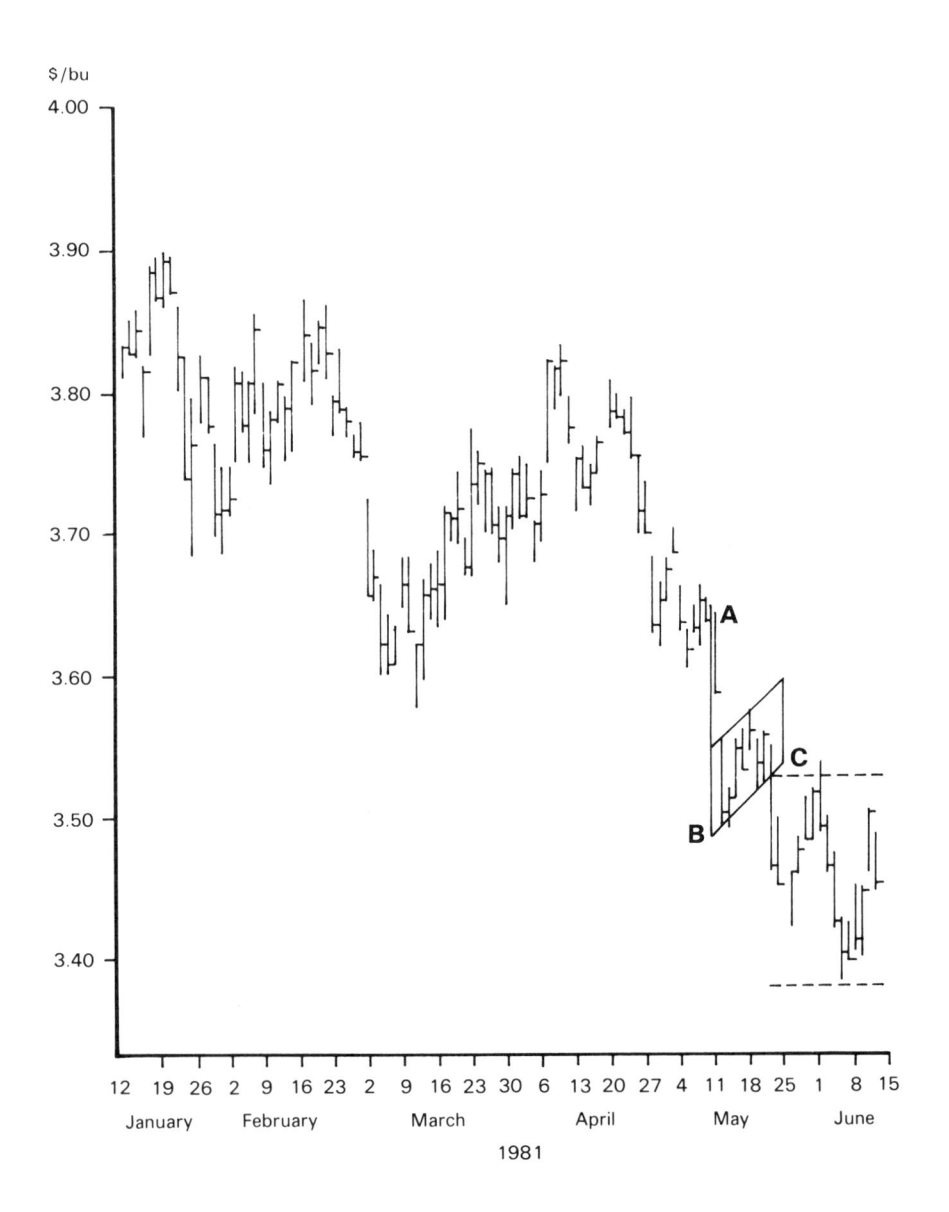

An example of a symmetrical triangle is shown in Figure 12-7. Note the sides of approximate equal length from which this pattern gets its name. Note also the coiling effect as the push-pull battle for direction creates price congestion.

The length of the vertical side of the symmetrical triangle, when added to the apex, or point, will give an estimate of the size of the next leg of the move. The vertical portion in our example is that distance from Point A to Point B, or $4.47 per cwt. The apex stands at approximately $71.30. Subtracting the length of the vertical side, $4.47, from the apex yields a price objective of $66.83. During the week of February 6 the market made a low of $66.65.

Ascending and descending triangles are found rather frequently in most agricultural commodities. Their structure consists of a long flat level of price support or resistance and a trendline that slowly descends or ascends (hence, its name) into this support or resistance, thus appearing as a right triangle.

Figure 12-8 shows an ascending triangle in the daily continuation chart for soybean meal futures. The resistance level held strong for almost four months when an upside breakout finally occurred. The up-trend line also survived numerous tests in that time. Ideally, as a triangle such as this is formed, volume will decrease as the coil is made and a false breakout can be expected. This particular example is somewhat different from a "textbook" example in that prices were very near to the apex before a breakout occurred. It is usually assumed that the breakout will take place about two-thirds of the way from the beginning of the triangle to its apex. In fact, if prices wait too long before a breakout occurs, the reliability of the triangle diminishes.

In using the ascending (descending) triangle as a measuring device, simply project the vertical height of the triangle at its beginning to an equal distance above (or below) its resistance (support) level. This vertical height in our example is the distance from Point A to Point B, or $173 - $153 = $20. Adding this to our resistance level of $173 gives us a price objective of $193.

Figure 12-7. JUNE 1981 LIVE CATTLE (Chicago Mercantile Exchange) Weekly Futures.

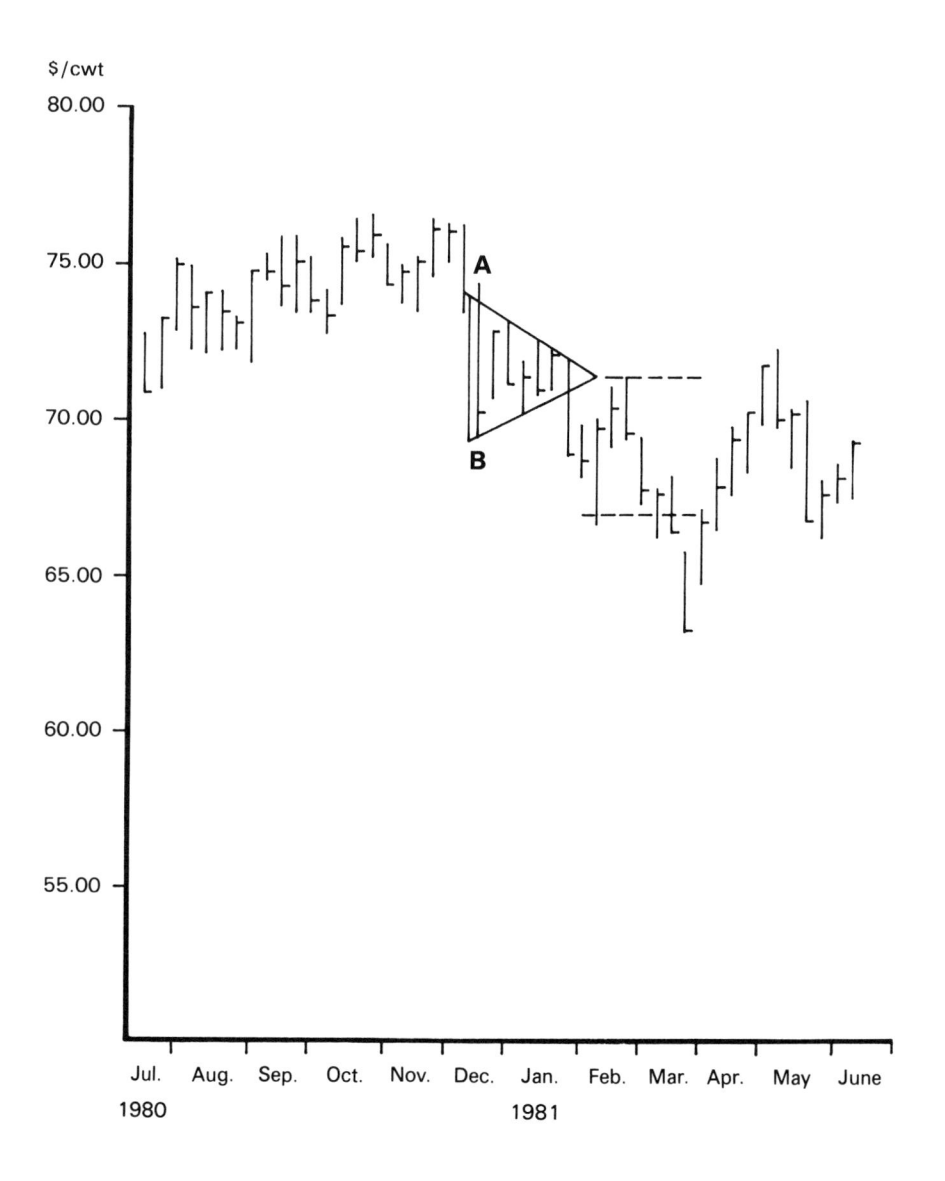

Technical Price Analysis

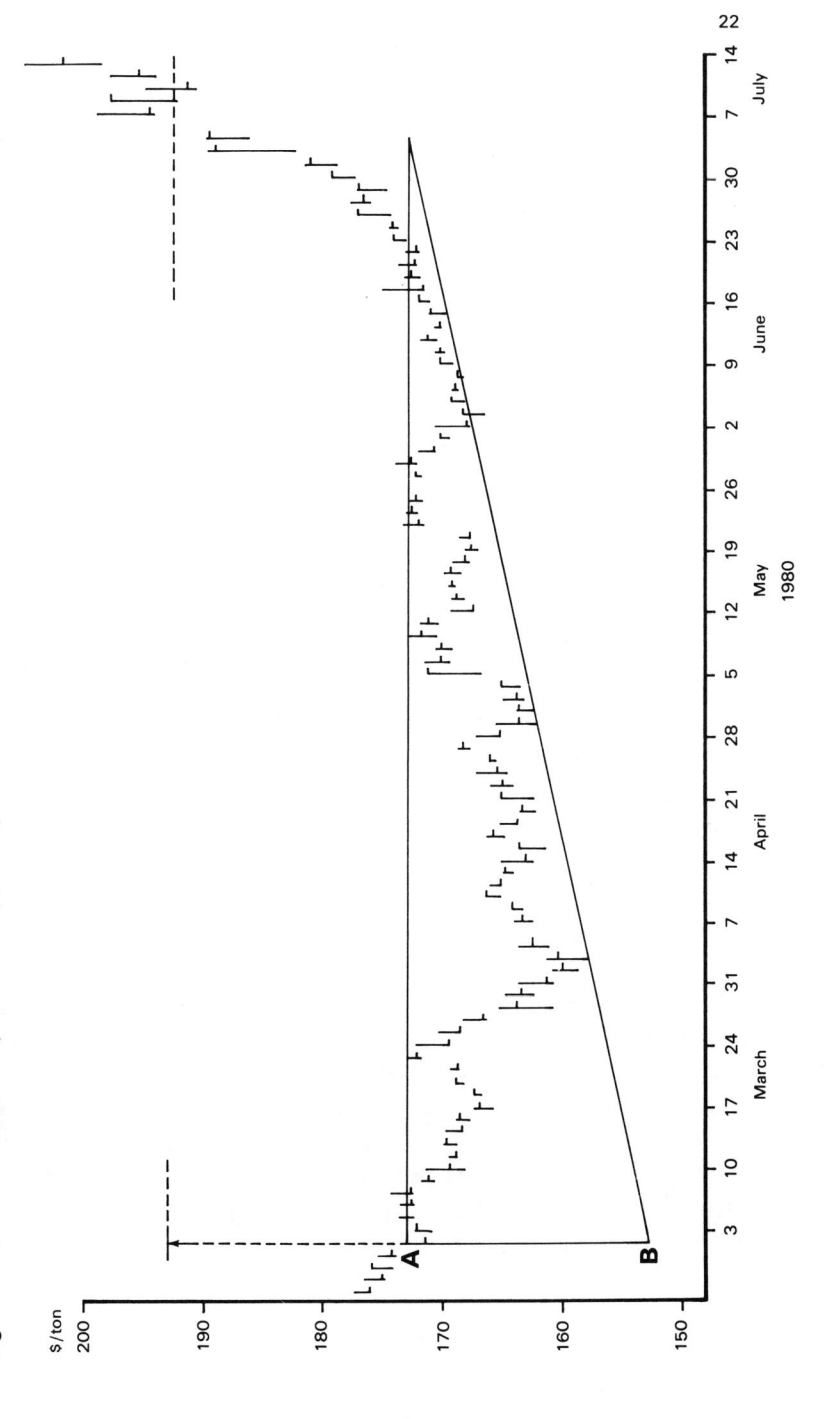

Figure 12-8. SOYBEAN MEAL (Continuation) (Chicago Board of Trade).

Other Formations

A very popular chart formation often referred to in the market literature is the *head-and-shoulders*. The head-and-shoulders is regarded as a top formation while the inverted head-and-shoulders is considered a bottom formation. The name comes from its usual three-peaked appearance with a protruding "head" situated between two lesser "shoulders." This is the most common configuration, although two or more shoulders may exist on each side. If the "multiple shoulder" variety occurs, the same number of shoulders will appear on both sides of the head.

Figure 12-9 is a good illustration of a head-and-shoulders formation. The left shoulder was formed in mid-to late September while the head appeared in October as a moderate uptrend in prices prevailed. A severe reaction then occurred that dropped prices to the support level in the $78 area. Profit-taking by shorts and an attempt by the bulls to resume the ascent in prices resulted in an unsuccessful rally which not only failed to make new highs, but barely made a 50% retracement of the previous collapse in prices. This rally is the right shoulder.

It is important for the reader to be aware that, at this point in the analysis, only a *potential* head-and-shoulders exists. We must now watch subsequent price action to see if, in fact, the formation will be confirmed. Confirmation comes with a close below the "neckline," the line connecting the "armpits," Points A and B. It is only then that a top in the market can be proclaimed and appropriate trading strategy determined. In establishing a position in the market the trader is given two opportunities to take his stance. The first is to go with the trend as soon as a close below or above the neckline occurs. Second, after the neckline is penetrated, the market will usually react to test the strength of resistance or support that lies there. A position could also be established at some point on this reaction.

The head-and-shoulders is a reliable tool in forecasting the extent of the new price direction. The vertical distance from the top (or bottom) of the head to the neckline must first be calculated. This is then added to that same point on the neckline to arrive at an estimated price goal. In our example, the vertical distance from the head to the neckline (Point C) is $5.40 per cwt. The price at the neckline (Point C) is $78.60. Subtracting $5.40 from $78.60, we predict that prices should drop to the $73.20 area. The low made on December 12 was $72.72.

Technical Price Analysis 245

Figure 12-9. MARCH 1981 FEEDER CATTLE (Chicago Mercantile Exchange).

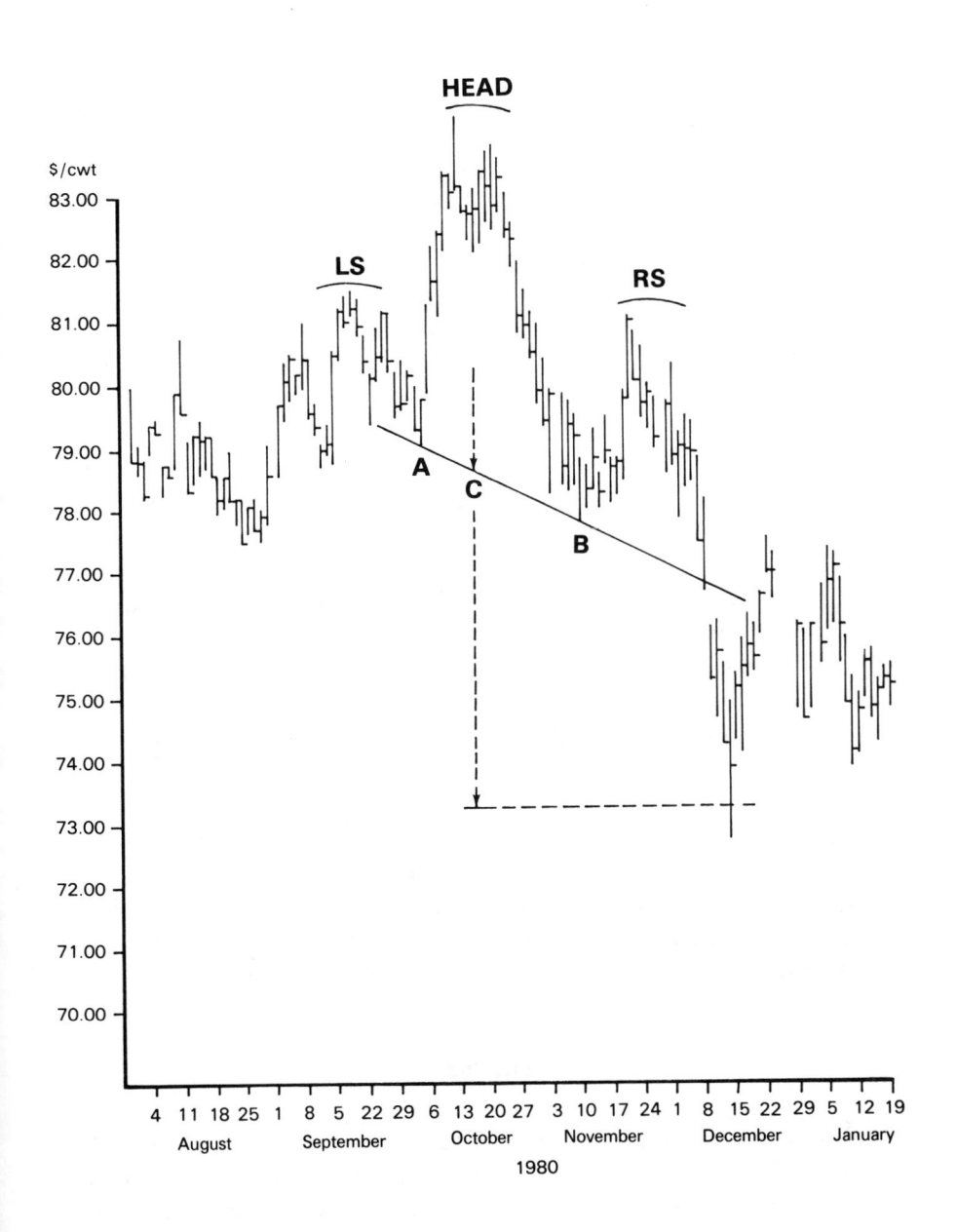

Double tops and double bottoms are highly dependable in forecasting the direction of a market. This should be obvious from their names. However, during their formation it is difficult to determine if such patterns are, in fact, developing. Take, for example, the double top in Figure 12-10. Even after the second top is made, you cannot be sure whether the market is taking a breather before the next leg up or if a top has, indeed, occurred. With a high degree of bullish enthusiasm prevailing in the marketplace, it is sometimes difficult to accept the notion that the end of the move is at hand. One source of assistance in arriving at an accurate conclusion is the trading volume. If volume at the time of the second top is low relative to that of the first, the trader should be wary. This is a signal that the upward pressure in the market is diminishing. The market is having difficulty making new highs. One should then be on the lookout for some other signal, such as the penetration of a trendline.

Double tops are noted for their appearance as the letter "M," a valley nestled between two peaks. (The double bottom resembles the letter "W.") The valley is formed as the market reaches some area of resistance during its ascent and profit taking occurs. Buying at some level of support suppresses any further descent in prices and the market rebounds. In our example the gap in the $9.30 area turned the market around for a test of the high. When the market's attempt at new highs fails and prices begin a second descent, a test of the reactionary (valley) low can be expected. *A double top is confirmed when the market closes below the low of the previous reaction, or valley.* In our illustration, the reactionary low appears at Point A. The double top was confirmed on December 4.

More than one attempt at new highs may occur, resulting in multiple top formations such as a triple top. As these tops are made and their subsequent reactions occur, resistance and support at these levels become quite intense, so that once a penetration and close below the reactionary lows occurs, a move of significant proportions ensues.

SUMMARY

Several general comments are necessary. First, all chart formations do not work equally well in all commodities. Each commodity possesses its own characteristics resulting from influences unique to that particular commodity or to those closely related. Therefore, individual price

Technical Price Analysis 247

Figure 12-10. MARCH 1981 SOYBEANS (Chicago Board of Trade).

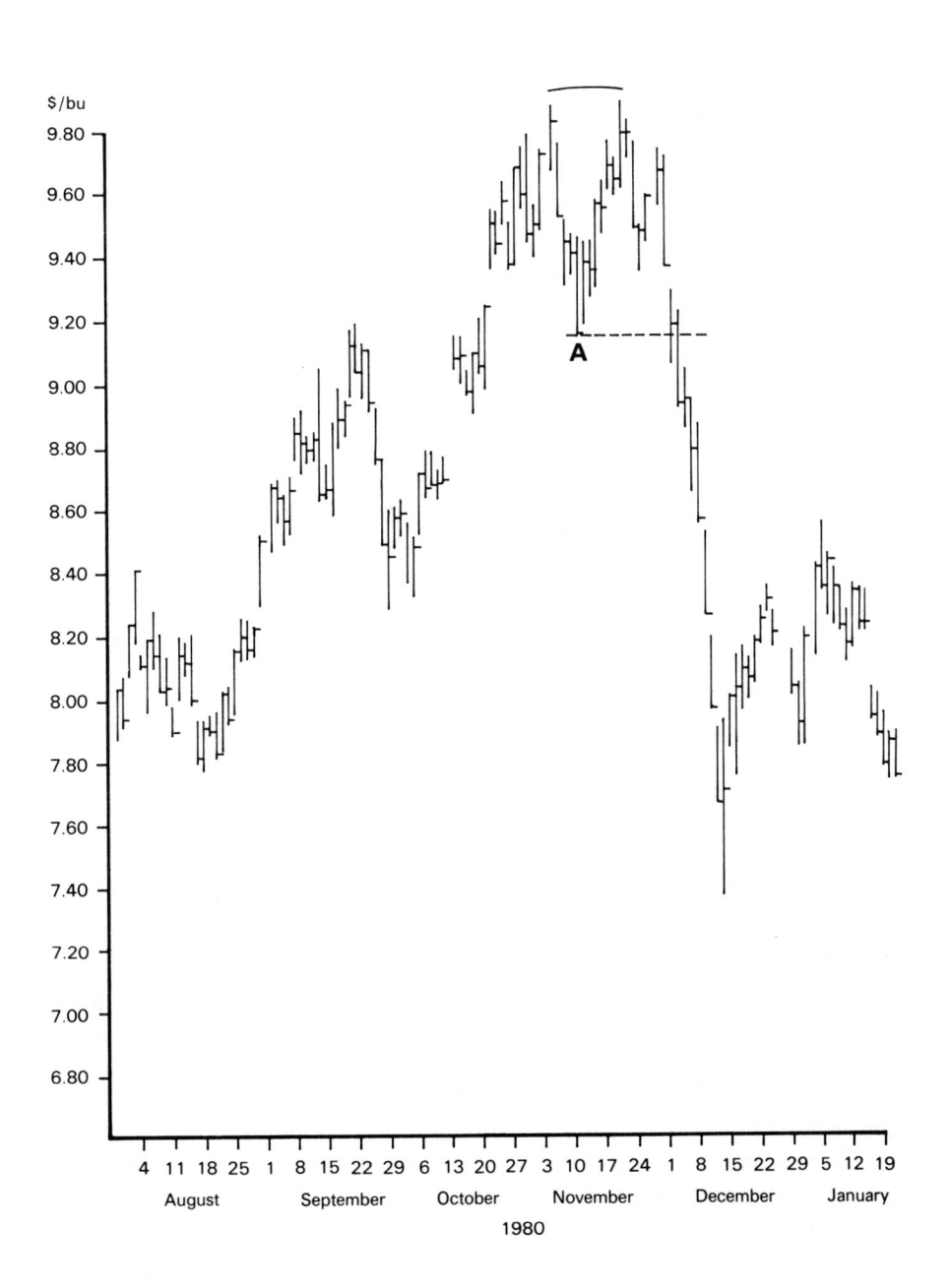

behavior differs, resulting in different predominant chart patterns. The more common a chart pattern is to a certain commodity, the more reliable it is. The chartist must keep this in mind as he watches the various scenarios unfold.

Second, do not base a trading decision solely on one chart. A head-and-shoulders in one delivery month does not necessarily mean that a bottom or top has been encountered in that commodity. Each contract, although closely related to all others in that commodity, is sensitive to its own factors regarding the time of its expiration. This may make it act somewhat differently than others. Look at several contracts and compare their price action. If a particular pattern is common to all, that pattern possesses a degree of reliability much greater than if it appears only in one or two months.

In the same light, do not base a trading decision solely on one pattern. Look for other signals which might aid in increasing the accuracy of the forecast. A key reversal is a good sign that prices may change direction. However, a key reversal at the test of a previous high (a potential double top) is an even better sign. To carry it one step further, a key reversal in a potential double top followed by a penetration and close below the uptrend line dramatically increases the chances of a successful trade by the chartist who establishes a position based on his new price prognosis. The whole point is that a chart formation, by itself, is a reliable indicator of price behavior. However, two or three chart formations together are even more reliable to the extent that you can establish yourself in the market with a good degree of confidence that your decision is correct.

This brings up the last point—the question of reliability. Charts are an essential tool for anyone whose income and/or profit is highly dependent upon the prices of the commodities in which he is associated. However, chart formations are not infallible. Their reliability is such that, as mentioned above, you can base a decision on them with a great degree of accuracy[3] and confidence; but things change quite fast in commodity markets, as most of you well know, and what may look good at one moment in time may turn sour soon after. Obviously, it is the prudent analyst-trader who keeps this in mind.

The chart patterns discussed above are those most commonly found in the price activity of agricultural commodities. There are other formations that occur. Some appear only infrequently, while others

---

[3]Studies have been made regarding the reliability of each individual chart formation. Their degrees of reliability range from 50% to 80%.

are of a somewhat more complex nature, beyond the scope of this discussion. If you understand this discussion, you have acquired the basic knowledge of charting and should be encouraged to pursue more advanced bar chart analysis. In addition, do not restrict yourself to bar charts only. As mentioned in the introduction to this chapter, technical analysis comprises a whole array of charts (bar, point-and-figure, moving average, etc.) and mathematical formulas to suit the skills and backgrounds of anyone willing to spend some time to learn them. Most important, these concepts possess high degrees of reliability so that it is worth taking the time to learn them.

Appendix A

HEDGER'S GLOSSARY

At the market - Term which instructs the broker to execute your order immediately at the current price at which the commodity is trading when the order enters the pit. Also referred to as **Market order.**

Basis - The difference between a futures price and a cash price which reflects the cost of transportation to the delivery point plus the cost of storage, interest and insurance until delivery date of the contract.

Basis quote - The differential between your local cash grain market quote and the corresponding futures market price. Usually stated as cents above (premium to futures) or below (discount to futures) the corresponding option price.

Bear - A person who expects lower prices.

Bear market - A market characterized by a declining price trend.

Bear spread - Simultaneous sale of a nearby option and purchase of a deferred, expecting the nearby to lose relative to the deferred.

Break - Quick drop in market price.

Bid - To be willing to buy a grain future or cash grain at a specific price subject to immediate acceptance unless otherwise stated.

Broker - A representative who is registered with the exchange and Commodities Exchange Authority and is responsible for execution of your purchase or sale order. (Need not be registered to execute trades in non-regulated commodities.)

Bulge - Quick rise in market price.

Bull - A person who expects higher prices.

Bull market - A market characterized by an advancing price trend.

Bull spread - Simultaneous purchase of a nearby option and sale of a deferred, expecting the nearby to gain relative to the deferred.

Buy in - Repurchase a short sale to liquidate delivery obligations and terminate a short trade. Also referred to as **Cover.**

C.A.F. (C & F) - Cost And Freight, usually to a port of exit. A trade term to describe delivery provisions of a cash grain purchase or sale which includes the purchase price and freight charges in the quoted price.

Carrying charge - A futures market condition where each succeeding option is quoted at a higher price to reflect costs of ownership of the physical commodity over a period of time such as warehouse charges, insurance and interest. Usually represents a surplus situation.

Cash commodities - Actual physical grain ownership. Referred to as "spot commodity" during a futures delivery month.

C.E.A. - Commodity Exchange Authority. Governmental body responsible for policing commodity trading on "regulated exchanges" and ensuring that all rules and regulations are adhered to by individual traders and exchange member firms.

Certificated stocks - Quantities of grain designated and certificated for delivery by the exchange under its grading and testing regulations at delivery points and/or warehouses specified and approved for delivery by the exchange.

C.I.F. - Cost, Insurance, and Freight. A trade term to describe a cash purchase or sale when these costs have been included in the quoted price.

Clearing house - The agency of the futures exchange that is responsible for matching purchases and sales, assuring proper conduct of delivery procedures and maintaining adequate financing by member firms.

Clearing member - An exchange member (individual or firm) who is also a member of the Clearing House or Association.

Clearing price - The price at which the Clearing House settles a trade. May be established by a referee if contracts are liquidated under exceptional circumstances. Also called **Settlement price.**

Appendix A

Close - The stated hour at which an exchange ceases trading during a day or the price at which a commodity is trading when time expires. Often a range of prices if buyers bid a lower price than sellers are willing to accept.

Commission - The brokerage fee for entering and liquidating one contract of a commodity future. See also **Round turn commission.**

Commission house - A business entity which employs registered representatives (brokers) and which acts as agent for the customer in buying or selling cash or futures and maintains records of customer transactions. The commission house also collects customers' margin deposits and disperses customer profits or collects customer losses based on trades executed at the customers' directions.

Commission house stops - See **Stop-loss order.**

Confirmation - A document sent by the clearing commission firm to its client when a futures transaction is conducted--either purchase or sale. Generally shows the date of the trade, the delivery month, the price and the quantity.

Contract - (Futures) The standardized unit (including size, quality, delivery points and delivery dates) of grain making up a single unit of trading on the major exchanges. Also referred to as a **Lot** or a **Car.**

Contract grades - A quality definition established by the exchange to represent the standard type of grain acceptable for delivery against a futures contract. Included in the specification is the premium or discount for delivery of a non-standard quality or type of grain.

Cover - See **Buy in** and **Sell out.**

Crop year - The period beginning about the harvest and extending 12 months, the beginning date of which varies by grain and is established by the Department of Agriculture for purposes of keeping records of production, disposition and stocks.

Day orders - Those orders entered on an exchange by your broker which expire at the end of trading that day if not executed.

Day trade - A trade which is entered and liquidated during the same trading session. The round turn commission is reduced and margin is not posted normally, although it may be required by the commission firm prior to entering the trade.

Deliverable grades - See **Contract grades.**

Deliverable stocks - See **Certificated stocks.**

Delivery - Settlement of a futures contract by tender of or receipt of the actual physical grain or a warehouse receipt covering a contract unit of grain.

Delivery month - That month during which a futures contract expires and becomes subject to delivery.

Delivery notice - A notice, in writing, to a long futures contract holder that the tender of physical grain is being made in provision with exchange rules.

Delivery points - Those locations (cities and/or elevators) designated by the exchange as authorized for placement of the physical grain in fulfillment of an expiring futures contract.

Delivery price - The settlement price designated by the Clearing House as the final price received or paid in fulfillment of a commodity contract.

Differentials - Premiums or discounts from the standard delivery grade or point specified by the exchange.

Discretionary account - A futures account in which the customer agrees (in writing) to allow a broker to enter trades without prior consultation.

Equity - The difference between the original price of purchase or sale and the current market price of a commodity contract.

Evening up - Reducing outstanding futures obligations by purchase or sale of the same option or by spreading to a different option.

Appendix A

Ex-pit - Trades which take place somewhere other than the regular exchange pit or ring.

F.A.S. - Free Alongside. A trade term to describe delivery conditions which include handling and shipping charges to export vessel berth.

F.A.Q. - Fair, Average Quality.

Floor broker - A registered representative who is physically present on the designated trading floor of the exchange.

Flat price - Current price for cash grain.

First notice day - The first day authorized and specified by the exchange on which notice of intention to deliver physical grain against a short futures position is permitted.

F.O.B. - Free On Board. A trade term describing a purchase or sale which includes the cost of loading grain on a ship, rail car, barge or truck.

Free supply - The supply of grain not owned or controlled by governmental agencies and not certificated for delivery against futures.

Futures - Common term representing a contract specifying the date, location, grade and quantity of a grain to be delivered at a later date which is traded or an organized commodity exchange.

G.T.C. - Good Till Cancelled. Those orders entered on an exchange by your broker which the broker will keep in effect until executed or cancelled. Also called **Open Order.**

Grades - See **Contract grades.**

Grading certificate - A paper issued by an authorized inspector which states the quality of grain presented for inspection at the time of inspection.

Heavy - A market condition characterized by inability of the market to advance.

Hedge - To reduce risk of cash grain ownership or delivery obligation due to market price changes by buying or selling an offsetting amount of futures. Also to lock in a satisfactory price, covering cost of production, by selling an amount of futures equal to anticipated production. See **Long hedge** and **Short hedge**.

Hedging margin - The margin deposit required by the exchange when a legitimate hedge sale of futures is made against physical inventory or production capacity. This margin is often less than for a normal speculative account.

Hedging plan - A written plan based on market fundamentals, established prior to placement of hedge which includes: objective of the hedge; outline of fundamentals; entry point (date and/or level); level for adding to hedge; provision for margin call; liquidation plans (date and/or level).

Inter-market spread - Simultaneous purchase and sale of the same commodity on different exchanges (such as Chicago/Kansas City/Minneapolis wheat) expecting a change in the price differential.

Inter-commodity spread - Simultaneous purchase and sale of related commodities (such as corn and oats) expecting a change in the price differential.

Initial margin - The margin deposit required by the exchange when a new futures trade is entered. See **Margin Deposit**.

Inverse or inverted market - A futures market condition where each succeeding option is quoted at a lower price. Usually represents a shortage situation.

Invisible supply - Stocks of grain held in other than regularly inspected and reporting warehouses. Includes afloat or intransit stocks.

Last trading day - The final day during which a futures contract may be traded on the exchange. Grain trading usually expires at noon on the final trading day and any contracts remaining open at the end of trading that day must be settled by delivery or receipt of physical grain or by agreement for cash settlement if delivery is not possible.

Appendix A

Life of contract - The period of time during which a futures contract is traded from the first trading day to the last trading day. (Usually about eleven months for grains.)

Limit move - The maximum change in price from the previous day's settlement as established by the exchange. Limits may change from time to time as market conditions dictate. (See **Variable limits.**)

Limit position - Maximum number of contracts which an individual may be long or short or which an individual may trade for his account during one day as established by the C.E.A.

Limited order - Those orders placed with your broker to which you have attached some restriction as to time or price for execution.

Liquidation - Cancellation of a future delivery obligation by the offsetting purchase or sale of the same futures contract.

Locals - Floor brokers who trade for their own accounts.

Long - To own (have bought) cash grain or futures contracts, and in the case of futures, to be obligated to accept delivery unless the position is offset before delivery date.

Long the basis - To own cash grain which is hedged in futures at a favorable basis in the prospect that the basis will widen, providing a hedge profit.

Long hedge - Purchase of futures to offset a cash delivery obligation (cash sale) rather than physical ownership of the grain and to reduce the risk of price change.

Lot - The contract unit. Also referred to as a **Contract** or **Car.**

Maintenance margin - The margin deposit required by the exchange to keep a futures trade in force, required when the initial margin has been depleted by adverse price movement. Maintenance margin is often 20% to 50% lower than initial margin.

Margin call - A notice that additional margin is required to keep the futures contract in force. Margin calls may result from a loss in the futures position or from increased exchange requirements due to higher price level or unusual market volatility.

Margin deposit - A "good faith" money deposit made by you with the brokerage house and in turn deposited by the brokerage house with the futures exchange. The minimum margin is determined by the exchange and is usually lower for hedgers than for speculators.

Margin to the market - A reverse margin call. When a profit accrues to your futures account, you may withdraw money from the account, reducing the balance to the minimum maintenance margin deposit requirement.

Market order - See **At the market.**

Members' rate - The commission charged to an exchange member. A lower commission fee than for non-member traders to reflect the cost of membership.

Negotiable warehouse receipts - Legal document issued by a warehousing firm which describes and guarantees the existence of a specified quantity (and sometimes grade) of grain in store.

Offer - To be willing to sell a grain future or cash grain at a specific price subject to immediate acceptance unless otherwise stated.

Offset - See **Liquidation.**

Open contracts - The total number of futures contracts in existence which has not been liquidated.

Opening - The designated hour of the day during which futures trading begins on the exchange floor. Major U.S. grain exchanges normally open at 9:30 a.m. Central Time. Also may refer to the opening or first price at which a commodity trades on a given day.

Open interest - The total of **Open Contracts** which includes both a long and a short for each open contract.

Appendix A						259

Open order - See **G.T.C.**

Option - Often used to refer to a grain futures month although technically, options are **Puts and Calls** which are not traded on regulated U.S. commodity exchanges.

Pit - The ring or designated area on the exchange floor where futures orders are executed.

Point - The price unit in which futures prices are expressed (usually eighths of cents per bushel for grains).

Position - The open commitment in a market, long or short.

Production hedge - A short hedge, placed prior to or during the growing season.

Public elevators - Bulk storage facilities open for rent to the public.

P & S - Purchase And Sale statement. A document sent by the clearing commission firm to its client when a transaction in futures is liquidated. Generally shows the dates of the trade, the delivery month, the price, the quantity, the profit or loss, the commission, the net trade profit or loss and and the new account balance.

Range - The difference between the low and high price of futures trading in a designated delivery month during the day, week, month or life of contract.

Reaction - A price change contrary to the current trend of prices.

Receipt - See **Delivery.**

Recovery - An upward movement in prices following a decline.

Regulated commodities - Those commodities (including U.S. grains) named in the Commodity Exchange Act over which the Commodity Exchange Authority has regulatory powers. The term does not imply price regulation.

Resting order - A limited open order on the exchange floor which is either to sell above or buy below the current futures price level.

Ring - See **Pit.**

Rolling the hedge forward - Liquidation of the original futures contract and the simultaneous purchase or sale of a more distant futures option to keep the hedge without holding into the delivery month.

Round lot - The full unit of trading, 5,000 bushels per contract for U.S. grains. See **Car, contract, or lot.**

Round turn commission - The brokerage fee for entering and liquidating one contract of a commodity future. Unlike stock trading, commodity brokerage fees cover both the cost of buying and selling one round lot. The commission is assessed only when the trade is liquidated.

Scale orders - Orders to buy or sell additional futures contracts as the price declines or advances from the initial trade level. For example, sell 5,000 May corn at each five cents up. Also referred to as selling on a scale or buying on a scale.

Scalp - A trade for small gains usually entered and liquidated during the day to take advantage of a daily price trend.

Sell out - Offsetting sale to liquidate a long futures trade.

Settlement price - See **Clearing price.**

Short - To have sold cash grain or futures and in the case of futures, to be obligated to make delivery unless the position is offset before delivery date.

Short the basis - To sell cash grain which is hedged in futures at a favorable basis in the prospect that the basis will narrow providing a hedge profit.

Short hedge - Sale of futures to offset cash ownership of grain and reduce the risk of price change.

Appendix A

Soft - Term used to describe a gradually declining market.

Speculator - A non-hedging trader. One who assumes risk positions with the hope of making a profit rather than protecting inventory or guaranteeing production costs.

Spot commodity - See **Cash commodity.**

Spot price - The value of the cash commodity at the current time.

Spread - Simultaneous purchase and sale of the same or related commodities with the expectation that the price differential will change. See **Bear spread, Bull spread, Inter-market spread, Inter-commodity spread.** Also referred to as Straddle.

Spread margin - The margin deposit required by the exchange when a futures spread position is entered. This is the lowest margin requirement, often only 10% to 20% of the initial net margin, in recognition of the lower risk nature of offsetting purchase and sale (spread) trades.

Squeeze - A technical situation in which lack of delivery supplies or transportation forces shorts to cover their delivery obligation by offsetting the futures contract rather than making physical delivery.

Stop-loss order - An attempt to limit market risk by placing a liquidation order to be executed if the price moves violently to the designated level. However, in actual trading, the movement may be so fast and the market so thin that the actual price may be over or under the stop-loss order price due to inability to execute at the designated price. Also referred to as Stops or Commission house stops.

Storage hedge - A short hedge placed following harvest with grain being stored on farm or in the country elevator.

Technical correction - Price change against the trend due to such considerations as chart formations, volume, open interest or delivery conditions rather than due to fundamental (supply-demand) reasons.

Tender - See **Delivery.** Also offer of cash grain to a buying agent.

Terminal elevator - Bulk storage facility located at a major grain marketing center such as Chicago, Kansas City or Minneapolis.

Terminal market - A major grain marketing center such as Chicago, Kansas City or Minneapolis.

Thin - Term used to describe a futures market with low volume of trading.

Trading limit - See **Limit move.**

Trading market - A market price pattern which is confined to a very narrow range between highs and lows for several weeks or months at a time.

Trending market - A market price pattern which has a well defined direction of price movement for several weeks or months with prices carried into new high or low ground consistently.

Variable limits - A new system of determining trading limits adopted in April 1974 by the Chicago Board of Trade whereby limits for grain futures will be increased to 150% of the normal level for the next three days if a commodity closed up or down the limit for three consecutive days in three or more contract months during the same crop year. The variable limits will remain in effect until at least three contract months fail to close up or down the limit during one day of any three day period. Limits will then revert to the original level.

Visible supply - Grain stocks which can be accounted for such as elevator and processor inventory.

Volume - Total number of contracts traded during a day.

Warehouse receipts - See **Negotiable warehouse receipts.**

Wire house - See **Commission house.**

Appendix B

LIVESTOCK FUTURES CONTRACT SPECIFICATIONS

Livestock futures contracts are traded on both the Chicago Mercantile Exchange and the Chicago Mid-America Exchange. Live slaughter cattle and live hogs are traded on both exchanges. Live feeder cattle contracts are traded only on the Mercantile Exchange.

Contracts on the Mid-America Exchange on live slaughter cattle and live hogs are identical to the Chicago Mercantile Exchange contracts, except that they are one-half the size. All other contract specifications are the same.

Details on contract specifications and tolerances are important on livestock futures because market conditions are sometimes favorable for producers to make or take delivery on the contracts. This is less likely in the case of farmer hedges on grains. The following provides details on the contract specifications and trading regulations for live slaughter cattle, live feeder cattle and live hogs on the Mercantile Exchange.

LIVE BEEF CATTLE

Size of Contract:	40,000 lbs. (up to 5% deviation permitted) (Chicago Mid-America Exchange—20,000 lbs.)
Daily Price Change:	No more than $1.50 per cwt from previous day's settlement price
Speculative Position Limit:	No more than 450 contracts long or short in any contract month
Brokerage Fee:	Negotiable between trader and broker
Initial Margin Deposit:	Minimum established by the exchange and normally related to price level
Contract Maturity:	On approximately the 20th calendar day of contract month (holidays may alter date by one or two days)
Delivery Period:	Monday, Tuesday, Wednesday and Thursday of contract month except on holidays or day preceding holiday
Contract Trading Months:	January, February, April, June, August, October and December

Par Delivery Unit:

Quality Grade:	USDA choice steers
Yield Grade:	USDA yield grade 1, 2, 3, 4, with no more than 4 head of yield grade 4 without discount
Weight:	Delivery unit must average between 1,050 and 1,200 lbs. with no steer weighing more than 100 lbs. above or below the average weight of lot.
Dressing Percent:	Delivery unit averaging from 1,050 lbs. to 1,125 lbs. must hot dress 62% or better.
	Delivery unit averaging from 1,125.6 lbs. to 1,250 lbs. must hot dress 63% or better.
Health:	All animals must be healthy. (Crippled, sick or bruised animals will not be accepted.)

Substitutions and Discounts:

Weight:	Steers averaging 100 to 200 lbs. over or under average are discounted $3 per cwt from par. No animals less than 450 lbs. or over 1,300 lbs. are allowed.
Dressing Percent:	For each ½% hot dress under par, the delivery unit is discounted 50¢ per cwt. No unit with an average dressing percent of less than 60% is deliverable.
Quality Grade:	Up to 8 head of Good grade steers are allowed at $3 per cwt discount.
Yield Grade:	Up to 8 head of yield grade 4 steers are allowed at a discount of 15% of the settlement price.
Delivery Points:	Par delivery at approved stockyards at Peoria, Ill., Joliet, Ill., Omaha, Neb., Sioux City, Ia., Guymon, Okla., and Greeley, Colo.
Inspection and Grading:	Quality grading, yield grading, estimating hot dressing percent and estimating weight of individual animals are performed by the designated USDA grader at each delivery point.
Delivery Costs:	Paid by seller and include yardage, commission fee, inspection and grading charges

LIVE HOG CONTRACT SPECIFICATIONS

Size of Contract:	30,000 lbs. (up to 5% deviation permitted) (Chicago Mid-America Exchange—15,000 lbs.)
Daily Price Change:	No more than $1.50 per cwt from previous day's settlement price

Appendix B

Speculative Position Limit:	No more than 750 contracts long or short by any one trader allowed and no more than 300 in any one contract month
Brokerage Fee:	Negotiable between trader and broker
Initial Margin Deposit:	Minimum established by the exchange and normally related to price level
Contract Maturity:	On approximately the 20th calendar day of contract month (holidays may alter this date by one or two days)
Delivery Period:	Monday, Tuesday, Wednesday and Thursday of contract month, except on holidays or day preceding holiday
Contract Trading Months:	February, April, June, July, August, October and December
Par Delivery Unit:	
Quality Grade:	USDA, No. 1, No. 2 and No. 3 barrows and gilts and no more than 90 head USDA No. 3
Weight:	Average weight between 200 and 230 lbs.
Health:	Sick, crippled or bruised animals not acceptable
Substitutions and Discounts:	
Weight:	Hogs weighing less than 200 lbs. and more than 230 are discounted 50¢ per cwt. No hog lighter than 190 lbs. or heavier than 240 is accepted.
Grade:	Delivery units containing more than 90 USDA No. 3 are discounted 50¢ per cwt. Delivery units containing up to 8 head USDA No. 4 are discounted $2 per cwt for each No. 4 hog.
Delivery Points:	
Par Delivery:	Peoria, Ill.
Alternate Delivery Points:	A discount of 25¢ per cwt for delivery at Omaha, Neb., Sioux City, Ia., E. St. Louis, Ill., and St. Paul, Minn. Discounts of 50¢ per cwt at Kansas City, Mo., and St. Joseph, Mo.
Inspection and Grading:	Grading, inspection and weight estimations are performed by designated USDA grader at each delivery point.
Delivery Costs:	Paid by seller and include yardage, commission fee, inspection and grading charges.

FEEDER CATTLE CONTRACT SPECIFICATIONS	
Size of Contract:	44,000 lbs. (up to 5% deviation permitted)
Daily Price Change:	No more than $1.50 per cwt from previous day's settlement price
Speculative Position Limit:	No more than 300 contracts in one delivery can be controlled by one trader.
Brokerage Fee:	Negotiable between trader and broker
Initial Margin Deposit:	Minimum is established by the exchange, normally related to price level.
Contract Maturity:	On approximately the 20th calendar day of the contract month (holidays may alter date by one or two days)
Delivery Period:	Monday, Tuesday, Wednesday and Thursday of contract month, except holidays or days preceding a holiday
Contract Trading Months:	January, March, April, May, August, September, October and November
Par Delivery Unit:	
Quality Grade:	Feeder steers grading medium frame with No. 1 muscle thickness and top one-third at No. 2 muscle thickness. Also, lower two-thirds of large frame, with No. 1 muscle thickness and top one-third of No. 3 muscle thickness. No more than 13 head at top one-third of No. 2 muscle thickness allowed without discount.
Weight:	A delivery unit of feeder steers averaging between 575 and 700 lbs. No steer in delivery unit may vary more than 50 lbs. from the average weight.
Other Limitations:	The following animal characteristics are not allowed: excessive fill, stag characteristics, blindness, horns or stubs over 5 inches, freshly dehorned, lameness, excessive finish, hump jaw, prominent dairy breeding or prominent hump on forequarter.
Substitutions and Discounts:	
Grade:	Over 13 head and up to 23 head of top one-third of No. 2 muscle thickness are allowed at $4 per cwt discount.
Weight:	An average weight of delivery unit up to 750 lbs. is allowed, but a discount of $3 per cwt for any unit weighing over 700 lbs. A delivery unit weighing over 750 and up to 800 lbs. is allowed at a discount of $5 per cwt for each lb. over 700 lbs.

Appendix B

Delivery Points:	Par delivery points are Omaha, Neb., Oklahoma City, Okla. and Sioux City, Ia. Delivery at Kansas City, Mo., St. Joseph, Mo. at 25¢ per cwt discount. Delivery at St. Paul, Minn., Greeley, Colo., Dodge City, Kan. and Amarillo, Tex. at 50¢ per cwt discount and Montgomery, Ala. at $6 per cwt discount.
Inspection and Grading:	Grading and inspection are performed by designated USDA grader at each delivery point.
Delivery Costs:	Paid by seller and include yardage commission fee, grading and inspection charges

Appendix C

COMMODITY PRICE DATA

The following pages show historical prices for the following farm commodities:

   Corn, No. 2, Chicago
   Grain sorghum, No. 2, Kansas City
   Wheat, No. 1 Hard Winter, Kansas City
   Wheat, No. 2 Soft Red Winter, Chicago
   Oats, No. 2, Chicago
   Barley, No. 2, Minneapolis
   Soybeans, No. 1, Chicago
   Soybean Meal, 44%, Decatur
   Choice Slaughter Steers, Omaha
   Good Slaughter Cattle, Omaha
   Choice Feeder Steers, Kansas City
   Choice Steer Calves, Kansas City
   Barrows and Gilts, 7-Market avg.
   Feeder Pigs
   Choice Slaughter Lambs, San Angelo
   Choice Feeder Lambs, San Angelo

Appendix C

CORN, NO. 2 YELLOW, CHICAGO
Price, Dollars Per Bushel

Year	Oct.	Nov.	Dec.	Jan.	Feb.	Mar.	Apr.	May	Jun.	Jul.	Aug.	Sep.	Avg.
1959-1960	1.15	1.13	1.12	1.17	1.15	1.17	1.22	1.23	1.22	1.21	1.20	1.17	1.18
60-61	1.10	.99	1.05	1.12	1.15	1.14	1.11	1.15	1.14	1.15	1.14	1.12	1.11
61-62	1.12	1.12	1.11	1.09	1.10	1.12	1.14	1.17	1.15	1.14	1.11	1.13	1.12
62-63	1.13	1.10	1.16	1.20	1.21	1.22	1.21	1.24	1.31	1.33	1.33	1.36	1.23
63-64	1.24	1.17	1.23	1.24	1.22	1.24	1.26	1.29	1.27	1.24	1.26	1.29	1.25
1964-1965	1.23	1.20	1.27	1.29	1.31	1.33	1.35	1.38	1.37	1.33	1.31	1.32	1.31
65-66	1.23	1.16	1.24	1.32	1.31	1.28	1.28	1.31	1.33	1.43	1.49	1.46	1.32
66-67	1.40	1.35	1.45	1.42	1.41	1.41	1.38	1.39	1.38	1.31	1.23	1.20	1.36
67-68	1.17	1.10	1.14	1.13	1.15	1.17	1.16	1.19	1.15	1.13	1.08	1.09	1.14
68-69	1.09	1.15	1.16	1.20	1.18	1.17	1.24	1.32	1.31	1.29	1.30	1.24	1.22
1969-1970	1.21	1.18	1.19	1.26	1.26	1.24	1.28	1.32	1.37	1.38	1.46	1.52	1.31
70-71	1.42	1.42	1.54	1.59	1.57	1.55	1.51	1.52	1.57	1.48	1.29	1.16	1.47
71-72	1.10	1.07	1.22	1.22	1.18	1.19	1.26	1.28	1.25	1.28	1.26	1.40	1.23
72-73	1.32	1.33	1.57	1.58	1.59	1.59	1.65	2.01	2.42	2.52	2.91	2.47	1.91
73-74	2.37	2.50	2.68	2.90	3.13	2.99	2.69	2.70	2.93	3.35	3.63	3.55	2.95
1974-1975	3.74	3.48	3.47	3.19	2.96	2.90	2.96	2.82	2.89	2.95	3.12	2.99	3.12
75-76	2.74	2.59	2.59	2.62	2.70	2.68	2.68	2.84	2.96	2.96	2.87	2.77	2.75
76-77	2.49	2.33	2.44	2.53	2.54	2.52	2.50	2.41	2.27	2.05	1.78	1.80	2.30
77-78	1.84	2.14	2.19	2.19	2.21	2.36	2.51	2.57	2.51	2.28	2.17	2.13	2.26
78-79	2.22	2.28	2.27	2.29	2.35	2.42	2.53	2.66	2.83	3.00	2.82	2.78	2.54
1979-1980	2.73	2.59	2.69	2.54	2.65	2.60	2.61	2.70	2.70	3.08	3.36	3.44	2.81
80-81	3.43	3.43	3.54	3.56	3.49	3.48	3.53	3.47	3.41	3.41	3.09	2.72	3.38
81-82	2.61	2.60	2.52	—	—	—	—	—	—	—	—	—	—

SOURCE: USDA Grain Market News

GRAIN SORGHUM, NO. 2 YELLOW MILO, KANSAS CITY
Price, Dollars Per Cwt.

Year	Oct.	Nov.	Dec.	Jan.	Feb.	Mar.	Apr.	May	Jun.	Jul.	Aug.	Sep.	Avg.
1959-1960	1.57	1.58	1.62	1.74	1.76	1.75	1.74	1.89	2.02	2.04	2.00	2.02	1.70
60-61	1.82	1.84	1.88	1.95	1.97	1.89	1.93	1.92	1.93	1.99	1.90	1.84	1.89
61-62	1.81	1.83	1.86	1.90	1.92	1.88	1.90	1.89	1.89	1.94	1.85	1.81	1.87
62-63	1.74	1.78	1.90	2.00	1.99	1.99	1.94	2.01	2.05	2.06	1.96	1.92	1.94
63-64	1.94	1.92	1.93	1.97	1.96	1.94	1.97	2.02	2.09	2.12	2.10	2.09	2.01
1964-1965	2.07	2.05	2.08	2.10	2.10	2.09	2.10	2.14	2.13	2.12	2.08	1.93	2.08
65-66	1.86	1.87	1.92	1.97	2.00	1.95	1.95	1.95	1.96	2.11	2.13	2.10	1.98
66-67	1.99	2.03	2.10	2.10	2.10	2.17	2.14	2.16	2.21	2.21	2.02	2.07	2.11
67-68	1.90	1.89	1.93	2.03	2.10	2.10	2.07	2.04	1.97	1.91	1.76	1.77	1.96
68-69	1.82	1.91	1.89	1.94	1.93	1.92	1.96	2.00	2.02	2.06	2.09	2.08	1.97
1969-1970	2.08	2.06	2.05	2.06	2.04	1.96	2.00	1.96	2.03	2.09	2.18	2.29	2.07
70-71	2.22	2.12	2.27	2.37	2.35	2.32	2.41	2.46	2.58	2.53	2.25	1.91	2.32
71-72	1.80	1.90	2.06	2.06	2.07	2.07	2.09	2.08	2.09	2.11	2.05	2.21	2.05
72-73	2.17	2.42	2.88	3.03	2.88	2.86	2.83	3.09	3.61	3.93	4.72	4.37	3.24
73-74	4.37	4.31	4.37	4.71	4.99	4.64	4.03	3.84	3.99	5.02	5.79	5.64	4.64
1974-1975	6.32	6.10	5.36	4.95	4.55	4.48	4.64	4.60	4.53	4.82	5.13	4.66	5.01
75-76	4.53	4.36	4.33	4.36	4.47	4.62	4.47	4.49	4.66	4.73	4.29	4.27	4.46
76-77	3.88	3.60	3.77	3.91	3.85	3.75	3.62	3.53	3.28	3.15	2.73	2.78	3.49
77-78	3.05	3.40	3.36	3.37	3.49	3.78	3.92	3.92	3.82	3.54	3.41	3.43	3.54
78-79	3.61	3.67	3.64	3.71	3.73	3.77	3.81	3.92	4.41	4.89	4.44	4.34	4.00
1979-1980	4.42	4.41	4.57	4.21	4.35	4.20	4.09	4.31	4.49	5.36	5.71	5.61	4.65
80-81	5.65	5.91	5.82	5.79	5.52	5.46	5.49	5.38	5.23	5.29	4.58	4.16	5.35
81-82	4.14	4.14	4.29	—	—	—	—	—	—	—	—	—	—

SOURCE: USDA Grain Market News

WHEAT, NO. 2 SOFT RED WINTER, CHICAGO
Price, Dollars Per Bushel

Year	Oct.	Nov.	Dec.	Jan.	Feb.	Mar.	Apr.	May	Jun.	Jul.	Aug.	Sep.	Avg.
1959-1960	1.87	1.90	1.92	1.94	1.96	2.01	2.00	2.03	2.01	2.06	2.11	2.07	1.99
60-61	1.91	1.85	1.88	1.93	1.97	2.02	2.08	2.15	2.14	2.07	1.93	1.88	1.98
61-62	1.89	1.94	1.90	1.98	2.01	2.05	2.09	2.06	2.04	2.08	2.13	2.17	2.03
62-63	2.17	2.15	2.11	2.07	2.05	2.10	2.13	2.13	2.11	2.11	2.16	2.13	2.12
63-64	1.96	1.84	1.83	1.97	2.15	2.17	2.20	2.24	2.21	2.03	2.12	2.03	2.06
1964-1965	1.53	1.43	1.46	1.49	1.52	1.55	1.52	1.53	1.53	1.51	1.49	1.46	1.50
65-66	1.44	1.48	1.55	1.58	1.59	1.66	1.69	1.71	1.71	1.63	1.64	1.66	1.61
66-67	1.79	1.90	1.90	1.86	1.72	1.76	1.80	1.71	1.70	1.80	1.73	1.67	1.78
67-68	1.58	1.50	1.49	1.51	1.52	1.45	1.46	1.49	1.51	1.50	1.41	1.38	1.48
68-69	1.30	1.28	1.22	1.20	1.25	1.32	1.33	1.38	1.36	1.32	1.32	1.33	1.30
1969-1970	1.28	1.30	1.27	1.31	1.36	1.41	1.48	1.49	1.55	1.53	1.55	1.48	1.42
70-71	1.41	1.45	1.52	1.67	1.74	1.77	1.74	1.75	1.74	1.70	1.67	1.61	1.65
71-72	1.64	1.54	1.45	1.45	1.53	1.60	1.71	1.69	1.61	1.62	1.66	1.63	1.59
72-73	1.46	1.53	1.76	2.02	2.11	2.28	2.60	2.65	2.47	2.37	2.45	2.71	2.20
73-74	2.82	3.08	4.75	5.11	4.75	5.47	5.84	6.30	6.50	5.59	4.33	3.48	4.84
1974-1975	3.91	4.40	4.34	4.41	5.03	4.86	4.69	4.02	3.84	3.62	3.63	3.25	4.16
75-76	3.03	3.42	3.82	4.06	3.84	3.49	3.32	3.45	3.78	3.66	3.34	3.30	3.54
76-77	3.47	3.37	3.01	2.89	2.72	2.60	2.66	2.73	2.74	2.63	2.53	2.35	2.81
77-78	2.29	2.20	2.08	2.20	2.27	2.59	2.65	2.69	2.64	2.82	3.11	3.14	2.56
78-79	3.18	3.22	3.32	3.42	3.51	3.68	3.68	3.73	3.88	3.79	3.60	3.86	3.57
1979-1980	4.36	4.39	4.23	4.28	4.30	4.13	4.26	4.36	4.39	4.18	3.96	4.04	4.24
80-81	3.96	4.17	4.21	4.38	4.70	4.92	4.54	4.57	4.34	4.15	4.18	3.80	4.33
81-82	3.60	3.70	3.70	3.87	3.97	4.08	3.86	—	—	—	—	—	—

SOURCE: USDA Grain Market News

WHEAT, NO. 1 HARD WINTER (Ordinary Protein), KANSAS CITY
Price, Dollars Per Bushel

Year	Oct.	Nov.	Dec.	Jan.	Feb.	Mar.	Apr.	May	Jun.	Jul.	Aug.	Sep.	Avg.
1959-1960	1.94	1.89	1.94	1.96	2.01	2.02	2.03	2.04	2.07	2.11	2.08	1.99	2.01
60-61	1.93	1.88	1.93	1.97	1.97	2.00	2.01	2.04	2.04	2.00	1.98	1.93	1.97
61-62	1.93	1.96	2.02	2.04	2.04	2.07	2.07	2.05	2.05	2.09	2.11	2.15	2.05
62-63	2.18	2.20	2.17	2.17	2.19	2.22	2.24	2.25	2.29	2.32	2.37	2.24	2.24
63-64	2.05	1.98	2.03	2.09	2.19	2.19	2.21	2.24	2.22	2.16	2.26	2.20	2.15
1964-1965	1.69	1.57	1.60	1.64	1.66	1.67	1.64	1.62	1.61	1.56	1.53	1.49	1.61
65-66	1.46	1.49	1.57	1.59	1.59	1.61	1.62	1.64	1.63	1.62	1.63	1.71	1.60
66-67	1.88	1.95	1.95	1.92	1.79	1.85	1.86	1.77	1.73	1.82	1.76	1.76	1.84
67-68	1.68	1.61	1.56	1.57	1.59	1.56	1.58	1.60	1.61	1.60	1.54	1.53	1.59
68-69	1.44	1.37	1.35	1.34	1.40	1.42	1.40	1.41	1.40	1.40	1.39	1.39	1.39
1969-1970	1.35	1.28	1.31	1.39	1.43	1.46	1.46	1.46	1.46	1.45	1.47	1.44	1.41
70-71	1.40	1.38	1.47	1.59	1.58	1.59	1.59	1.58	1.58	1.55	1.56	1.61	1.54
71-72	1.63	1.54	1.54	1.53	1.56	1.56	1.58	1.58	1.57	1.58	1.61	1.62	1.57
72-73	1.52	1.58	1.82	2.10	2.15	2.25	2.62	2.67	2.48	2.42	2.51	2.63	2.23
73-74	2.69	2.90	4.67	5.01	4.67	4.78	5.22	5.68	5.82	5.01	4.07	3.59	4.51
1974-1975	4.05	4.36	4.33	4.35	4.94	4.88	4.66	4.15	3.93	3.69	3.66	3.34	4.19
75-76	3.23	3.61	4.12	4.21	4.09	3.71	3.50	3.57	3.81	3.81	3.61	3.57	3.74
76-77	3.75	3.63	3.21	3.01	2.77	2.62	2.64	2.70	2.73	2.63	2.52	2.36	2.88
77-78	2.31	2.35	2.31	2.47	2.56	2.81	2.80	2.82	2.84	3.07	3.21	3.12	2.72
78-79	3.12	3.14	3.14	3.24	3.42	3.48	3.39	3.42	3.50	3.52	3.53	3.64	3.38
1979-1980	4.17	4.34	4.12	4.26	4.39	4.53	4.51	4.33	4.32	4.07	3.90	4.10	4.25
80-81	4.07	4.21	4.31	4.45	4.70	4.89	4.54	4.60	4.47	4.35	4.48	4.36	4.45
81-82	4.24	4.25	4.14	4.19	4.31	4.46	4.35	—	—	—	—	—	—

SOURCE: USDA Grain Market News

OATS, NO. 2 EXTRA HEAVY WHITE, CHICAGO*
Price, Dollars Per Bushel

Year	Oct.	Nov.	Dec.	Jan.	Feb.	Mar.	Apr.	May	Jun.	Jul.	Aug.	Sep.	Avg.
1959-1960	.76	.71	.70	.70	.74	.80	.79	.80	.80	.77	.78	.78	.76
60-61	.69	.73	.69	.66	.65	.62	.66	.69	.69	.64	.66	.70	.67
61-62	.69	.74	.69	.69	.67	.71	.73	.73	.69	.70	.72	.74	.71
62-63	.73	.68	.66	.68	.67	.72	.77	.77	.76	.76	.75	.74	.73
63-64	.65	.70	.68	.71	.71	.70	.73	.75	.70	.68	.68	.67	.70
1964-1965	.75	.65	.69	.71	.72	.73	.76	.79	.74	.74	.78	.76	.74
65-66	.76	.73	.72	.72	.69	.72	.77	.78	.78	.77	.75	.75	.75
66-67	.77	.77	.76	.76	.77	.79	.78	.80	.77	.78	.76	.76	.77
67-68	.76	.75	.74	.73	.74	.74	.78	.81	.83	.80	.80	.81	.77
68-69	.64	.67	.60	.62	.61	.68	.72	.76	.75	.68	.68	.68	.67
1969-1970	.71	.64	.63	.63	.60	.61	.63	.69	.67	.63	.65	.70	.65
70-71	.79	.69	.74	.79	.75	.83	.84	.82	.84	.78	.76	.76	.78
71-72	.77	.71	.69	.69	.74	.76	.78	.79	.79	.76	.70	.75	.74
72-73	1.03	.77	.80	.82	.85	.89	1.01	.96	.95	.92	.98	1.02	.92
73-74	1.55	1.04	1.27	1.30	1.33	1.38	1.49	1.71	1.80	1.63	1.41	1.47	1.45
1974-1975	1.64	1.77	1.74	1.78	1.87	1.90	1.90	1.73	1.76	1.56	1.71	1.75	1.76
75-76	1.77	1.53	1.53	1.47	1.37	1.52	1.55	1.61	1.64	1.59	1.54	1.53	1.55
76-77	1.51	1.65	1.50	1.50	1.53	1.59	1.76	1.86	1.90	1.83	1.82	1.76	1.68
77-78	1.45	1.28	1.13	1.16	1.14	1.36	1.43	1.42	1.43	1.46	1.52	1.52	1.36
78-79	1.62	1.32	1.25	1.26	1.30	1.32	1.37	1.41	1.45	1.42	1.43	1.47	1.39
1979-1980	1.88	1.60	1.42	1.45	1.43	1.52	1.71	1.64	1.65	1.64	1.71	1.83	1.62
80-81	1.88	1.90	1.75	1.84	1.90	2.08	2.22	2.33	2.35	2.31	2.26	2.28	2.09
81-82	2.08	2.29	1.83	1.93	2.09	2.25	—	—	—	—	—	—	—

SOURCE: USDA Grain Market News
*No. 2 Heavy White, beginning November, 1975.

BARLEY NO. 2 OR BETTER FEED, MINNEAPOLIS*
Price, Dollars Per Bushel

Year	Oct.	Nov.	Dec.	Jan.	Feb.	Mar.	Apr.	May	Jun.	Jul.	Aug.	Sep.	Avg.
1959-1960	1.07	1.10	1.04	1.02	1.00	1.03	1.00	1.01	.99	.99	1.00	1.03	1.02
60-61	.99	.93	.95	.90	.95	.90	.91	.92	.95	.95	1.01	1.03	.95
61-62	1.02	1.23	1.21	1.22	1.30	1.28	1.26	1.30	1.23	1.22	1.20	1.15	1.22
62-63	1.15	1.09	1.01	1.01	1.04	1.07	1.06	1.05	1.06	1.07	1.07	1.09	1.06
63-64	1.06	.96	.92	.99	.98	.96	.97	1.00	.96	.96	1.01	1.03	.98
1964-1965	1.01	.97	.96	1.08	1.09	1.10	1.09	1.12	1.15	1.15	1.18	1.22	1.09
65-66	1.21	1.12	1.12	1.16	1.19	1.20	1.20	1.23	1.29	1.28	1.23	1.21	1.20
66-67	1.20	1.20	1.19	1.22	1.23	1.23	1.22	1.21	1.18	1.20	1.21	1.24	1.21
67-68	1.23	1.20	1.16	1.14	1.14	1.13	1.12	1.16	1.15	1.13	1.12	1.14	1.15
68-69	1.10	.99	.92	1.02	1.04	1.02	.98	.99	1.02	1.02	1.04	1.06	1.02
1969-1970	1.02	.98	.87	.94	.95	.96	.96	.95	.95	1.00	1.03	1.08	.97
70-71	1.08	1.01	1.00	1.08	1.16	1.08	1.13	1.16	1.22	1.15	1.13	1.15	1.11
71-72	1.08	1.00	.95	.99	1.04	1.04	1.04	1.07	1.07	1.05	1.06	1.08	1.04
72-73	1.05	.96	.98	1.11	1.10	1.14	1.27	1.34	1.20	1.19	1.25	1.36	1.17
73-74	1.51	1.67	2.12	2.12	2.02	1.80	2.12	2.34	2.51	2.32	1.74	2.10	2.03
1974-1975	2.36	2.36	2.69	2.48	3.07	3.17	2.89	2.82	2.59	2.26	2.24	2.05	2.58
75-76	1.67	2.04	2.77	3.00	2.83	2.42	2.23	2.11	2.26	2.36	2.39	2.50	2.38
76-77	2.62	2.45	2.48	2.68	2.46	2.21	2.05	2.20	2.35	2.29	2.28	2.13	2.35
77-78	1.76	1.63	1.50	1.58	1.66	1.65	1.65	1.65	1.65	1.66	1.91	1.90	1.68
78-79	1.84	1.71	1.68	1.77	1.81	1.88	1.79	1.71	1.69	1.86	1.89	1.96	1.80
1979-1980	2.16	2.39	2.15	2.22	2.34	2.11	2.15	2.09	2.04	2.06	2.12	2.09	2.16
80-81	2.15	2.48	2.39	2.43	2.77	3.03	2.75	2.81	2.90	2.63	2.51	2.39	2.60
81-82	2.09	2.26	2.35	2.21	2.26	2.31	2.05	—	—	—	—	—	—

SOURCE: USDA Grain Market News
*Prior to June 1977, No. 3 or Better Feed Barley.

Appendix C

SOYBEANS, NO. 1 YELLOW, CHICAGO
Price, Dollars Per Bushel

Year	Oct.	Nov.	Dec.	Jan.	Feb.	Mar.	Apr.	May	Jun.	Jul.	Aug.	Sep.	Avg.
1964-1965	2.70	2.73	2.81	2.91	2.96	3.03	3.01	3.04	2.86	2.97	2.89	2.75	2.88
65-66	2.68	2.49	2.54	2.66	2.84	2.91	2.86	2.98	3.08	3.38	3.59	3.73	2.98
66-67	3.19	2.96	2.99	3.00	2.96	2.91	2.91	2.88	2.87	2.90	2.83	2.81	2.93
67-68	2.69	2.60	2.61	2.64	2.69	2.73	2.71	2.71	2.74	2.71	2.71	2.72	2.69
68-69	2.61	2.46	2.53	2.59	2.63	2.64	2.64	2.69	2.72	2.69	2.70	2.61	2.63
1969-1970	2.49	2.38	2.42	2.47	2.55	2.59	2.58	2.64	2.70	2.81	2.90	2.79	2.61
70-71	2.81	2.95	3.00	2.93	3.03	3.06	3.04	2.91	3.03	3.21	3.38	3.29	3.05
71-72	3.12	3.12	3.00	3.08	3.09	3.18	3.37	3.49	3.49	3.47	3.51	3.55	3.29
72-73	3.38	3.33	3.64	4.13	4.49	5.81	6.24	6.53	8.99	10.87	8.60	9.08	6.26
73-74	6.50	5.62	5.65	5.95	6.17	6.39	6.23	5.56	5.42	5.47	6.97	7.55	6.12
1974-1975	7.57	8.33	7.58	7.28	6.33	5.68	5.56	5.76	5.23	5.15	5.58	5.97	6.34
75-76	5.55	4.97	4.70	4.59	4.65	4.74	4.66	4.71	5.21	6.25	6.64	6.30	5.25
76-77	6.59	6.23	6.58	6.86	7.08	7.25	8.33	9.74	9.50	8.18	6.29	5.66	7.36
77-78	5.21	5.05	5.77	5.87	5.65	5.57	6.53	6.81	7.09	6.79	6.54	6.43	6.11
78-79	6.47	6.76	6.66	6.79	6.85	7.28	7.47	7.30	7.16	7.67	7.49	7.17	7.09
1979-1980	7.04	6.52	6.38	6.40	6.22	6.38	6.06	5.80	6.02	6.13	7.19	7.36	6.46
80-81	7.87	8.06	8.71	7.71	7.49	7.32	7.32	7.72	7.53	7.09	7.28	6.95	7.59
81-82	6.50	6.30	6.30	6.19	—	—	—	—	—	—	—	—	—

SOURCE: USDA Grain Market News

SOYBEAN MEAL, 44% BULK, DECATUR
Price, Dollars Per Ton

Year	Sep.	Oct.	Nov.	Dec.	Jan.	Feb.	Mar.	Apr.	May	Jun.	Jul.	Aug.	Avg.
1965-1966	76.80	70.80	75.75	71.40	78.80	77.30	71.50	75.50	80.30	92.70	97.20	97.90	80.49
66-67	88.40	82.20	78.90	84.60	81.70	79.50	76.60	74.50	73.70	78.10	78.20	78.70	79.59
67-68	79.20	71.80	71.90	73.40	75.10	74.50	75.00	74.60	75.00	79.50	82.80	84.40	76.43
68-69	85.10	78.20	73.50	71.60	69.80	69.90	72.60	73.30	76.10	77.50	77.30	76.90	75.15
1969-1970	72.70	75.40	69.90	82.90	87.50	85.25	71.80	74.60	71.20	74.70	82.90	84.00	77.74
70-71	81.20	77.25	77.90	82.00	80.25	77.50	77.00	74.25	78.25	81.50	84.25	78.75	79.18
71-72	73.25	74.75	73.80	86.00	82.60	84.80	90.90	94.50	95.50	95.00	101.40	101.00	87.79
72-73	107.75	109.00	123.20	174.00	188.40	218.75	199.90	203.25	314.60	412.50	311.20	285.00	229.00
73-74	208.10	159.60	167.00	192.00	172.00	160.00	147.10	117.20	109.25	100.00	138.10	155.90	152.19
1974-1975	138.10	168.20	141.00	143.40	129.20	117.25	117.75	122.00	118.50	120.90	124.00	134.40	131.23
75-76	133.70	125.90	119.90	125.10	128.25	132.60	127.90	127.10	152.25	187.90	193.90	173.30	143.98
76-77	179.20	169.60	181.20	197.60	207.00	211.00	226.20	275.60	258.25	225.30	162.00	140.30	202.77
77-78	143.60	135.00	161.70	160.10	162.20	152.90	171.90	173.00	177.40	169.75	172.00	162.90	161.87
78-79	163.90	176.80	177.10	188.75	184.90	190.90	194.50	191.10	188.00	209.60	201.60	188.90	188.00
1979-1980	188.60	181.40	183.10	188.00	180.20	174.25	164.60	154.20	166.50	160.90	187.90	207.40	178.09
80-81	234.50	246.40	261.40	223.70	223.50	212.50	210.40	222.00	221.00	200.90	204.10	202.25	221.89
81-82	190.00	180.75	178.40	187.50	—	—	—	—	—	—	—	—	—

SOURCE: USDA Feed Market News

Appendix C

900-1,100 LB. CHOICE STEERS, OMAHA
Price, Dollars Per Cwt.

Year	Sep.	Oct.	Nov.	Dec.	Jan.	Feb.	Mar.	Apr.	May	Jun.	Jul.	Aug.	Avg.
1961	26.74	26.15	25.52	24.87	23.22	22.42	22.34	23.87	23.78	23.96	24.83	25.51	24.43
62	25.76	25.95	26.36	26.81	25.50	25.07	25.68	27.41	28.83	28.46	29.12	28.12	26.92
63	26.49	24.47	22.88	23.10	22.27	22.52	24.57	24.40	23.98	23.74	22.92	21.64	23.58
64	22.20	21.36	21.38	20.88	20.28	21.33	22.69	24.23	24.75	23.66	23.45	22.79	22.42
1965	22.98	22.53	23.17	24.38	26.00	26.69	26.05	26.28	26.19	25.33	24.93	25.38	24.99
66	25.91	27.16	28.25	26.94	25.94	25.25	25.27	25.76	25.54	24.70	23.92	23.92	25.71
67	24.62	24.32	23.92	23.89	24.75	25.45	26.18	26.57	26.63	25.98	25.34	25.48	25.26
68	25.69	26.37	26.60	26.50	26.30	26.39	27.37	27.54	27.27	27.05	27.38	27.94	26.87
69	27.74	27.50	28.81	30.14	32.79	33.63	31.29	30.04	28.66	27.60	27.44	27.77	29.45
1970	28.38	29.30	30.99	30.79	29.57	30.36	31.12	30.09	29.21	28.47	27.22	26.82	29.36
71	29.10	32.18	31.89	32.41	32.86	32.35	32.44	33.10	32.58	32.23	33.30	34.28	32.39
72	35.63	36.32	35.17	34.52	35.70	37.91	38.38	35.70	34.92	34.92	33.59	36.85	35.80
73	40.65	43.55	45.65	45.03	45.74	46.76	47.66	52.94	45.12	41.92	40.14	39.36	44.54
74	47.14	46.38	42.85	41.54	40.52	37.98	43.72	46.62	41.38	39.64	37.72	37.20	41.89
1975	36.34	34.74	36.08	42.80	49.48	51.82	50.21	46.80	48.91	47.90	45.23	45.01	44.61
76	41.18	38.80	36.14	43.12	40.62	40.52	37.92	37.02	36.97	37.88	39.15	39.96	39.11
77	38.38	37.98	37.28	40.08	41.98	40.24	40.94	40.11	40.35	42.29	41.83	43.13	40.38
78	43.62	45.02	48.66	52.52	57.28	55.38	54.59	52.40	54.26	54.93	53.82	55.54	52.34
79	60.35	64.88	71.04	75.00	73.99	68.53	67.06	62.74	67.84	65.81	67.00	68.72	67.75
1980	66.32	67.44	66.88	63.07	64.58	66.29	70.47	73.31	69.68	67.18	65.05	64.29	67.05
81	63.08	61.50	61.40	64.92	66.86	68.26	67.86	66.37	65.37	61.45	59.81	59.46	63.86

SOURCE: USDA Livestock Market News.

900-1,100 LB. GOOD SLAUGHTER CATTLE, OMAHA
Price, Dollars Per Cwt.

Year	Sep.	Oct.	Nov.	Dec.	Jan.	Feb.	Mar.	Apr.	May	Jun.	Jul.	Aug.	Avg.
1961	24.31	23.87	23.34	22.80	21.30	20.88	20.92	22.43	22.43	22.68	23.36	23.66	22.66
62	23.52	23.73	23.72	24.08	23.26	22.93	23.53	24.67	25.86	26.05	26.58	25.71	24.22
63	24.17	22.62	21.30	21.42	20.65	20.99	22.80	22.82	22.59	22.25	21.10	19.54	21.86
64	20.18	19.43	19.49	19.08	18.30	19.04	20.47	22.00	22.67	21.58	21.06	20.22	20.29
1965	20.56	20.27	20.72	21.90	23.18	24.09	23.78	24.14	23.80	23.00	22.74	23.06	22.60
66	23.68	25.02	25.89	24.93	24.02	23.63	23.71	24.02	24.04	23.53	22.83	22.76	24.00
67	23.42	23.03	22.60	22.28	23.09	24.02	24.88	25.31	25.05	24.46	23.45	23.35	23.74
68	23.24	24.11	24.52	24.42	24.44	24.62	25.48	25.77	25.40	24.87	25.14	25.44	24.79
69	25.15	25.28	26.40	27.47	29.86	30.91	29.34	28.00	26.32	25.51	25.63	25.88	27.14
1970	26.03	27.06	28.26	28.48	27.38	27.77	28.49	27.60	26.72	26.29	25.53	24.93	27.05
71	26.53	29.43	29.24	29.77	29.92	29.46	29.28	29.88	29.64	29.65	30.66	31.42	29.58
72	32.62	33.36	32.83	32.34	33.23	34.73	35.31	33.50	32.89	33.33	32.34	33.45	33.33
73	37.61	40.34	42.79	42.46	43.31	44.06	44.83	50.31	43.32	39.92	38.29	37.77	42.09
74	44.87	43.78	40.08	39.12	37.54	33.54	38.43	41.91	38.26	37.00	35.55	34.77	38.71
1975	33.09	31.43	32.93	38.92	44.00	45.85	43.34	39.52	41.09	41.39	41.19	40.65	39.45
76	37.75	36.14	33.77	39.78	38.26	37.88	34.72	33.52	33.28	34.10	35.12	36.11	35.87
77	34.81	34.75	34.34	36.84	38.25	36.77	37.02	36.24	36.24	37.89	37.93	39.34	36.70
78	39.81	40.70	44.30	47.70	51.96	50.60	50.06	48.59	50.02	50.67	49.97	51.40	47.98
79	56.01	61.18	66.46	70.15	69.86	64.55	61.31	57.48	62.30	61.27	62.35	63.66	63.05
1980	61.89	62.54	62.85	59.06	60.25	61.04	63.79	65.44	63.52	62.77	61.53	61.28	62.16
81	59.71	58.48	58.62	60.33	61.76	62.43	62.95	61.60	60.93	58.36	57.21	55.74	59.84

SOURCE: USDA Livestock Market News.

Appendix C

600-700 LB.* CHOICE FEEDER STEERS, KANSAS CITY
Price, Dollars Per Cwt.

Year	Sep.	Oct.	Nov.	Dec.	Jan.	Feb.	Mar.	Apr.	May	Jun.	Jul.	Aug.	Avg.
1960	26.21	26.94	28.61	29.06	28.18	26.64	25.98	25.20	24.30	24.20	25.28	25.74	26.36
61	25.86	26.28	26.51	26.81	26.25	25.62	24.98	25.66	25.40	24.35	25.92	25.68	25.86
62	25.34	26.03	26.52	26.68	26.18	26.31	26.87	27.25	27.86	28.05	28.80	28.15	27.00
63	27.24	26.48	26.13	26.62	26.00	26.38	26.85	26.31	25.42	24.63	24.19	23.15	25.78
64	23.21	22.64	23.32	22.74	21.54	21.74	21.36	21.30	21.74	21.24	21.25	20.90	21.92
1965	21.43	21.92	22.70	23.66	25.18	25.85	25.44	24.72	24.68	24.32	24.43	25.13	24.12
66	26.29	28.12	29.64	28.28	28.45	27.56	26.70	27.42	27.51	27.07	26.35	25.80	27.43
67	26.16	26.28	26.44	26.39	27.04	27.34	27.68	27.84	26.74	26.38	25.89	26.03	26.68
68	25.82	26.94	27.60	28.64	28.90	29.69	29.75	28.40	27.74	27.09	28.11	28.42	27.92
69	28.30	29.04	30.34	32.64	35.18	35.74	32.46	31.76	31.29	31.15	31.12	32.38	31.78
1970	32.83	34.44	35.85	35.01	35.00	34.92	34.54	33.28	32.86	32.66	31.79	31.28	33.70
71	32.20	34.24	34.26	34.46	34.52	34.52	34.36	35.18	34.97	35.64	36.88	37.20	34.87
72	37.92	38.86	38.64	38.54	40.43	41.94	42.02	42.07	43.29	44.15	43.17	45.77	41.40
73	47.33	50.98	54.01	51.82	54.55	54.85	56.49	62.40	55.06	51.86	51.02	47.71	53.17
74	50.58	47.95	44.81	44.15	40.14	35.10	36.72	36.70	30.49	30.94	28.71	28.27	37.88
1975	26.45	26.96	28.75	31.69	35.50	36.81	34.70	34.34	37.59	38.09	38.26	37.83	33.91
76	37.46	40.42	39.69	44.62	44.21	42.83	39.18	38.94	36.18	36.72	36.26	36.23	39.40
77	36.49	37.86	38.95	41.69	41.72	39.90	40.64	41.99	40.85	40.82	39.94	41.33	40.18
78	44.07	47.60	52.00	55.08	60.36	58.56	60.60	63.08	64.46	64.88	64.85	69.83	58.78
79	75.29	80.26	87.25	89.98	88.32	82.19	82.48	79.31	85.34	81.29	82.44	82.80	83.08
1980	80.52	83.18	77.62	69.87	69.18	72.25	73.32	76.40	77.60	76.05	73.75	72.98	75.23
81	72.58	70.40	68.80	68.94	65.79	65.12	63.22	65.75	66.16	64.07	64.02	61.18	66.34

*Simple average of Choice price quotations, 600 to 700 pound weights 1972 to present; 500 to 800 pounds 1960 through 1965; 550 to 750 pounds 1966 through 1971.

400-500 LB.* CHOICE STEER CALVES, KANSAS CITY
Price, Dollars Per Cwt.

Year	Sep.	Oct.	Nov.	Dec.	Jan.	Feb.	Mar.	Apr.	May	Jun.	Jul.	Aug.	Avg.
1960	27.18	29.28	30.44	30.01	29.52	28.52	27.44	25.97	25.50	26.04	27.56	27.05	27.88
61	27.44	27.69	28.11	28.32	28.35	27.58	26.96	27.72	27.86	27.73	28.00	27.45	27.77
62	25.86	26.76	27.14	27.62	27.13	27.19	27.63	27.63	28.56	28.94	29.24	28.62	27.69
63	28.09	28.30	27.78	27.94	27.47	27.82	28.32	26.97	26.32	25.62	25.40	24.20	27.02
64	24.50	24.58	24.75	23.72	22.74	22.60	21.86	21.32	21.56	21.13	21.24	20.80	22.57
1965	21.30	21.44	22.20	23.49	24.12	24.58	24.40	23.93	24.62	24.61	24.46	25.30	23.70
66	26.38	28.53	29.86	28.92	29.46	28.78	27.42	28.23	28.90	28.57	27.94	27.54	28.38
67	27.74	27.70	27.84	27.73	28.60	28.62	28.44	29.00	28.28	27.98	27.00	27.08	28.00
68	28.69	29.52	30.46	31.04	32.95	32.54	32.50	32.10	31.42	30.89	31.50	31.50	31.26
69	31.15	32.26	34.39	36.74	38.26	38.62	35.79	35.66	35.91	35.77	35.21	35.60	35.45
1970	36.82	38.55	39.74	39.40	40.61	41.48	41.24	39.50	38.66	37.60	36.08	35.49	38.76
71	36.18	38.48	38.17	38.62	39.19	39.15	39.10	39.36	39.33	39.95	41.70	41.81	39.25
72	41.50	43.94	44.69	45.16	46.67	47.32	47.10	48.32	48.70	49.81	48.37	49.90	46.79
73	51.95	56.10	62.72	60.42	62.59	62.42	64.40	72.52	62.80	59.46	56.42	52.59	60.36
74	54.66	54.45	54.02	50.30	45.48	39.96	37.72	36.84	32.40	30.47	27.31	26.54	40.85
1975	25.55	26.29	29.14	31.45	34.66	35.82	32.58	31.70	35.15	36.04	36.26	35.94	32.55
76	37.47	41.40	44.01	47.01	47.58	44.81	40.64	41.13	38.18	39.81	38.46	38.22	41.56
77	37.99	41.69	44.36	45.72	45.20	42.46	43.14	45.27	46.06	44.48	42.95	43.84	43.60
78	46.15	51.78	57.64	61.10	68.17	67.00	68.42	71.61	74.51	72.30	73.03	78.27	65.83
79	85.19	94.70	101.04	105.62	106.88	96.38	98.72	98.39	104.29	94.04	92.99	93.84	97.66
1980	91.64	98.08	90.39	83.99	81.00	79.65	77.12	83.65	87.90	84.32	80.57	77.38	84.64
81	77.45	77.30	77.65	77.45	72.50	72.02	69.04	70.95	71.52	66.56	67.05	64.00	71.96

SOURCE: USDA Livestock Market News.

*Good and Choice Grade prior to 1968; and 300 to 500 lbs. prior to 1972.

Appendix C

SLAUGHTER BARROWS & GILTS, AVERAGE 7 MARKETS
Price, Dollars Per Cwt.

Year	Sep.	Oct.	Nov.	Dec.	Jan.	Feb.	Mar.	Apr.	May	Jun.	Jul.	Aug.	Avg.
1961	17.33	18.13	17.53	17.04	16.37	16.60	17.87	18.33	18.18	16.85	15.97	16.70	17.24
62	16.98	16.69	16.31	15.81	15.51	16.87	18.30	18.50	18.82	16.87	16.50	16.16	16.94
63	15.65	15.14	14.07	13.78	15.01	17.10	18.44	17.55	15.89	15.47	14.47	14.21	15.56
64	14.70	14.70	14.48	14.16	14.84	15.83	17.11	17.05	16.76	15.39	14.43	15.55	15.42
1965	16.06	17.01	16.98	17.63	20.29	23.38	24.27	24.67	22.92	23.36	24.33	28.07	21.58
66	27.93	27.80	24.41	22.26	23.16	24.72	25.09	25.75	23.16	21.57	19.87	19.67	23.78
67	19.46	19.38	18.43	17.62	21.83	22.29	22.58	21.05	19.46	18.16	17.36	17.29	19.58
68	18.31	19.41	19.07	19.00	18.88	20.43	21.48	20.08	19.93	18.29	17.92	18.76	19.30
69	19.77	20.41	20.69	20.38	23.14	25.16	26.05	26.91	25.94	25.53	25.77	26.93	23.89
1970	27.40	28.23	25.94	24.02	23.53	24.04	25.13	22.12	20.35	17.91	15.69	15.67	21.95
71	16.25	19.43	17.13	16.19	17.43	18.38	19.84	19.05	18.91	19.80	19.39	20.85	18.45
72	24.84	25.61	23.56	22.89	25.32	26.74	28.57	28.86	29.10	28.09	27.79	30.78	26.67
73	32.51	36.23	38.13	35.56	35.89	38.55	46.64	56.68	43.79	42.12	40.97	39.79	40.27
74	40.59	39.73	34.88	30.52	26.09	27.40	36.31	37.67	35.79	38.90	38.34	39.93	35.12
1975	38.93	39.61	39.52	40.69	46.44	51.19	57.17	58.10	61.23	58.52	49.74	48.33	48.32
76	48.40	48.85	46.71	47.89	48.89	50.80	48.26	44.00	39.39	32.66	32.05	38.05	43.11
77	39.52	40.18	37.53	36.97	41.79	43.86	45.76	44.38	41.40	40.83	39.33	43.99	41.07
78	45.99	48.83	47.50	46.04	49.17	48.31	46.78	48.77	50.00	52.23	48.36	49.57	48.49
79	52.13	54.42	49.38	45.04	43.79	40.29	38.73	38.21	38.62	34.74	36.01	38.45	42.06
1980	37.49	37.51	33.94	28.86	29.50	35.17	43.16	48.30	47.24	48.15	46.38	44.80	39.48
81	41.42	42.43	39.54	39.79	42.05	49.04	50.66	50.92	49.68	45.62	42.20	39.94	44.44

SOURCE: USDA Livestock Market News.

FEEDER PIG PRICES*
Price, Dollars Per Cwt.

Year	Sep.	Oct.	Nov.	Dec.	Jan.	Feb.	Mar.	Apr.	May	Jun.	Jul.	Aug.	Avg.
1961	17.70	18.80	18.40	18.20	17.10	16.80	17.60	18.30	18.70	17.50	16.80	17.30	17.80
62	17.70	17.50	17.30	16.80	16.80	17.70	18.50	19.20	20.30	18.90	18.80	18.60	18.20
63	18.40	17.90	16.90	16.90	17.90	16.00	18.30	17.80	16.60	16.40	15.50	15.00	17.00
64	15.70	15.50	15.30	15.20	16.70	17.30	18.30	18.00	18.40	17.30	16.10	16.90	16.70
1965	17.50	18.60	18.50	18.80	21.90	24.70	32.70	34.10	32.90	35.80	36.60	40.00	35.40†
66	46.40	46.40	45.00	44.00	42.50	39.60	38.10	39.60	38.40	36.30	35.60	34.80	40.55
67	33.10	33.70	33.50	33.20	34.00	33.30	34.20	36.00	36.00	33.60	31.20	30.60	33.53
68	30.50	32.90	33.60	34.90	33.40	33.50	33.70	34.50	35.00	33.10	30.90	30.00	33.00
69	31.10	32.00	35.00	37.50	39.50	39.50	40.00	42.00	42.50	43.10	43.30	44.50	39.17
1970	48.10	57.00	57.00	55.60	50.00	41.00	43.30	40.00	40.00	31.00	27.00	24.50	42.90
71	22.90	28.50	31.00	28.70	29.70	27.50	28.90	29.30	29.00	32.50	32.20	35.50	29.60
72	43.70	47.60	50.60	50.10	51.70	47.00	52.50	53.40	57.10	54.30	51.50	49.70	50.80
73	54.60	65.70	78.00	70.00	72.80	62.10	82.10	90.00	78.80	73.90	76.20	67.90	72.20
74	86.75	83.13	81.25	80.48	55.25	43.28	53.75	47.25	46.88	60.25	52.83	64.38	62.96
1975	75.25	89.38	99.38	107.63	110.00	111.63	110.25	116.88	149.53	141.38	122.35	110.48	112.01
76	115.73	124.60	119.80	128.20	111.43	97.13	76.13	77.55	69.23	54.38	52.93	60.10	90.60
77	59.60	83.10	96.45	103.73	102.28	87.95	92.25	99.60	91.15	87.35	80.80	75.95	88.35
78	89.70	110.30	129.08	136.43	135.20	113.40	113.03	127.08	132.28	129.60	117.53	111.23	120.41
79	105.65	131.35	132.85	127.10	102.23	75.28	60.35	63.83	73.25	57.75	65.88	65.20	88.36
1980	73.80	87.10	74.93	59.65	50.93	55.60	61.20	83.65	83.13	94.38	93.00	94.35	75.98
81	78.75	92.15	90.83	98.33	90.25	94.70	82.20	96.38	100.58	85.50	79.70	68.60	88.16

SOURCE: USDA Agricultural Prices and Livestock and Meat Situation, USDA.

*1961 through June 1965 derived from price reports on 100 to 160 lb. feeder pigs in Sioux City and St. Paul markets; beginning July 1965, based on data derived from reports in 15 states on prices paid for pigs weighing 40 to 60 lbs.; from January 1966 through 1973, based on data for 27 states; beginning January 1974, based on prices for 40 to 50 lb. pigs in Southern Missouri.

†July-December average.

Appendix C

CHOICE SLAUGHTER LAMBS, SAN ANGELO
Price, Dollars Per Cwt.

Year	Sep.	Oct.	Nov.	Dec.	Jan.	Feb.	Mar.	Apr.	May	Jun.	Jul.	Aug.	Avg.
1967	21.50	19.56	22.15	24.25	25.60	24.34	23.56	22.25	21.90	22.19	22.60	23.13	22.75
68	22.94	24.19	26.88	28.80	27.40	26.13	25.25	23.81	25.38	25.75	26.31	25.33	25.71
69	25.56	28.00	30.69	31.05	29.44	29.00	29.05	28.19	28.00	28.35	28.62	28.50	28.79
1970	28.81	28.06	31.06	28.35	27.75	27.41	27.00	27.06	26.85	27.19	25.81	24.00	27.45
71	24.06	24.12	28.05	29.06	29.69	30.05	29.06	28.12	25.70	25.06	26.00	25.49	27.27
72	27.19	28.69	32.00	32.12	33.75	32.88	33.31	31.92	29.44	28.75	28.90	30.42	30.49
73	35.06	37.08	43.65	39.50	36.70	38.46	37.31	39.42	—	35.50	38.13	38.33	38.13
74	39.50	40.75	40.38	42.25	47.15	46.25	37.94	42.50	36.12	36.44	37.58	39.25	40.51
1975	38.25	39.31	45.88	46.65	47.62	46.06	45.25	40.75	43.50	44.50	46.83	48.75	44.45
76	49.25	49.00	56.25	62.95	62.12	50.81	47.81	39.92	42.88	44.25	45.50	47.69	49.87
77	52.00	51.25	55.70	59.62	55.56	52.10	50.42	51.46	53.75	55.69	55.06	58.75	54.28
78	61.44	64.88	76.69	73.12	72.85	61.44	60.62	59.70	62.88	62.50	62.00	65.83	65.33
79	73.80	69.12	64.00	78.62	73.20	68.83	65.83	62.65	67.75	66.50	66.63	68.12	68.75
1980	67.40	66.31	68.02	65.50	61.75	69.00	69.00	69.25	68.25	66.19	—	61.75	66.64
81	57.50	57.75	56.75	63.20	65.38	67.76	64.38	61.62	52.30	54.25	48.50	52.00	58.45

SOURCE: USDA Livestock Market News.

CHOICE FEEDER LAMBS, SAN ANGELO
Price, Dollars Per Cwt.

Year	Sep.	Oct.	Nov.	Dec.	Jan.	Feb.	Mar.	Apr.	May	Jun.	Jul.	Aug.	Avg.
1967	21.62	20.00	20.10	20.19	22.05	21.12	20.86	20.95	21.56	21.67	22.00	23.08	21.27
68	22.35	23.75	24.81	27.50	24.30	22.88	22.90	22.88	23.81	24.30	24.75	25.58	24.15
69	26.12	27.62	30.69	29.55	26.88	25.81	26.57	26.56	29.00	28.70	29.81	29.00	28.03
1970	29.81	29.50	30.88	28.50	27.12	26.25	25.25	25.44	26.60	26.19	24.56	23.50	26.96
71	24.00	24.75	28.05	27.44	26.76	25.65	24.69	25.75	24.95	25.19	26.44	26.69	25.86
72	27.69	28.38	32.25	32.00	32.55	29.81	29.88	29.70	29.50	29.50	30.45	31.33	30.26
73	33.94	37.44	40.10	40.75	36.05	35.31	34.50	38.40	35.06	35.50	36.56	37.75	36.78
74	39.55	38.12	40.88	41.56	42.00	37.08	31.25	32.58	30.75	31.75	36.25	36.42	36.52
1975	34.12	35.31	43.50	43.65	43.00	39.69	40.25	38.75	41.25	42.62	46.33	48.38	41.40
76	48.38	49.69	56.30	62.71	59.56	48.56	49.38	45.94	46.65	47.31	49.67	51.19	51.28
77	53.56	54.81	56.25	59.19	51.38	46.15	47.33	50.75	54.31	55.75	63.19	68.83	55.12
78	67.00	76.31	80.85	73.33	75.05	68.75	69.33	76.10	80.38	78.00	79.88	82.33	75.61
79	86.30	84.50	84.25	89.75	76.15	71.12	70.25	71.00	74.25	70.00	73.00	79.83	77.53
1980	77.88	79.00	70.50	64.00	57.42	65.38	65.38	65.44	67.62	69.75	68.67	69.33	68.36
81	61.75	62.25	59.00	61.30	60.69	62.92	56.62	54.56	51.40	51.62	49.33	51.08	56.88

SOURCE: USDA Livestock Market News.

Index

Terms listed in Appendix A (Hedger's Glossary) are not included here.

A

advisory services, commercial   132-3
Agricultural Outlook   209
assets and liabilities   256
auction markets   138
auctions, special   139

B

bar chart analysis   229
bar charts   226, 229-46
bargaining associations   141
barley, historical prices table   274
basis   96-102
   chart development for   99-101
   chart interpretation for   101-2
   current data for   99
   definition of   96, 99
   historical data for   99
basis, local   96-7
bearish hook reversal   236
bearish key reversal   236
bearish signals, an example of   228
bear market   227
bull market, major, early stages   226-7
bear move   102
bears   91
beef calf crop chart   136
beef cattle, live, contract regulations, Chicago Mercantile Exchange   263-4
beef cattle, live, short hedge on   182-3
beef consumption trend   202-3
beef demand, seasonality of   214
beef steers, cost of gain   166-7
benchmark reports   106-8
bottom in the making, an example of   228
breakaway gap   237-8
brokerage fee, livestock   178
broker   88
   fees of   93
   table showing commissions of   95
   selection of   110-2
bullish hook reversal   236
bullish key reversal   236
bullish signals, an example of   228
bull market   103
bull move   102
bulls   91

C

call price   132
calves, Choice steer, 400-500 pound, table   280
carcass grade and yield selling   146-8
carcass weight selling   146
cash contracts   75-85
cash-flow breakeven   27-8
cash forward sales contracts   75-7
cattle and calves data from USDA   206
"Cattle and Calves on Feed"   208
cattle
   cyclical price and supply tendencies of   218-20
   par weight   193
cattle delivery points   193
"Cattle, Hogs and Sheep Slaughtered by Class"   207
"Cattle Inventory"   208
cattle, live slaughter, delivery months for   190-1
cattle market discounts   163
cattle marketing, formula for   168-9
cattle on feed data from USDA   206
cattle on U.S. farms by cycles, table   220
cattle price forecasting   222-4
cattle selling, by carcass grade and yield   146-7
cattle selling, carcass vs. live   148-9
cattle yield grades   163
channel lines   234
chart formations, geometrical   239-46
chartists   225, 232
Chicago Mercantile Exchange   190-2, 194, 263
   as source of livestocks futures report   208
Chicago Mid-America Exchange   191-2, 194, 263
Choice feeder lambs, historical prices table   284
Choice feeder steers, 600-700 pounds, table   279
Choice slaughter lambs, table   283
Choice steer calves, 400-500 pound, table   280
Choice steers, 900-1,100 pounds, table   277
commercial advisory services   132-3, 210
commodity exchanges   88-9
commodity markets   2, 13, 88
   variability of   2
commodity prices   2
computerized marketing   140
"Confirmed Direct Sales"   207
consumer demand for livestock products   203, 205
continuation chart   230
contracts, cash   75-85
   vs. hedging with futures   83-4
contracts, cash forward sales   75-7
contracts, deferred payment   82-3
contracts, deferred pricing   79-82
contracts, fixed basis   79
contracts, futures, how they work   87-8
contracts, offsetting   88, 191
contracts, service charge for   79-82
cooperative selling and shipping associations   139
corn
   computing shrink for   47-8
   drying and conditioning   40-1
   historical prices table   269
   local basis for   98
   sample hedging problems   112-4
   storing of   40-1
   when to sell   41-3
corn, economics of drying   46-58
corn feed purchase, hedging of   109-10
Corn Husker Economics   209
corn moisture discounts   48

corn price prospects 131
corn, seasonal price index 44
country commission firm or feedlot marketing 139
country dealers 138
cow-calf production, effect of feed on location 135
cow herd price expectations 221
Crop Production Report 208
crop reports, monthly, from USDA and private forecasts 123-4
cycles in livestock supply 201

D

debt to asset ratio 26
deferred payment contracts 82-3
deferred pricing contracts 79-82
double bottoms 246
double tops 246

E

electronic auction marketing 140
elevators, *see* grain elevators
"Estimated Federally Inspected Slaughter" 207
exchanges, commodity 88-9
exhaustion gap 237-8
export demand indicators 126-7

F

farm commodities, historical prices for 268-84
Farmline 209
fed cattle marketings chart 137
fed cattle prices, seasonality of 214
feeder cattle 192-3
feeder cattle contract, limitations of 193
feeder cattle contract regulations, Chicago Mercantile Exchange 266-7
feeder cattle hedge, short 185-7
feeder cattle, hedging purchases of 192-3
feeder cattle marketing
  channels 141
  seasonality of 213-4
Feeder Lamb Summary 208
feeder pig historical prices table 282
feeder pig marketing channels 141
feedgrain exporting countries 127-8
feed purchases, hedging of 109-110
fill shrink 155
fixed basis contracts 79
flags 239
fundamental analysis 225
futures contracts, how they work 87-8
futures markets, price determination in 89-90
futures price movement 102-3
futures prices as forecasts 103-4
futures traders 90-3
futures trading
  costs of 93-6
  tax treatment of 104

G

gaps 236-8
Good grade steers 191
Good slaughter cattle, 900-1,100 pound, table 278

government policy, effect on livestock 205
grain
  demand for U.S. production of 8-11
  drying and conditioning of 40-1
  figuring local basis of 97-8
  for export 8
  futures markets for 87-119
  projected season average farm prices of 130-1
  quarterly stocks reports of 124
grain balance sheets 128-32
grain elevators 12-3, 102
grain exporting and importing countries 127-8
grain harvest pricing 34-5
grain market, analysis of information on 128-33
grain marketing alternatives, table 37
grain marketing objectives 17-37
grain marketing plan 22-34
grain marketing system 7-16
grain marketing tools 34-7
Grain Market News, a USDA publication 125
grain markets 121-33
  price fluctuations in 121
  information sources on 121-2
grain postharvest pricing 35-6
grain preharvest pricing 36
grain price breakeven levels 32-3
grain price outlook 33-4
grain price patterns, seasonal 33
grain prices, seasonality of 43-5
grain pricing 13, 15-6
  when to price 20-2
grain production characteristics 7-8
grain production hedge 104-5
grain sorghum, historical prices table 270
grain storage 39-73
grain storage return, probability of 45
grain, stored, price protection for 108
grain supplies, U.S., estimates of 122-6

H

head-and-shoulders 244
hedge, lifting of 93, 188-90
hedge, long, on feeder cattle 187-8
hedge on livestock, when to lift 196
hedge, short, on feeder cattle 185-7
hedge, short, on live beef cattle 182-3
hedge, short, on live hogs 183-5
hedge, storage 108
hedgers 92-3
  definition of 90
hedging 39
  how to 104-10
hedging feeder cattle 192-3
hedging feed purchases 109-10
hedging Good grade steers 191
hedging heifers 191
Hedging Matrix 114-5
hedging of non-par cattle 192
hedging, selective 39
hedging vs. cash contracts 83-4
"Hide, Pelts and Variety Meat Prices" 207
hog delivery limitations 192
hog futures contracts 191-2

INDEX

hog number cycles 220
hog packers 148
hog price expectations and forecasting 221-4
hog prices, seasonal index for 216
hog production, effect of feed on location of 135
hogs
   contract sizes for 191-2
   cost of gain 166
   market discounts for 163
   marketing formula for 167-8
hogs and pigs data from USDA 206
"Hogs and Pigs Report" 208
hog selling by carcass weight and yield 147-8
hog selling, carcass vs. live 148
hogs, live, contract regulations,
      Chicago Mercantile Exchange 264-5
hogs, live, short hedge on 183-5
hook reversal 236
hotlines 111

I

"Import and Export Volume" 207
import/export prospects for livestock 210
initial margin 94
interest costs, effect on livestock price 202-3
Iowa Farm Outlook 209

K

key reversal 234, 236, 248

L

lamb crop and marketings, seasonality of 214
lambs, Choice feeder, historical prices table 284
lambs, Choice slaughter, historical prices table 283
"Lambs on Feed" 208
liabilities and assets 25-6
live beef cattle contract regulations,
      Chicago Mercantile Exchange 263-4
"Live Feeder and Slaughter Prices" 207
live hog contract regulations,
      Chicago Mercantile Exchange 264-5
live sort and select 145
Livestock and Meat Situation 209
livestock basis 194-9
livestock brokerage fee 178
livestock carcass grade and weight selling 142
livestock, choosing to hedge 179-80
livestock, cost of gain 166-7
livestock data series 207-9
livestock data sources, private 206
livestock-delivery marketing costs 177-8
livestock delivery point discount 178
livestock, forward pricing of 170-1
livestock futures contract specifications 263-7
livestock futures markets
   cash and futures positions in 174
   cash basis in 174
   characteristics of 173-5
   hedging in 174-6

localized futures prices vs. basis 180-1
localizing factors for 177-9
   price-quality relationships in 175
   vs. those for grains 181
livestock hedges, limitations of 190-4
livestock hedging 181-90
   vs. forward pricing 171
livestock import/export prospects 210
livestock, market advisory services for 210
livestock market discounts 163
livestock market outlet table 143
livestock marketing 135-50
livestock marketing channels and patterns 137-44
livestock marketing, developing a plan 151-72
livestock marketing formulas 167-9
livestock marketing methods 144-9
livestock marketing's future 150
livestock marketing strategy of timing 158-69
livestock market premiums 163, 166
livestock market regulations 149-50
livestock market risk 169-70
livestock markets 201-24
livestock market, selection of 153-8
livestock market shrink 154-5
Livestock Meat and Wool Market News 207
livestock price expectations 221-4
livestock price forecasting 224
livestock price patterns and cycles 159-62
livestock pricing plan 169-72
livestock production 205-10
   location of 135
livestock products, demand for 203, 205
livestock publications 207-9
livestock quality discount 178
livestock, seasonal supply and price patterns 213-6
livestock, seasonal price index tables 215-6
livestock shrink adjustment 177
livestock, slaughter, marketing patterns 141-4
livestock slaughter, location of 135, 137
"Livestock Slaughter Reports" 208
livestock sorting and selecting 157
livestock statistics, interpretation of 210-2
livestock supply 201-3
livestock supply data from USDA 206
livestock supply forecasting 224
livestock transportation costs 154, 177
liveweight marketing 144-5
local basis 96-7
local markets and concentration yards 138
lock up procedures 123
long in the market 92

M

maintenance margin 94
margin 93-6
margin call 93-6
margin deposit, interest on 179
market information sources 125
market supplies of livestock 201-2
Market Viewpoints 209
marketing alternatives 3
marketing fees 156
marketing services 156-7
marketing without use of services 157

market information system, USDA   122-7
markets, commodity   2, 18, 88
market shrink, livestock   154-5
measuring gap   237-8
meat, poultry, and fish consumption table   204
meat prices, projection of   221
meat storage stocks   202
Mercantile Exchange   190-2, 194, 263
Mid-America Exchange   191-2, 194, 263
Missouri Agricultural Outlook,   209

N

National Farmers Organization (NFO)   141
National Feeder Cattle and Calf Summary   208
National Feeder Pig Summary   208
net worth breakeven   28-33
net worth statement   25, 29, 31-2

O

oats, historical prices table   272
offsetting contracts   88, 191
offsetting futures position   181
oilseed supplies, U.S., estimates of   122-6
open interest   227
   and volume, used together   228
order buyers   139

P

packer buyers   138
Packers and Stockyard Act   149-50
packing plants and packer buying stations   139
paper profit   96
par contract   178
pencil shrink   155
pennants   239
pig farrowing and pork production seasonality   214
pigs, crop chart for   136
pigs, feeder marketing channels   141
pork consumption trend   202-3
pork demand, seasonality of   214
possible top   228
poultry consumption trend   202-3
price forecasting for cattle or hogs   222

R

"Range and Pasture Conditions"   208
ready asset accounts   96
release price   132
resistance, area of   230

S

seasonal patterns in livestock supply   201
service charge contracts   79-82
"Sheep and Lamb Inventory January 1"   208
sheep and lambs data from USDA   206
sheep flock and band number changes   220
slaughter barrows and gilts, historical prices table   281
slaughter cattle, Good, 900-1,100 pound, table   278
slaughter lambs, Choice, price index for   216
slaughter steers, Choice, price index table   215
soybean importing nations   128
soybean meal, 44% bulk, historical prices table   276
soybean moisture discounts   60-1
soybean price prospects   131
soybean production hedge   105-6
soybean shrinkage from drying   58-60
soybeans, economics of drying   58-73
soybeans, No. 1 yellow, historical price table   275
soybeans, seasonal price index   44
speculating hazards for farmers   91-2
speculator   90-2
speculator vs. businessman   23-5
steer calves, 400-500 pound, price table   215
steers, Choice feeder, 600-700 pound, table   279
steers, Choice, 900-1,100 pound, table   277
steers, Good grade   191
storage hedge   108
supply-demand balance sheet   128
support, area of   230

T

technical developments, effect on markets   225-6
technical price analysis, 225-49
teleauction   140
teletype auction   140
terminal public markets   138, 142
top, possible   228
tissue shrink   155
trading strategy with trendline analysis   232
trading volume   226-7
trendlines   230
   construction and violation of   232
triangles and triangular formations   239-41

U

USDA livestock data   205-6
USDA publication, *Grain Market News*   125
USDA's mailing list   132
USDA's market information system   122-7
USDA's *Weekly Weather and Crop Bulletin*   124-5
U.S. livestock production   205-10
U.S. Meat Export Federation, a data source   210

V

video auctions   140
volume and open interest used together   228

W

weather as a livestock supply determinant   201-2
"Weekly Outlook" (Illinois)   209
"Weekly Receipts of Salable Livestock at 39 Public Markets"   207
Weekly Weather and Crop Bulletin, USDA   124-5
Western Livestock Roundup   209
wheat exporting and importing countries   128
wheat, No. 1 hard winter, table   272
wheat, No. 2 soft red winter, table   271
wheat, seasonal price index   44-5
"Wholesale Dressed Meat Prices"   207